HAMMERED
MARK WARD

HAMMERED
MARK WARD

'I PLAYED FOOTBALL FOR WEST HAM, MAN CITY AND EVERTON... THEN THE POLICE CAME CALLING AND MY LIFE FELL APART.'

JOHN BLAKE

www.johnblakepublishing.co.uk

First published in paperback in 2010

ISBN: 978 184358 272 4

British Library Cataloguing-in-Publication Data:

A catalogue record for this book is available from the British Library.

Design by www.envydesign.co.uk

Printed in Great Britain by CPI Bookmarque Ltd, Croydon

1 3 5 7 9 10 8 6 4 2

Papers used by John Blake Publishing are natural, recyclable products made from wood grown in sustainable forests. The manufacturing processes conform to the environmental regulations of the country of origin.

Every attempt has been made to contact the relevant copyright-holders, but some were unobtainable. We would be grateful if the appropriate people could contact us.

I am dedicating this book to the memory of my late
father, William Joseph Ward. To my mother, Irene Ward,
and my daughter, Melissa.
Also, my Uncle Tommy and Auntie Helen and my brothers
and sisters, Susan, Billy, Tony, Irene, Ann and Andrew.
My four grandchildren, Deri, Zach, Isabella and Frankie.
I love you all.

ACKNOWLEDGEMENTS

I couldn't have written this book without the help of the following people and I'd like to personally thank them all:

Tony McDonald and his partner Susie at Football World, for their support and encouragement and for publishing my story.

Howard Kendall for contributing the foreword.

Mick, Danny and Gary Tobyn, Nick Harris, Peter McGuinness, Tony Murphy, Paul McGrath, Richie Harrison, Paul Downes, John Blake, Duncan Ferguson, Tommy Griffiths, Kevin Hayes, Tony Gale, Alvin Martin, Tony Cottee, Alan Dickens, Billy Bonds, Liam Daish, Paul Tait, Father Giles Allen, my niece Faye Butterworth, Murray Lyall, Yvonne Lyall, Nicola Kelly, Frankie Allen, Dave Davies, Jimmy Keogh, Steve Surridge, Ian Snodin, Phil King, Phil Banks, Braddy, Dave Hunter and Dave Small, who sent me copies of the Birmingham City fanzine, *The Zulu*.

I've met hundreds of decent prisoners during the past four years, too many to mention here. With their help and friendship, it has made my stay behind bars that bit easier. Thank you, in particular, to: Paul Dunn, Jimmy Sanders, Peter Wilson, Warren Cox, Andy Rogan, Lee Bonney, Nicky Ayres, Marvin Kane, Richie Harrison Senior, Little George, Big Danny, Big Leroy, Tony Molloy, Marzy, Ian Longy and John Young.

And to the one screw who helped me out when I needed it, he is a true fan of the 'People's Club'.

And to Paul Hill, framework director of GB Building Solutions for having the strength and character to employ me and to give me a second chance.

My publishers and I would also like to acknowledge and says thanks to the following for their assistance:

Danny Francis, Steve Blowers, Terry Roper, Jack McDonald, Anne Walker, Alison and Darron McDonough, Danny Judge, Gerry Dignan,

Mark Robertson, Dave Evans, Tony Hogg, Tim Crane, Dave Alexander, Terry Connelly and the lads at Lynhurst Press (Romford). References: John Laidlar, webmaster at: www.altrinchamfc.co.uk and www.lusa.u-net.com

Our thanks go to Nick Harris and *The Independent* for allowing us to reproduce the Barry Fry and Joe Royle quotes, plus Stuart Pearce and Headline, publishers of Stuart's autobiography *Psycho*.

Finally, I would like to thank my partner Michelle Hall for her love and support.

With apologies to anybody who may have been overlooked.

CONTENTS

FOREWORD

By Howard Kendall

BY pure coincidence, I had just finished watching an episode of the TV police series *The Bill* when Mark's publisher phoned me at home and asked if I would contribute this foreword. How timely!

I was obviously shocked when I heard that Mark had been arrested and then subsequently sentenced. I don't want to go into what he was guilty of and why he ended up in prison for the past four years but when it happens to someone you know well and have become close to over the years, it's obviously very disappointing.

But once I knew how long he would have to spend inside, I had no doubts whatsoever that Mark would be able to handle it. His outstanding qualities of resilience and determination that characterised his performances for me, firstly at Manchester City and then Everton, have again stood him in good stead.

Mark first came to my attention some eight years or so before I actually signed him. He was playing for Everton in a testimonial at Halifax one night in May 1981, just after he had been given a free transfer by manager Gordon Lee, who was in fact sacked later that day. I'd just been appointed as Lee's successor when I was sat next to my assistant, Colin Harvey, at the game.

Despite being shown the door by the club he'd supported as a kid, Mark gave a typically honest performance that caught my eye at The Shay that night. I asked Colin if he thought the club was doing the right thing by letting 'Wardy' go and he mentioned that Lee had based his decision on Mark's size and stature and doubted whether he had the strength to fully make the grade.

Although I accepted Lee's verdict at the time and didn't intervene, I made a mental note of Mark's ability and the decision to let him go ultimately proved an expensive one for the club – I brought him back to Everton 10 years later at a cost of £1million.

HAMMERED

After being released by Everton in the early 80s, Mark went on to show what he was all about. Instead of feeling sorry for himself and giving up on his dream, he worked hard to improve his game, kept plugging away and got his reward via a non-league spell with Northwich Victoria that took him back into pro football at Oldham Athletic and then West Ham United. For this achievement I always use him as the perfect example of a youngster who showed the hunger and determination required to bounce back from a big setback early on in his career.

For me, Mark's best qualities were his consistency and the 100 per cent commitment he guaranteed with every game he played. Some players don't attain that level of consistency but he always did. Add that attitude to the lad's other abilities – his strength and willingness to get up and down the wing and a good crosser of the ball – and here was a player you wanted on your team-sheet every week.

It was those fighting qualities that made me sign him when I returned to England after managing Athletic Bilbao to take over at Man City towards the end of 1989. The team was struggling in a relegation battle and not only did I need to bring in players of quality, but ones who would fight to dig us out of that hole to ensure survival in the top flight.

One of the first games I saw on my return from Spain was Blackburn Rovers against West Ham – and I knew then that Wardy was ideally suited to help us get out of the situation we were in. I swapped him for two players, Ian Bishop and Trevor Morley – plus money – to form a central midfield partnership alongside another reliable Scouser called Peter Reid, and City eventually pulled clear of trouble.

I found myself in a similar predicament when I went back to Everton to manage there for the second time, in the summer of 1991 – and I again turned to Mark because I knew he would do the job we needed from him. This time, he was asked to play on the left of midfield, but it didn't matter where I put him in midfield because I knew I'd always get the same consistent level of performance and wholehearted endeavour.

I never really liked to play with out-and-out wingers anyway. I preferred wide players who would attack and then also get back to defend when needed – and Wardy could perform both roles very well.

After he had recovered from a badly broken leg during my second spell as Everton manager, I didn't hesitate to put him straight back in the side as soon as he was fit enough to play again. He had a winning mentality, on and off the field.

I saw more evidence of this soon after he'd joined City, when I took the lads on a mid-season break to Tenerife. I challenged Wardy to a game of tennis after we'd all spent the previous night enjoying drinks in the hotel bar. There was a £100 side-stake on the match and I managed to beat him two sets to one.

He could never stand to be beaten, though, so he insisted on a double-or-quits re-match the next day. This time he got his revenge – he must have caught me at a weak moment!

I got him back a few years later, though, on Everton's summer trip to Mauritius. Wardy had got up to something – I can't remember what – so I punished him by making him stand up on stage at our hotel and sing *Summertime* to the whole squad. It probably proved to be more a punishment for the other lads who had to listen to him perform!

These bonding tours did much to boost morale among the players. There were no cliques and they always had a positive effect. We'd invariably win our next game after a mini-break, although the players had to pay for their own fun. If any of them stepped out of line during the season I'd fine them for it and put the money into a kitty that went towards our next trip.

I'd keep a log of all the miscreants and what they had paid into the fund. Before going away I'd read out the list of contributors and the sums they had raised. The lads would all clap and cheer as I went down the list but, inevitably, Wardy's name would be at or somewhere near the top and I'd be informing him that it was his turn to get the champagne in again!

Not that he has had any champagne to enjoy in the past four years. I visited Mark in prison, along with Duncan Ferguson and my pal Tommy Griffiths, and I didn't know what to expect when we arrived there. But I was very pleased to see that he looked well and as fit as he did during his playing career.

It wasn't for me to probe him about what had happened or ask how or why he got himself into such a mess. The main thing is that he has paid the price for his mistakes and done his time like a man.

I understand that Mark would now like to rebuild his life and career by getting back into football in a coaching or management capacity. My advice to him would be to apply himself fully and gain the necessary coaching qualifications, so that any prospective chairman can see that he means business and has a clear intent to progress in coaching and management. If he can show desire and commitment, the same qualities that made him an integral part of my teams at both Manchester City and Everton, then people will sit up and take notice of him.

I wish Mark good luck in the future and look forward to seeing him back at Goodison Park again soon, where he will always be made welcome by me.

Howard Kendall
Formby, Merseyside
November 2010

INTRODUCTION

THE radio in the van taking me from court to prison was tuned to the local station and it blasted out the bad news I never wanted to hear: 'Former Everton player Mark Ward has been remanded in custody on a drugs-related charge.'

I'd obviously heard my name mentioned countless times before on radio and TV during my years in top flight football, but this was a surreal moment.

I could just manage to see out of the prison van window and recognised what was a familiar route. We had to pass Everton's famous ground on the way to the jail and I reminisced to myself about the many carefree days when I'd driven to Goodison, eagerly looking forward to the really big games playing for my hometown team. I remembered the day I was acclaimed a hero by nearly 40,000 fellow Bluenoses for scoring twice on my debut against the mighty Arsenal. And also my goal against our big city rivals Liverpool.

Now I was on my way past Everton's famous football ground in Walton, to HMP Liverpool Walton. To me, they were a world apart.

The dreadful enormity of what I'd got myself into hit me hard and fast. Being refused bail in the magistrates' court that morning came as a shock and bitter disappointment. It was looking bad for me.

I was worried for my family. I'd let them down terribly. How would they cope with all this bad publicity? I knew my daughter Melissa would be devastated. I'd looked across at her and the rest of the family in court that morning and the sight of Melissa's tears rolling down her face will haunt me forever.

Her dad, her hero, was going to prison.

As I stepped down from the dock, I heard her say, 'I love you, Dad.' I couldn't look back, I was too emotional, trying as hard as I could to fight back tears. I didn't want her to see me losing it.

So much was going on in my head. I was living out my very own nightmare.

That short journey to Walton in the confined space of the meat wagon was very uncomfortable. How on earth larger prisoners could travel any great distance in such cramped conditions was beyond me.

There were four other prisoners on my journey and the awful stench of p**s was overwhelming. There are no toilets on board where prisoners can relieve themselves, so they just p**s on the floor of their own tiny individual cubicle.

When the van came to a halt, a screw came aboard and handcuffed himself to me before escorting me in to Liverpool's notorious prison. I was led to the main reception desk, where I was confronted by three screws. I could already sense some resentment towards me. The youngest of the screws said, 'We've been waiting for you. You're gonna be here for a long time.'

I didn't react – I was still in a state of shock at being refused bail, although I knew I had to try and retain my dignity as best I could and not take any bait from prison staff trying to further humiliate me.

After confirming my name and date of birth, I was led away to an area set aside for stop-searches. I had to take off all my clothes and put them in the box set in front of me. A screw told me to turn around, spread my legs and open the cheeks of my a***. I did as I was instructed before being given back my clothes.

Undressing in front of anybody has never been a problem. As a footballer, taking off your kit in the dressing room is an everyday occurrence. But to be told to bend over, spread the cheeks of your a*** and lift up your b******s so that prison officers could check to see if I was hiding anything, was a degrading experience.

They then asked if I had any valuables on me. The only thing I had to disclose was a Gucci watch, a present from my former West Ham team-mate Alan Devonshire for playing in his testimonial match in 1987. They logged it down on my property card and gave it back to me.

I was then escorted to a larger room where other prisoners were waiting to be told which wing and cell they would be allocated to. I sat down and looked around at the others – all of them looked dog-tired, restless and in need of a good feed. Some of the lads knew each other and were talking about prison and other establishments where they had stayed. Time dragged on and, having not slept properly since my arrest two days earlier and the hours of police interrogation that followed at St Helens nick, I felt shattered.

The door opened and a screw asked if we wanted a welcome pack of tobacco or sweets. Everybody asked for tobacco except me.

The screw left us and soon returned with 11 packets of Golden Virginia and a small bag of 'goodies' for me. A young lad asked the screw why it was taking so long sort out our cell allocations. He explained that the prison was full to the rafters.

The same kid approached me and asked if I was Mark Ward, the former Everton player, and I answered 'Yes'. He told me he also came from Huyton and knew some of my cousins. He was quick to tell me that I'd be looking at eight-to-ten years inside. 'Get yourself a good QC and watch yourself when you get on to the remand wing – that's B-wing,' he added.

As he offered me this advice the skinniest prisoner came up to me and asked for a bar of chocolate. I gave him a small Milky Way and watched him scoff it down as if he'd not seen food for weeks.

The door opened yet again and this time we were asked by a nurse if any of us wanted to see the doctor for medication. Everyone except me joined the queue to see the prison doctor. When the rest had all been given their medication I soon sussed that most of the lads – drug addicts – had been given methadone to calm them down.

The room stank of tobacco smoke and, being a non-smoker, I began to realise that I could soon be banged-up with one of these lads.

Then the youngster from Huyton started to tell everybody that we would be put on K-wing. 'If that's the case,' he said, 'tell them to f*** off.'

I asked him what was wrong with K-wing and he just laughed out loud. 'Wardy, lad, that's where all the nonces are. The scum all get put there.'

Another prisoner approached me for a bar of chocolate. I gave him a Snickers before the Huyton kid told me to stop giving away my bag of treats. 'You're gonna have to learn fast,' he warned. 'Some prisoners will take the eyes out of your head for a deal of smack.'

We'd been waiting around for four hours and I was feeling overwhelmed with absolute mental and physical exhaustion. Finally, a screw opened the door and my name was called out. I followed him into another room where he told me to sit down. He took my photograph and put the passport-sized picture in a plastic cover with my prison number underneath it.

I used to be proud to wear No.7 on my back in my playing days. Now I was NM6982 – a number I'll never forget until the day I die. 'Don't lose that Ward and always wear it around your neck,' he told me.

I was then shuffled along to see a more senior screw, who informed me that I was to be put on the lifers' wing – A-wing. He pushed a bundle of clothing and bedding into my arms but I nearly dropped my belongings at the thought of what he'd just told me. Lifers' wing! F*****g hell – I hadn't killed anybody!

I knew that although the drugs and paraphernalia were not mine, and nor were they put there by me, I'd be held responsible because the property they had been discovered in was rented in my name.

What a dickhead I'd been.

1. BORN IN THE ATTIC

REACHING the top in football became my goal very early in life, so it was perhaps appropriate that I was born in the attic of 25, Belton Road, Huyton, Liverpool on October 10, 1962.

My sister Susan had arrived a year before me. As the eldest of seven children, we became very close as kids. Like all families in the large Ward clan, Mum and Dad kept very busy and seemed to produce a baby almost once a year. Billy turned up just nine months after me, then Tony, followed by Irene, Ann and Andrew. Mum lost a child somewhere in between, so there should really have been eight of us.

In later years I asked Dad why, as his eldest son, I was named Mark William Ward and not Billy, after him. He explained that it was deemed unlucky in our family to name the eldest boy after the father. Apparently, there had been a series of tragic deaths in previous generations of our family, so Dad chose to name his second son Billy instead.

Billy Ward senior came from a large Catholic family of 13 children, with him and Tommy the two youngest. Tommy – who has been a father-figure to me and my brothers since Dad died – tells me that my grandfather had been a stoker in the merchant navy, travelling to Russia in the first world war. My mother, Irene, was one of six kids in a family of Protestants. I've got so many cousins and relatives, I've never even met half of them.

Dad's family originated from County Cork in the Republic of Ireland. He used to tell me about his grandmother, Mary McConnell, who came to Liverpool on the boat from Cork. She was blind and he and the other children would have to carry her to the toilet or bathroom.

Ward is a very common name in Ireland. I found out from my Uncle Paddy that they were tinkers – or 'knackers' as they were also sometimes called. Many a time on my visits to Ireland as a footballer I'd be asked if I was a knacker. They were not well thought of and were widely regarded as trouble-makers who loved a scrap. That doesn't sound like me!

Ireland has always been one of my favourite destinations. I love the place and the people who make it so special. I've made so many friends in the Emerald Isle and I could happily live there. Dublin is Liverpool without the violence.

I can't remember much about living in Huyton as a kid, although I do recall my first visit to hospital. I was three or four years old and Mum would allow me to go to the shop at the top of our road – Keyos – that sold just about everything.

I always had a football to dribble to and from the shop. I remember being nearly home, as happy as Larry with my pockets stuffed with sweets, when, all of a sudden, I was hit from behind. It felt like one of the worst tackles I've ever experienced. A large Alsatian dog attacked me and caused me to hit the pavement so hard that my head split wide open, with blood gushing everywhere. Luckily, Dad was at home and he picked me up before carrying me all the way to Alder Hey Hospital, where I had the first of many stitches I'd need throughout my life.

I was told the next day that the dog wouldn't be attacking any more children. Dad had taken his revenge on the beast with a metal pipe.

However, this painful childhood experience did not dampen my desire for sweets. In fact, this mishap effectively became my first-ever coaching lesson. From then on, whenever I went to the shop I'd dribble the ball but with my head up, so that I could see and be aware of everything around me. Instead of looking for my next pass, I was alert to the opposition – the dogs. I'd learned the hard way and didn't want to go back into hospital again. I wasn't going to be caught out by any more vicious dogs and there were plenty of them around. Huyton, in the L36 postcode district of Liverpool, was such a tough area, the locals used to reckon that even the dogs would hang around in pairs! In fact, Huyton was also known as 'Two Dogs Fighting'.

Before he met and married Mum, Dad was a PT instructor in the army and always kept himself extremely fit. Dad was only a small man – 5ft 4ins – but incredibly strong and athletic. At 5ft 6ins, I'm hardly much taller than he was but, more importantly, I inherited his strength and athleticism too. Without those two assets, I could never have made it as a footballer. He would say to me: 'Strength and speed equals power.' Although I had to work on my fitness as much as everyone else, I had the capability to reach the levels needed to play at the top level.

As a small child, I remember gazing in admiration at Dad's trophies on display in the cabinet in our living room. He won medals for football, running, cricket and weightlifting. Signed by Don Welsh, he was a promising left-winger for Liverpool in 1953-54, playing a number of games for the reserves. Uncle Tommy tells me that he once saw a photograph of the entire Liverpool squad lined up on the pitch at Anfield, with his brother stood proudly next to a young lad called Roger Hunt.

But compulsory National Service spoilt Dad's hopes of becoming a pro. He was shipped out to Hong Kong, where he played for the battalion along with quite a few pro footballers. After completing two years in the army he was demobbed in 1956.

Over the years he'd tell me all about this magical place called Hong Kong. He really enjoyed his time out there and would say: 'If you ever get the chance, son, visit Hong Kong.' I would eventually play in Hong Kong for a short period at the end of my career.

* * * *

My parents married at St Columbus Church in Huyton on Grand National Day in April 1960. Dad's sister, Chrissie, was Mum's best friend and it was through her that they met.

One special talent I didn't inherit from Dad was his wonderful left foot. He was actually a two-footed player. If I'd inherited his left peg, I'd have been a far better player – my left foot was hopeless.

As well as making around 10 appearances for Liverpool's reserve team, Dad also played for South Liverpool, Skelmersdale United and some of the top Sunday League teams in our area, notably the Eagle and Child and the Farmers Arms in Huyton. Comedian Stan Boardman played at centre-forward in the same Farmers Arms team. I'd have a famous fall-out with Stan years later.

Uncle Tommy would take me to watch my father play. Apparently, I was a real handful and would try and run onto the pitch to join in. Although eight years separated them, Tommy was very close to Dad and he, too, was a very good player – as he's still fond of reminding me to this day! He held the local league scoring record and once netted nine goals in one game, including six with his head.

I'm very close to Tommy and his wife, Helen, who have both always been there for my brothers and I since Dad died in 1988.

Dad taught Tommy how to tie his shoe laces, basic arithmetic and the art of kicking a ball with both feet. He also showed him how to look after himself with his fists, which was a handy skill to have around our way.

Huyton, in the borough of Knowsley, is not only known for being a rough area, though. A number of famous names are also associated with my birthplace. Harold Wilson was the MP for Huyton and the week after my birthday he became Prime Minister. Being a staunch socialist himself, Dad voted for him.

In the second world war, Huyton was home to an internment camp for German and Austrian prisoners of war. Goalkeeper Bert Trautmann was held there before going on to become a Manchester City legend.

Football and Huyton go hand in hand. Over the years there have been many debates among locals as to who would be included in a best-ever Huyton XI. Four definite starters would be Peter Reid, Steven Gerrard, Joey Barton and, of course, myself! What a formidable midfield quartet that would have been.

Reidy played for the Huyton Schoolboys team that won the English Schools Trophy, which was no mean feat. In my fictional Huyton all-time team I can just imagine Reidy commanding the centre of the midfield and pulling the strings with Gerrard powering forward to destroy the opposition, ably supported by the combative Barton and Ward.

Despite my true blue allegiance, I rate Steven Gerrard as the best midfielder I've seen in my time – a truly amazing player who has served Liverpool and England with distinction.

* * * *

4

As the size of our family increased, Mum and Dad decided to move on – to nearby Whiston, which is just a stone's throw to the east of Huyton, on the other side of the A57. In the summer of 1967 we moved to a bigger, four-bedroom council house at 23 Walpole Avenue. I remember a happy and loving childhood and feeling secure in a very close-knit family. Not that we had much money. Dad was a labourer who found himself in and out of employment, although he always worked hard to provide for us as best he could.

I realised from an early age how relatively poor we were compared to most other kids in our area, and that we weren't going to get a new bike at Christmas or go on holidays in the summer. We knew better than to ask for things our parents clearly couldn't afford. I wore the cheapest football boots money could buy and never had a replica Everton kit as a kid. We just didn't have the money for such luxuries. It didn't used to bother me much, although it hurt my feelings a bit when I'd go to play for the under-nines and I'd turn up in football boots with holes in them while other kids, who couldn't even kick a ball properly, were wearing the flashiest boots going.

But I honestly wouldn't have swapped what we had as a family unit for anything. It was character-building. The most important thing was that there was always food on the table. Although how my parents managed at times I'll never know.

You had to be smart and fight for everything in our house. If you were last out of bed to get your breakfast, there was a very good chance that there would be no Weetabix or Shredded Wheat left after six hungry kids had devoured it. Even if there were still a few cereal crumbs left at the bottom of the box, the chances were that there would be no milk left to pour on them.

Despite the harsh economics of home life, Mum tried her best to provide a special birthday present for her kids. The only way she could purchase these surprises was by means of the catalogue, paying for items in weekly instalments. On my 10th birthday I received a brand new 12-gear racing bike, which became my pride and joy. I knew that the weekly amount Mum had to re-pay the catalogue company was more than she could really afford but she still made sure I had this special bike to treasure.

I was oblivious to most of the everyday goings-on at home, though, as I fully immersed myself in football. You see few kids doing it today, but playing out in the street was my life. Our house was on the corner and instead of a fence or wall, there were hedges surrounding the garden. They reminded me of the Grand National fences – and they were ideal for smashing a football into. Over the years they got some hammer and the constant daily bombardment from my ball took its toll. While our neighbours' hedges were all lush and green, ours were bare.

One day I was asked to run an errand for a man called Billy Wilson, who lived opposite. He and his wife May treated me like their own son – I was the spitting image of their grandson Karl who had emigrated to Australia years before I arrived in the street and whom they missed terribly. I had white blond hair just like him, too.

A miner who loved his garden, Billy became a great friend to me and I'd happily run to the shops nearly every day for him to get the *Liverpool Echo*. He was so generous, he'd give me a threepenny bit almost every time I went to the shops for his Woodbines and papers, which made me well off compared to the other kids in the street.

My first real mate was a lad called Colin Port, who lived in our street and was a couple of years older than me. He became my sparring partner and we competed against each other at everything. Once a week there was always a fall-out between us and it would inevitably end up in a scrap. The truth is that I hated losing at anything – still do – and my attitude to defeat usually sparked a fist-fight.

The first school I attended was Whiston Willis Infants, next door to the junior school. The two playgrounds were adjacent and I'd constantly be caught on the junior school premises playing football with the older lads. Looking back, competing against more senior boys played a massive part in my development as a young player.

After moving up into the juniors, I was picked for the football team two years above my age group, which was unheard of. My first cup final was in 1969 – Whiston Willis Juniors v Bleak Hill at the neutral

St Lukes venue. It's a game that will always remain with me – not for the fact that we won and I scored the equaliser in our 2-1 victory, but because it earned me a pound note. Alan Moss – a lad I still know well – had watched me play from an early age and, before kick-off, he promised to give me a quid if I managed to score.

It seemed like a fortune and when the final whistle blew, as everybody ran on to the pitch and started hugging all the players, I was too busy looking around for 'Mossy'. He sneaked up behind me, picked me up and placed my first football-related payment in my little hand. My best mate Colin scored the winner to cap a great day.

Alan Moss always had faith that I'd go on to become a pro. Whenever we meet up now, we still talk about the day he paid me a pound for my goal and made the smallest kid on the park feel 10ft tall.

* * * *

My father had his own way of toughening up his eldest son. He would take me with him to visit his brother – my Uncle Joey – two or three times a month. Joey and Aunt Ivy also lived in Huyton but I think Dad took me along more as 'insurance'. When he left me there to go out drinking with Uncle Joey, he knew he'd have to pick me up at his brother's place later on and take me back home, which meant he couldn't stay out all night.

He'd leave me to play with my cousin Kevin Ward, who became the elder brother I never had. Of all my countless cousins, he was the closest to me, even though he was four years older. Kevin had a fearsome reputation around Huyton. No sooner had our fathers sloped off to The Quiet Man or the Eagle and Child for a pint or six then Kevin was lining me up for a fight with one of the local kids – even though these hand-picked opponents were usually older and bigger than me. If they were getting the better of me, as they often did at first, Kevin would come to my aid by giving my rival a slap before sending him on his way.

This went on for years. At first I'd try and hide from Dad when I knew he was planning to visit Uncle Joey's. He'd always find me, though, and while he never said as much, I'm sure he told Kevin to harden me up a bit. It worked, because I'd gained in confidence when I returned to my hometown of Whiston. I never backed down to any of the local kids and was always in trouble for fighting.

Mr Boardman, the disciplinarian headmaster at Whiston Willis Juniors, had enough of my ongoing battles with a lad called David Maskell, the youngest of six brothers in a family of boxers. One day the Head organised a boxing match between David and myself in the school hall, in front of all the other kids. David knew how to box but I'd never even pulled on a pair of boxing gloves before. I knew I could beat David in a straightforward street fight but the boxing ring was a different matter.

My fears that our bout was going to be one-way traffic proved correct – he boxed my head off. I managed to butt him in the nose and there was blood all over his face but it was so one-sided. When the Head raised David Maskell's hand to signal his victory at the end of the fight, he barked: 'I hope this is the end of your fighting.'

Who was he trying to kid? I was so absolutely gutted to have lost to David in the ring that I waited for him after school to exact my revenge – in the street. I just couldn't let him think that he was better than me at anything. I was never a bully but having this inner drive and sheer will to win became a key part of my make-up from an early age.

My class-mates would ply me with Mars bars, sweets, apples and cans of Coke, just so I'd pick them in my team at play-time. I quickly realised that being good at football made me popular with other kids – including the girls. This continued when I left the Juniors and moved on to Whiston Higher Side Comprehensive school.

* * * *

Life in the Ward household was chaotic at times. Being the eldest lad, it was my job to ensure the younger ones behaved themselves properly when our parents were not around. Our Billy and Irene argued like cat and dog, constantly at each other's throats over anything and everything.

One day Billy and I were playing darts in our bedroom. The dartboard was hanging from the back of the door but there was a constant distraction in the form of Irene, who was the cheekiest and naughtiest sister you could imagine. She kept running in front of the dartboard to put us off until Billy told her: 'I'll throw this dart at you if you don't go away.' But Irene being what she was, continued to wind him up all the more.

Before I could say anything, Billy let fly with the dart – and it entered Irene's head. She had a mass of curly hair and to my horror, the red dart was sticking out of the top of her head. I panicked, knowing I'd get a good hiding if Dad found out. I rushed over to Irene to try and extract the dart but she already had her claws out and was chasing Billy around the bedroom like a raging bull.

As she was about to pounce on my brother, I pulled the dart from her head and got in between them. It was only then that the tears and screams started – not because of the pain caused by the dart, but the fact that she couldn't get her revenge on Billy!

My brothers and sisters get together occasionally and we reminisce about how violent we were towards each other as kids. Although we'd argue and fight with each other, if any outsiders ever tried to harm any of us, we'd stick together like glue.

* * * *

I was probably about six years old when Dad called me in off the street and told me to run to the bookies for him. If ever he told you to do something, you daren't refuse or even make him wait.

The nearest betting shop to our house was about half a mile away. Kicking a football in the street had obviously improved my fitness and speed, but running as fast as I could to the betting shop to place Dad's bet definitely enhanced my aerobic capacity. Many a time I'd been in the middle of a game in the street and be summoned by Dad to go to the bookies as fast as I could because he had a runner at Haydock Park or some other racecourse. Sometimes I'd only have 10 minutes to get there before the 'off' and then hope that I wouldn't have to wait long for a punter to agree to my urgent request to put the bet on.

Regulars in the bookies got to know me as Billy Ward's lad, so it was never a problem sneaking inside the door. As soon as the bet was placed and I had the receipt slip in my hand, I'd run like the wind to get back and resume playing football in the street. Looking back, I think I ran faster than Dad's bloody horses – he never gave me a winning ticket to take back to the shop! On the rare occasions that he did back a winner, I think he must have collected his own winnings and then headed straight off to the pub.

The positive from my regular sprints to the bookies was the fact that, from a young age, I learned to run very fast over a fair distance. The downside was that my early introduction to the betting shop and horseracing probably led to my own gambling habit in later years.

I admit, I did develop a big gambling problem in adult life – I'd say after I joined West Ham in 1985. It's well documented that gambling was, and still is, a footballer's disease and I'd agree with that because it goes with the territory. Then again, maybe I would still have gambled even if I hadn't been asked to place Dad's bets at the bookies.

* * * *

Junior football clubs started to develop around the area where we lived and I was soon signed up to play for a Sunday side called Whiston Cross – later re-named Whiston Juniors – who had, and still have, a big stronghold on all the best young players in the area. Steven Gerrard is their most famous graduate but I also came through the Whiston Juniors system, along with a dozen or so others who went on to make the professional grade, including Karl Connolly (Queens Park Rangers), Ryan McDowell (Manchester City) and John Murphy (Blackpool).

We all owe so much to the managers who looked after the Whiston teams. In my time, without pioneers like Steve Hughes and Brian Lee giving up their spare time to run the clubs, a lot of us wouldn't have developed into the players we became.

I made more friends from other parts of Whiston and the surrounding areas because football brought us together. Even though we didn't attend the same schools, we'd hang out together. One of my best mates – and he still is – was a goalkeeper called Kevin Hayes. We nicknamed him 'The Egg' because he was brilliant at finding birds' nests and had a great egg collection. I still call him The Egg to this day.

Peter McGuinness was our left-back with a great left foot. We became close friends and remain so to this day.

Our Whiston Cross team was so successful that we were invited to play at Everton's Bellefield training ground against the best kids on their books. It proved to be a big turning point in my life. Dad came along to watch but he wasn't like all the other fathers. He wouldn't go religiously every week to see me play, whereas some fathers would kick every ball for their boys from the sidelines.

I reckon that Dad knew I had qualities, although he never, ever told me I was good. I'd score four or five goals in a game and dominate the opposition but he'd never tell me afterwards that I'd played well. It was only quite a bit later in my career, when I was at West Ham, that he ever lavished any praise on me. I'll never forget it. We were sat together in a pub, on one of my home visits, when he suddenly commented I was a far better player than he ever was. I nearly fell off my chair in shock.

Dad didn't coach me and never told me to do this or that. He just let me develop in my own way. He knew my size would be an obstacle I had to overcome but he also knew I had the qualities of strength and speed that I'd inherited from him.

That game against Everton's kids was a real lesson. They murdered us 6-0 but – and don't ask me how – some of our players still came out of the game with credit. Afterwards Everton youth coach Graham Smith approached my father and asked if it would be okay for me to go to Bellefield after school every Tuesday and Thursday night for proper coaching.

Dad agreed and going home that night he told me to just go along and enjoy it. Kevin Hayes – 'The Egg' – was also invited back by Everton even though he'd conceded six. It still amazes me how they saw any positive play from me that day, because I hardly kicked the ball – Everton's kids were that good. But Graham Smith said that it was my never-say-die attitude, even when we were being hopelessly outclassed, and the fact that I kept trying to do the right thing and never hid, that caught his eye.

Dad presumably felt chuffed to see his lad attracting the attention of

Everton – the club he'd supported all his life – but if he was, he never showed it.

Training twice a week at Bellefield improved my technique and it was the first time I'd had the benefit of proper coaching. Playing for my school, then Whiston Cross on Sundays and the St Helens Schoolboys district side meant that hardly a day went by without me playing a game. I couldn't get enough of it.

My mate Colin Port and I would go to Goodison to watch Everton play one week and then see Liverpool at Anfield the next. I was brought up as an Evertonian while Colin was a Rednose.

It was around this time that I was called in to see Ray Minshull, Everton's youth development officer. I was concerned that I might have done something wrong but he counted out my expenses for travelling to training and they gave me a pair of brand new Adidas boots. They were size six, and a little big for me, but it was a wonderful gesture and made me feel good.

Ray then asked if I'd like to become a ball-boy at Goodison for first team games. Wow! In those days it was every schoolboy's dream to play for his hometown club and being a ball-boy provided a great opportunity to at least get onto the hallowed turf. The feeling I had while running out with the other nine ball-boys before the opening game of the 1974-75 season was magical. I remember the deafening noise from the crowd, the *Z-Cars* music and every hair on my body standing up as players such as Bob Latchford, Andy King, Mick Lyons, George Wood and Martin Dobson ran out of the tunnel. It wasn't the greatest side in Everton's history but it felt fantastic to be so close to the action and able to take it all in at the age of 11. I realised then, more than ever, that there was nothing I wanted more than to run out with the blue shirt on my back.

Other clubs who showed interest in me included Blackburn Rovers, Manchester United and Liverpool. Jimmy Dewsnip, the local Liverpool scout, invited Dad and I to be Liverpool's guests at Anfield, where I was dying to meet my idol Kevin Keegan. Even though I was an Evertonian, I loved to watch him play. I can't remember much about the game itself but I was introduced to Kevin outside the changing rooms afterwards. I was a star-struck 15-year-old as the England star, wearing a vivid red polar neck jumper, shook my hand. The first Cup final I recall watching on telly as a kid was Liverpool's 3-0 win over Newcastle in 1974, with Keegan scoring twice.

Liverpool were definitely pushing the boat out in an effort to impress. Soon after our visit to Anfield they arranged for me to travel down to Wembley, with a number of other schoolboy players they had their sights on, to watch the 1977 FA Cup final. Liverpool lost 2-1 to Manchester United and the mood on the journey back to Merseyside was very glum, but Bob Paisley's Reds were destined to lift the European Cup for the first time in Rome just four days later.

Everton got word of my trip to Wembley with their Merseyside rivals and quickly offered me schoolboy forms, much to the annoyance of Jimmy Dewsnip who arrived at our house hoping he'd done enough to convince me to sign for the Reds. The truth is, I was never going to sign for any club other than Everton. I was determined to live my dream and playing for my club would mean everything to me.

Although football dominated my every waking hour, it was around this time that I started to become more aware of my parents' badly deteriorating relationship. Dad was a proud man and he found it difficult to come to terms with being out of work and unable to provide properly for his family.

He also had a terrible jealous streak where Mum was concerned. It's so sad, but this was the main cause of their marriage problems.

I couldn't stop them from breaking up. All I could do was focus all my efforts on becoming a footballer. I lived and breathed the game and my burning desire was to play well enough to earn myself an apprenticeship at the club when I left school at 16. Bill Shankly famously said that football was more important than life or death. That's how I felt too.

2. JOY AND SORROW

HOW ironic that my first-ever appearance as a player at Goodison Park, on September 12, 1978, was largely thanks to . . . Merseyside Police!

The same constabulary whose officers arrested me in May 2005 were responsible for giving me and my team-mates at Whiston Cross (Juniors) the experience of a lifetime. Our local police force organised a five-a-side competition throughout Merseyside in the summer of '78 – and the reward for reaching the finals was the opportunity to play at Goodison. It was a huge competition and winning it was no mean feat.

Our team comprised goalkeeper Kevin Hayes ('The Egg'), skipper Peter McGuinness, hatchet man Carl Thomas and the two playmakers, Andy Elliot and myself. Andy was the best player at our rival school St Edmund Arrowsmith and we became good pals. The early rounds of the competition were played locally and we comfortably swept through the games and advanced to the semi-finals at the police training grounds in Mather Avenue.

Our journey by minibus to the semi-finals was one full of excitement and nervous expectation for our team of 15-year-olds. We'd all known each other from having played in school matches over the years and we were very confident of going all the way.

I travelled to the game in a pair of bright red Kickers boots that Mum had bought me. Nobody else around our way had them at the time and I thought of myself as a bit of a trend-setter. Dad was none too pleased to see his son strutting around in red boots but I was very much my own man even in those days. Just because my family are all Bluenoses, it didn't deter me from wearing what I wanted – even if they were in the colours of our big Mersey rivals. In fact, I wore those boots until they fell off my feet and was forever gluing the soles back on them. This was the era of baggy jeans and I must have looked ridiculous.

HAMMERED

My choice of music was different to that of my mates. I was influenced by my eldest sister Susan's boyfriend at the time, Les Jones. He was into Earth Wind & Fire and I'd borrow his records and listen to this magnificent American R&B band. In later years I was lucky enough to see them perform live on two occasions.

I also loved listening to Elvis Presley. Not too many lads my age would admit to admiring Elvis but he really was the king in my eyes. One Christmas Mum bought me the Elvis Greatest Hits double album and I wish I had a pound for every time I played it. I'll never forget the day Elvis died – August 16, 1977 – because I was at the FA's coaching headquarters at Lilleshall having trials for England Schoolboys. I was there for a few days and I recall coming down for breakfast that morning, picking up a newspaper and reading the shock front-page headline 'Elvis is Dead'.

Peter McGuinness and The Egg started to listen to Northern Soul and visited Wigan Casino, which was voted 'Best Disco in the World' by American music magazine *Billboard* in 1978 and was definitely the place to be seen. You had to be 16 to get in and, being five-feet nothing and baby-faced, I'd not plucked up the courage to try and sample the unbelievable atmosphere at this famous dance venue. I'd always thought it would be a wasted journey until my curiosity got the better of me one night and I jumped on the train for the short journey to Wigan.

I'd borrowed a blue velvet jacket from an older lad called Brian McNamara. As I stood in front of him and tried it on, he said: 'It's a bit big for you but you'll get in – no problem.' But looking back on it, I must have looked pathetic. Brian was a lot bigger than me and his jacket probably looked like an overcoat.

Stepping down from the train and walking to the dance venue, I started to have second thoughts. There was no way I looked 16. As we arrived I was amazed by the size of the queue – there seemed to be young girls and lads from all parts of England talking in different accents. I was in a gang of about 10 lads and as I neared the front of the queue, I was trying to remember my adopted false date of birth that would hopefully convince them that I really was old enough to be allowed in.

Just as I approached the entrance, a big bouncer tugged at my arm and pulled me to one side. 'Sorry, son, you have to be 16 to get in here – not 12.' I turned red with embarrassment, as everybody heard his humiliating put-down.

All the other lads entered the Casino okay, leaving me feeling gutted and alone outside. I was angry with myself for having believed that I might get in. I took off the oversized blue velvet jacket, tucked it under my arm and started the solitary journey back to Liverpool.

These knock-backs were very common at the time. My diminutive size and youthfulness made it very difficult for me to socialise with my mates of the same age. Another similar example occurred one night at Prescot Cables FC, where they held very popular Saturday dance nights in the bar area known as Cromwells. The disco was organised by the Orr brothers – Robbie and John – who also ran the football team. The venue was just up the road from where I lived and all the lads of my age were flocking there every weekend.

Peter McGuinness, who played for Prescot Cables, and The Egg were regulars and the stories they told of the girls they had pulled on their nights out there gave me the urge to join them. As I queued to get in, I was amazed by the quality of the local talent – the lads were bang on with their assessment. Standing between Peter and The Egg, I watched anxiously as Peter paid his 50p entry fee and as I went to give my coin to the bouncer, he said: 'Sorry, no midgets tonight.'

With a lot of sniggering from way back in the queue, once again I felt totally humiliated at this rejection. Only this felt even worse than being turned away from Wigan Casino, because Cromwells was in my own back yard.

That night, Peter mentioned my problem to Robbie Orr, who said that if I approached him at the door the following week, he'd let me in. I didn't really believe what Peter told me but there I was again the very next week, just hoping that Robbie would be on the door to let me in as promised. True to his word, after Peter introduced me to Robbie at the entrance, he just shook my hand and said 'come in'. He never even charged me admission.

It turned out the Orr brothers were both Evertonians. This was the first instance of me being given special treatment simply due to my association with Everton. Ironically, although I never had to pay whenever I went back there again, Peter and The Egg both continued to have to fork out 50p every week!

At this time I'd been courting a girl from Whiston Higher Side school called Jane Spruce. She was two years younger than me and I was very keen on her. She wasn't like the other girls her age – she was very confident and had an arrogance that attracted me to her.

Jane and her friends would also go to Cromwells on Saturdays. Although she wasn't from a wealthy family, Jane's parents, Barbara and George, worked hard for a living and ensured their daughter had the best in clothes. Always immaculately dressed, Jane was despised by some of the other local girls, which I put down to jealously. She was always the girl I fancied more than any other but she was no push-over and I soon realised that we were both strong characters. I was eventually to fall madly in love with her.

* * * *

The five-a-side tournament semi-finals at the police training grounds reached a dramatic finale. The whistle blew at full-time and then the cruel reality hit both teams – the golden chance to progress to the final at Goodison all came down to a penalty shoot-out.

Our manager Steve Hughes brought the lads together and told us not to worry about missing a penalty. In his eyes, we had already achieved great success just by getting this far.

I took our first penalty and slotted it comfortably home. Every penalty hit the back of the net, so it was left to the keepers to decide it. The Egg stepped up to take his and blasted it past their keeper. One last save from The Egg and we'd be in the final. Their keeper struck his spot kick very hard and straight but The Egg had his measure and turned the ball around the post. We all ran to Kevin, lifted him off the ground and the feeling was one of unbelievable elation.

On the way home in the minibus, Steve Hughes asked if any of us wanted a biscuit. But as he reached into his coat pocket, he suddenly laughed out loud. The digestives were no more. Steve had been so engrossed and stressed during the penalty shoot-out, he had crushed the whole packet of biscuits into tiny crumbs. The dream of stepping out onto the pitch at Everton meant as much to our manager as it did to his players.

Tuesday, September 12, 1978 was my swansong playing with my mates in the final of the Merseyside Police five-a-side competition at Goodison. That night was special and I remember scoring a couple of goals in a 4-1 victory. Everyone in our team played brilliantly and it was the last trophy I won with the lads I'd grown up with. Soon after, I was offered a contract by Everton and signed as an apprentice professional in 1979.

* * * *

Billy Ward was a very proud Dad when he left our house in Whiston to accompany me on the bus to sign the paperwork at Goodison. Dad had been a massive Evertonian all his life. He'd tell me about greats like the 'Golden Vision' Alex Young, Alan Ball and the other stars of the 1970 championship-winning side.

One of his big mates was Eddie Kavanagh, a legendary Evertonian who famously ran on to the Wembley pitch during the 1966 FA Cup final against Sheffield Wednesday and had to be wrestled to the ground by a number of coppers. They used to call Eddie 'Tit Head' because he took so many beatings in his time that one of the scars on his head looked like a nipple. Eddie ended up being a steward at Goodison.

I remember the look of pride and joy on Dad's face as I signed my first Everton contract in front of Jim Greenwood, the club secretary. He was beaming – little was he to know that, just an hour later, our whole world would be turned upside down.

I'd been full of excitement on the return bus journey and couldn't wait to get home and tell Mum what it was like behind the scenes at Goodison, to be part of the inner sanctum. But, strangely, when we arrived back at the house, she wasn't there to greet us.

As Dad walked straight into the kitchen to put the kettle on, I noticed an envelope on top of the mantelpiece with 'Billy' written on it. I picked it up and gave it to Dad without even thinking – I assumed it was probably just a note from Mum to say that she had gone shopping.

HAMMERED

As I sat in front of the telly, dreaming about the future . . . playing in front of massive crowds and scoring in the Merseyside derby . . . I felt a tap on the shoulder. With tears running down his face, Dad passed me the letter. And as I read Mum's words, I realised the enormity of what she had written.

She was apologising for leaving him and their children. Dad and I looked at each other and we started to cry, not wanting to believe the terrible truth that the most important woman in both our lives had left us.

Dad adored Mum but, looking back on their time together, I don't think she could cope with him anymore. The relationship between my parents was volatile at times, due mainly to Dad's insane jealousy. It was a terrible disease of his mind and he couldn't control it. He was never violent towards Mum but he constantly accused her of being disloyal when, in truth, she hardly went anywhere without him. I loved the pair of them dearly.

He was devastated by the break-up and, because of the hurt it caused him, I took Dad's side. In fact, I never spoke to Mum again for 16 years.

But there was never any doubt that she loved her seven kids. Just six months after moving to Wolverhampton, she decided to return to Liverpool – with another man. Dad went crazy. I remember him screaming all sorts of threats one night after he'd found out she was living back in Liverpool with a new partner. He was making verbal threats to kill Mum's boyfriend – and he meant it.

Even though I was just 16, Billy 15 and Tony 13, the next day we made a point of warning Mum's boyfriend – I never did find out his name – to get out of town or else he'd definitely come to some serious harm. When we barged past Mum at her front door, her new partner sat there on the sofa. I just blurted it out: 'Do yourself the biggest favour, mate. Get out of Liverpool before my father gets you.'

Mum was shouting and screaming but the three of us just walked straight past her and out through the front of the house, hoping we'd done enough to convince her new man to see sense. And thankfully he did. He moved out the next day and Mum followed him to start a new life together in the Wolverhampton area, where she still lives today.

Dad passed away in 1988, aged 52. It was a heart attack that killed him but I've always maintained that he really died of a broken heart, because he never got over losing Mum. I don't blame her at all, though. That's life, many couples divorce – I've been there myself – and if it hadn't been for certain flaws in their relationship, who knows, they might still have been together today.

I'll never forget, though, the stark contrast of emotions Dad felt on the day his eldest son signed for his beloved Everton. How, one minute, he was the proudest man in the whole of Liverpool and, just an hour later, he found out he'd lost the only woman he ever loved. Why she chose *that* day of all days to leave, I'll never know. Mum told me years later that, with Dad out of the house and on his way to Goodison with me, she had an unexpected opportunity to leave. Feeling as desperate as she did at the time, she said it was a chance she simply had to take.

Her leaving the family home affected us all. My sisters, Susan, Irene and Ann, eventually set up home in Wolverhampton with Mum, while Billy, Tony, Andrew and myself stayed with Dad in Liverpool. From being a very close-knit family, the break-up of our parents also split us right down the middle. It knocked me for six at first.

Dad was a broken man but he cared about my future and gave me one bit of sensible advice: 'Just concentrate on being a winner and give it your best shot at becoming a footballer,' he told me. An old saying of his was: 'Quitters never win and winners never quit.' How right he was.

It was unbearable, at times, to hear him crying at night after coming home drunk from the pub again. I felt helpless, as most kids do when their parents split up. I think it did affect my football for a while but I was so determined to succeed in the game, I had to think of myself and try and forget about the troubles at home.

3. SLAVES TO THE PROS

ALTHOUGH I was at the bottom of the ladder and knew I had a mountain to climb, I was on my way. The summer of '79 was to be one of sheer hard work. I was still very small and needed to work on building up my strength in the battle to make the grade.

I was taken to Huyton Leisure Centre by Les Jones, my sister's boyfriend, who worked out regularly with me and over the next eight weeks I developed muscles that appeared from nowhere. It was hard going but I was determined to give myself every possible chance of making it at Everton.

The club took on 12 new apprentices that year. The most notable, and the two who became the biggest stars for the Toffees in later years, were Gary Stevens and Kevin Richardson. When we all got together, I was as good as, if not better, than them technically. It was just my stature that caused others to doubt whether I'd make it and it was for that reason that I didn't get through trials for both England and Liverpool Schoolboys.

To be fair, the FA coaches at Lilleshall encouraged me at the end of the trials by saying that I'd bypass a lot of the taller, more powerful lads during the growing process. Tommy Caton, who went on to play for Manchester City, was also at the England trials and, even at 14, he looked like a fully developed adult. The scouts and management of Liverpool Schoolboys saw what I could do when I scored the winner against their team while playing for St Helens Schoolboys.

Gary Stevens was a big, powerful lad, the 200m, 400m and 800m champion of Cumbria. Kevin was also strong and I struck up a good relationship with this likeable Geordie. Although we were all team-mates playing in the 'A' and 'B' Central League teams, we were also competing with each other for a professional contract in the months ahead.

HAMMERED

Mind you, the job of an apprentice footballer in the early 80s gave you no time to rest on your laurels. Not only did we have to train and play matches, but there were a number of menial chores that had to be finished each day – as slaves to the older professionals. It was a tough regime that would either make or break you. There was no youth academy set-up like those which exists at all top clubs today. Apprentices were part of a feudal system in which young players were ritually bullied and verbally abused by senior pros.

The apprentices and young professionals had their own dressing room and each apprentice was allocated a number of first team players to serve on demand. Among the group of players I had to care for was Andy King, the club's star midfielder. Cockney 'Kingy', a fine player and a crowd favourite, took a shine to me and instead of bullying me would want me to tend to his needs.

Everton were not a brilliant side at that time but they had some good players. Bob Latchford scored goals for fun, Dave Thomas was the winger I admired, Asa Hartford was the heartbeat in midfield and Steve McMahon, who I'd played with at Everton in the 'A' and 'B' teams, was challenging for a starting place in the first XI.

Our duties included cleaning boots, showers, toilets, dressing rooms and anything the pros asked us to do. The senior players commanded respect and the treatment they dished out to the youngsters at their beck and call would not be tolerated today.

At Christmas, each apprentice was stripped naked and a pair of football socks stretched over their eyes to form a blindfold. The entertainment was provided by two apprentices who were ordered to fight blindfolded in front of the senior pros. As the fight was in progress, the pros would smear each youngster in boot polish. When the fight had ended, the blindfolds were removed and then the duo had to further entertain the first-teamers with a Christmas song.

I remember it being a very humiliating experience but this initiation ceremony was part of becoming a footballer and had been for many years. It was regarded as a test of character. Intimidation was all part of the process.

It was all a question of respect and knowing your place. If you disrespected a senior player, the older pros had a way of dealing with you among themselves. At the end of the training session they would capture the cheeky upstart, strip him naked and make him gather up all the balls that had been used in that morning's training session – and there would be at least 40 to 50 footballs to collect, depending on the severity of sentence. I witnessed one of my fellow apprentices being tied to a tree, with not a stitch on, and having to suffer the pain of having a number of players fire balls at him.

It was a question of respect. I was always mindful to knock on the door of the first team's dressing room before entering to gather up all their sweaty kit, which was always scattered everywhere. I remember once picking up the last sock and then being set upon. In the shower area there were two huge baths, one filled with cold water that was used as a cold plunge for the players after their sauna.

I was picked up and thrown, head-first, into the icy water, followed swiftly by all the kit I'd just collected up off the dressing room floor. Two or three of the players stood guard while I shivered in the water. My next problem was getting all the kit dry in time for the players' afternoon training session. I always managed to survive the intimidation process, although it helped that star midfielders Andy King and Asa Hartford both took me under their wing.

Kingy become a law unto himself at times. He was routinely late for training once or twice a week – he wouldn't have lasted five minutes in today's game – but he was a character as well as a great footballer. He once approached me half an hour before kick-off at Goodison. He took me outside the dressing room, stuffed £200 in my hand and told me to put it on a horse. I tried explaining to him that if I got caught leaving the ground, I'd be in big trouble. He just shrugged his shoulders and said: 'Not to worry, I'll sort it out.'

I rushed across to Stanley bookmakers and, with what seemed to me like an enormous amount of money in my hand, wrote the name of his horse on the slip and pushed it towards the woman at the till. She looked at me bemused and asked: 'Is this your money, son?'

I told her straight: 'No, it's Andy King's – the Everton player.' There were hundreds in the betting shop at that time and at first I didn't think she was going to accept the bet. But, thankfully, she put the slip through the machine and I took off clutching the bet receipt and managed to get back inside the stadium unnoticed just before kick-off.

This was to become a regular occurrence but Kingy looked after me with a tenner here and there. In fact, I'd earn more for putting on a bet for him than I did as an apprentice footballer. My weekly wage was £16 per week. The club gave the household where you lived £25 towards your food and upkeep, so you were always well fed.

Gaining the trust of the senior players made me feel good. One afternoon Scottish international Asa Hartford sent me to the passport office in Liverpool and rewarded me for the errand with £20, which was a lot of money to me at that time.

Being close to the players and watching them train and play only made me want to become a footballer even more. It was a tough baptism, though, and my cause wasn't helped when I picked up a back injury that put me out of action for four months. It was a massive setback, as I had to impress manager Gordon Lee and his staff by the end of the season in order to earn the full-time professional contract I craved. I had a trapped nerve – sciatica was diagnosed – and it was as if I didn't exist anymore. When you're injured, you are useless to the club.

My injury eventually cleared up, though, and I travelled to Holland with the youth team to take part in the Groningen under-19s international youth tournament. I knew it would have an important bearing on my future at Everton, so I was determined to play well and put the months spent recovering from my back injury behind me.

It was a truly big tournament featuring clubs such as FC Hamburg, Sparta Rotterdam and PSV Eindhoven, to name just a few. I loved the atmosphere and build-up to the games and was starting to believe in myself more and more as we progressed through the competition. Our team was full of future Everton stars: Gary Stevens, Graeme Sharp, Steve McMahon and Kevin Richardson. Kevin Ratcliffe was due to travel with us but had to withdraw because he had first team commitments with Everton and was also selected for Wales in the Home International Championships.

I played on the right-wing in every game in which we achieved one draw and four victories to earn a place in the final against the mighty PSV. Despite dominating the game, we struggled to score against the Dutch, who managed to make it 1-1 with their only shot of the game. We'd played so many matches in such a short period of time that the players were very tired.

With only a few minutes remaining in the second period of extra-time, something inside my head told me to chase what seemed like a lost cause. The PSV defender was running back towards his own goal and I was just hoping he'd make a mistake – and he did. He tried to nudge the ball back to his keeper but under-hit his pass. I seized on it in a flash and buried the ball into the net.

I was surrounded by my jubilant team-mates and before we knew it, the whistle blew and we'd won the tournament. I'd scored the winner. How fortunes can change so quickly in football. Unbelievably, I was voted player of the tournament. I'd been picked out ahead of some brilliant players. It was quite an achievement and I thought this was just what I needed if I was to earn a full-time contract.

That night, I remember getting drunk for the very first time and how I suffered for it afterwards. After our victory we were allowed out to celebrate and the lads ended up in a lively bar, where I drank a small glass of cold beer that I didn't much like the taste of. Inevitably, I was p****d within the hour and, along with a couple of the other lads, was in a terrible state by the time we got back to the hotel, where I became violently sick.

Arriving back in Liverpool the next day, somewhat hungover, it was great to hear our success being reported on radio and television. And my personal award meant I found myself in the limelight for the first time. The press came to our house and it was well documented in reports that Everton's future was in good hands with young players of the calibre of Steve McMahon (who made his first team debut in the opening game of the following season), Gary Stevens, Graeme Sharp and Kevin Richardson – and I was being mentioned along with them.

When Everton played Nottingham Forest at home at the start of the 1980-81 campaign, I was thrilled to be pictured on the front cover of the match day programme along with some of my team-mates from the Groningen tournament, plus youth development officer Ray Minshull and coach Graham Smith. And there, on page 3, was a photo of me holding my player of the tournament trophy alongside a decent write-up of our victory.

As well as Ray and Graham, I should also give credit to the efforts of Ray Deakin, who became my youth coach. He gave me so much sound advice and encouragement in my first spell at Goodison, making me realise that, due to my size and weight disadvantage, I had to go into every tackle twice as hard as my opponent. I was saddened to hear that he died of cancer on Christmas Eve 2008, aged just 49.

If it hadn't been for my performances in the Dutch tournament in the summer of 1980, I don't think Everton would have offered me a full-time contract as a professional. But they did and Dad was made up. Not that there was any chance of him allowing my success to go to my head. He would knock me back down by saying things like 'don't get carried away' and 'you still have such a long way to go.'

Once again, he was dead right.

4. GOODISON HEARTBREAK

EVERTON became a poor team under manager Gordon Lee, who came in for plenty of stick from the press. I witnessed at first hand how he had lost the dressing room and failed to control certain players. Even at that young age I realised none of the senior pros respected him. And no-one undermined Lee's authority more than Andy King, our prolific goal scoring midfielder, who really gave the beleaguered manager the run-around towards the end of his first spell at Goodison.

Looking back, Kingy was a total rebel and, as his apprentice and the one responsible for cleaning his boots, I had a bird's eye view of his antics.

The other players would be halfway through their warm-up when you'd hear the screech of Kingy's brakes as he belted in to Bellefield – late, as usual. And then, as he emerged from his car, I'd hear that familiar voice: 'Wardy, come here.' I'd jog towards him as he began to undress while walking from the car park to the changing rooms.

'What's going on? What's being said?' he'd ask me.

As usual, I'd ensure his kit was laid out neatly for him on arrival. Half the time he'd still be drunk from the night before but he wasn't bothered. A very talented attacking midfielder who was once being touted for England honours, he knew that whatever he said around the club and no matter how badly he behaved by gambling and drinking too heavily, he was always going to keep his place in the first team. Everton's squad was so small and p**s-poor back then that nobody could even get near to replacing him in the side – and Lee knew it, too.

After arriving late, Andy would often start to argue with Lee about one thing or another, even telling the manager to 'f*** off' before skulking off to train with the reserves and apprentices. Lee never ordered Kingy to train apart from the first team – it was the player's choice. I can't imagine any manager today tolerating this kind of petulance and blatant disrespect from any of his senior players.

The 1980-81 season was a mixed one for me. With a glut of midfield players at the club and first-teamers given priority when dropping down to play in the reserves, I was in and out of the second XI. Andy King left in September 1980 to join QPR in a £400,000 deal but returned to Everton, via West Bromwich Albion, two years later. Before I knew it, the season was over and it was D-Day – the moment I'd learn whether I would be offered another pro contract or be released. All the other young lads at the club were telling me not to worry, so convinced were they that Everton would give me another year, or maybe even two.

Dad saw me off to training, telling me not to worry but I was nervous. I sat quietly in the dressing room at Bellefield, waiting for the call summoning me to the manager's office. It was like waiting to be sentenced – or reprieved – by a judge. My football future was in one man's hands. After all my hard work in trying to make the grade, it all came down to his judgement.

Lee had hardly spoken a word to me in the previous two years – he showed no interest in the younger players. He was dour in both demeanour and words. As I nervously stepped inside his office, he told me to take a seat. I'll remember his next words for as long as I live. He came straight to the point: 'Mark, we believe you're never going to be big enough, strong enough or quick enough to establish yourself at the highest level. There is no doubting your ability but we have decided to let you go.'

He didn't even make eye contact as he delivered his damning verdict. A voice inside me kept saying: 'Tell him he's making the wrong decision. Tell him you're getting stronger and that you *will* become quicker in time.'

But no words left my lips. I was stunned, in a state of deep shock.

I left Lee's office and headed for the stairs, where I was met by my team-mates, Steve McMahon, Kevin Richardson, Gary Stevens, Dean Kelly and Brian Borrows, who were clearly upset for me. They were full of support and commiserations but, as I choked back the tears, I just wanted to get home.

Waiting for the No.75 bus on Eaton Road, I felt emotionally shattered. I paid my fare, made my way upstairs and sat on the empty top deck, where I cried. I was angry and frustrated with myself. I should have told Gordon Lee he was making a terrible mistake and that I'd prove him wrong.

My thoughts then turned to Dad, who was still struggling badly to come to terms with Mum having walked out on him. Now that his son had been dumped by his beloved Everton, it was another major body blow for him to handle. By the time I got home I felt more in control of my emotions. I stepped into the living room, where Dad looked up from his *Daily Mirror*. He knew my fate from the sadness written all over my face. And as he grabbed hold of me, I broke down in his arms.

He did his best to try and reassure me that Everton had made a big mistake in letting me go, and that he knew I was good enough, but his words were of no comfort to me at the time. We just sat together for a couple of hours drinking tea. He made me promise him one thing: not to give up on my dream of becoming a professional footballer. 'Mark, you *will* get stronger and quicker,' he reassured me. 'By the time you're 21 you'll have these two ingredients to make you a better player. With your skill and the extra power you gain, you'll become a footballer of some quality.'

I gathered myself together to reassure Dad that I was more determined than ever to prove Everton wrong.

A couple of hours later that afternoon we heard some amazing news on the radio.

Lee had been sacked.

Dad and I both looked at each other. We couldn't believe that the man who had turned my world upside down just a few hours earlier, had now also been given the boot by Everton.

The sacking of the colourless Lee – appointed as Billy Bingham's successor in January 1977 – had been on the cards for a good while. After a good start, the former Newcastle United manager had seen his

HAMMERED

Toffees team finish 19th and 15th in successive seasons before the Goodison board decided his time was up.

Little did the football world know then that Lee's replacement, Howard Kendall, was about to revive Everton's glory days and become the greatest manager in the club's history.

Even though I was shown the door at Goodison in May 1981, Howard was to play a major part in my football development. In the short term, he threw me a lifeline I was determined to grab. Although the season had officially finished, there were still a couple of friendlies to be played. He wanted to see me play even though the decision had already been made to let me go, so I was given one half of a testimonial match against Halifax Town at The Shay in which to try and impress him. For Howard to offer me hope in this way, I was going to have to play the best 45 minutes ever. The pressure was enormous.

Alongside me in the team that day were seasoned senior pros including Bob Latchford, Asa Hartford and Mick Lyons. End-of-season testimonials are never easy games to play in – players don't want to risk injury and most are already thinking of lazing on a beach while knocking back the San Miguels.

For the first time nerves got the better of me. I was trying too hard and although I had some success against the Halifax full-back and managed to provide a few decent crosses, I sat in the dressing room afterwards knowing that I hadn't done enough to excite Howard. On the team bus journey back to Liverpool, Bob Latchford and one or two other senior pros tried to lift my spirits by saying they thought I'd done enough to impress the new boss.

It wasn't to be, though. My dream had been shattered. Lee's sacking had come too late for me and I felt devastated that I was no longer an Everton player.

But Howard Kendall never forgot me.

Ironically, when he signed me from Manchester City 10 years later and brought me back to Goodison, I was amazed when he mentioned that nondescript game at Halifax. He had questioned the judgement of Lee and his coaches in their decision to release me. For Howard to remember a low-key testimonial match from a decade earlier, it just showed his fantastic knowledge of the game and the attention to detail he always brought to management.

Showing me the Goodison exit door would ultimately prove a costly decision for Everton, although, realistically, I accept that I was still some way off playing for the first team in that summer of '81. Leaving the club I loved hurt very badly at the time but it was to be the making of me – as a player and as a man. I'd embark on a 10-year rollercoaster ride, a journey of blood, sweat and tears to get back to *my* club.

5. THE KING AND I

AFTER being released by Everton, the 1981-82 season quickly became a reality check for me. For a start, I didn't even have a club to play for as the new campaign loomed. Everton had promised to arrange practice matches against lower league teams, to give me the chance to impress other clubs, but nothing materialised.

The only contact I had with anyone at Goodison was from Geoff Nulty, one of the first team coaching staff and a former senior player who lived near me in Prescot. He arrived at the house one day in the summer to reassure my dad and I that he believed I had what it took to become successful. It was good to hear and gave me some much-needed encouragement at a time when I really needed it.

Then, out of the blue, a telegram arrived at the house – the first we'd ever received. It was addressed to me and I was excited as I opened it, praying for good news and the offer of a trial by a league club.

The telegram read: 'Can you contact Tony Murphy, who is a player at Northwich Victoria FC, so he can bring you along for a trial at Drill Field, Northwich, to play against Bolton Wanderers'. Tony's address was printed at the bottom of the message.

At first, I mistakenly thought it said 'Norwich', so I immediately assumed the telegram had been sent from Norwich City (who had just dropped from the first to the second division). I must admit, I felt deflated when I realised it was Northwich, a non-league club in Cheshire. Dad told me to go and knock at Tony Murphy's house, which was just a short distance from us, to find out all I could about the Alliance Premier League side.

I hadn't heard of Tony before our first meeting but he is still a good friend of mine to this day. We always reminisce about the first time we clapped eyes on each other. I knocked on his front door and was greeted by the most unlikely looking footballer you could imagine. My first impression of Tony, who had a big, round face and legs like tree trunks, was that he was too fat to play football! He always says that when he first saw me, he thought I was too small and looked like a young teenager.

He invited me in, I handed him the telegram I'd received from the club's new manager, Lammie Robertson, and he read it to himself. Tony was friendly enough and told me not to be late on Saturday because he would take me to Northwich with him.

He chauffeured me to my first trial game in his Hillman Imp and it was the first time I realised how close Northwich was to Liverpool. I took an instant liking to Tony, who was 25 at the time and in his third stint with Vics after spells with Runcorn and Bangor City. He never shut up all the way there and was good entertainment.

Before leaving home that morning, Dad advised me to treat the game as a training session and, no matter what happened, I should not sign for Northwich under *any* circumstances.

On arrival at Drill Field I was disappointed to be told that I'd only be one of the substitutes. I watched the first half and was surprised at the quality of the Northwich lads, who were holding their own against the strong full-time pros of Bolton Wanderers. Tony Murphy played at left-back and he had a great left peg and tackled anything that moved. As expected, he was slow but he read the game amazingly well. Not many got past him – he'd take out anyone who dared to try.

There was a crowd watching and I was itching to get on and show everyone what I could do. Scotsman Lammie Robertson, who had a brief spell at Leicester City and a 400-game career with various lower league clubs, told me to warm up with 20 minutes to go. He told me to go on and enjoy myself. And I certainly did.

I felt no pressure at all and was instantly picking the ball up and flying past the opposition. We were a goal down but within minutes I made the equaliser with a dribble and a neat cross. My two previous full seasons spent training every day at Everton had seen me attain a very high standard of fitness. I scored the winner with five minutes to go and didn't want the game to finish.

As I walked off the pitch at the final whistle, Tony put his arm round me and said: 'Don't sign for us, son, you're too good'. I took his kind comments with a pinch of salt but I knew I'd done well.

I got changed and enjoyed the buzz of the dressing room, where it soon became obvious that Tony was the joker in the pack. I was asked to go and see the manager in his office before I left. Lammie came straight to the point: 'Mark, you have done really well today,' he told me. 'We would like to sign you on a two-year contract.'

He went on to tell me how easy it was to drift away from football and become forgotten. Northwich could offer me £45 per week and a platform to bounce back into the Football League. I was getting £22 per week on the dole by this time and whatever possessed me to reach out for the pen and sign, I'll never know to this day. But I'm glad I did.

Lammie looked as pleased as punch at getting my signature. It was only when Tony and I were nearing Liverpool, on our way home from the trial game, that I remembered Dad's last words before I left the house that morning.

The Watchmaker was the nearest pub to Tony's house and it also happened to be Dad's local. Tony asked if I fancied a shandy as I told him my father would be in what I called his 'second home'. He was keen to meet him, so we made our way to the bar in The Watchmaker and, sure enough, there was Dad, standing in his favourite place . . . drunk.

I introduced him to my new team-mate and Tony immediately went into detail about how well I'd played and told my father that he had a good footballer for a son. I was praying that Tony wasn't going to let slip the fact that I'd actually signed for Northwich that day. I wanted to tell Dad myself later, when he'd sobered up, as I knew he'd kick off on me for ignoring his advice.

I'd just taken a sip of shandy when Tony told Dad: 'I told him not to sign for us, he's too good.'

'Have you signed for Northwich?' Dad snarled.

'Yes,' I replied, waiting for the inevitable eruption.

He lurched forward but I was already poised to make my escape. Dad chased me out of the bar into the street, shouting obscenities and telling me I'd ruined my career, while Tony made his diplomatic exit through the other door. Having seen Billy Ward in one of his infamous tempers, he was wise to beat a hasty retreat. Dad was drinking too much by this time. He still hadn't got over losing Mum – he never would – and so he found salvation in the bottom of a beer glass. He could become very aggressive and unpredictable through drink.

The next day, however, he eventually came around to the fact that I'd lowered my sights to non-league level. Little did either of us know then that Northwich Victoria were going to be an excellent club to propel me back into full-time football. They were a great, little non-league outfit with a proud history. There was a warmth and friendliness running right through the club and I felt instantly at home there. The people embraced me as the Greens' youngest player and they looked after me in every way.

Our team was a good, interesting mixture. The Vics players all had full-time jobs, so the wages they earned at Northwich was their secondary income. Kenny Jones, the captain who had been with them for 10 years, was a brickie.

His sidekick and centre-half partner was Jeff Forshaw, who worked as a joiner. They were a formidable pair of Scousers.

We had a school teacher in Philly Wilson, a building society manager in Dave Fretwell and just about every other job description you could think of. Tony Murphy worked at the Ford motor factory in Halewood.

One thing I quickly noticed was their unbelievable team spirit. It was a team that bonded on and off the pitch – in spectacular fashion. After matches, it was all about drinking and shagging! The motto of the team was: 'Win or lose, on the booze'. And didn't we just.

Some of the lads were on good wages and used their football earnings to fund a very enjoyable and active social life. After every game, home and away, the lads went out together in Northwich and they introduced me to drinking in a big way. We had some long away trips – to Weymouth, Enfield and other far-flung fixtures in the south – and I was regularly p****d by the time I got off the team bus back at Drill Field on a Saturday night.

Then we would continue drinking in local haunts – the Martin Kamp nightclub and the famous Cock Inn pub. Even though Northwich Victoria were only non-leaguers, the players still attracted their share of local groupies. The same women hung around us every week. And the lads would share them, especially two of the more desirable ones, named Pat and Debbie. I was gobsmacked by how flirtatious these women were. They just wanted a good shagging – and the lads never liked to disappoint them!

Kenny Jones, our inspirational skipper and defensive rock, was having an affair with a local woman known to us as 'Louby Lou'. She would be waiting for him religiously after every game. Some of the messages she left on Kenny's car windscreen were outrageous.

There was always fun and games after matches and there were some legendary party animals, namely strikers Colin Chesters and Paul Reid plus goalkeeper Dave Ryan.

But the team didn't make a good start to the 1981-82 season and poor Lammie Robertson was sacked after just six matches. I was injured in a game against Barnet – who were managed by Barry Fry – just before his dismissal.

It was definitely more competitive at this level of football compared to what I'd been used to in the youth and reserve teams at Everton. I was up against strong, experienced footballers each week and getting clobbered regularly. But then I always did enjoy the physical side of the game.

The lads tried to look after me on the pitch. The nasty injury I suffered against Barnet resulted from an horrendous tackle. Their cocky midfielder had been mouthing off all through the game, telling me what he was going to do to me.

And, true to his word, he topped me and I thought he'd broken my leg. I was in agony and as I waited to be attended to by the physio, I heard Kenny Jones arguing with Barnet's hatchet man. I wanted my revenge but the blood was pumping from my leg wound and I was forced to leave the field.

Kenny told the beefy Cockney that he was a coward. The Barnet player replied: 'F*** off, old man.' I heard Kenny add: 'I'll show you how old I am in the bar afterwards . . . '

HAMMERED

I thought nothing of this spat but these careless words from the mouthy Barnet player would soon backfire on him. I was bandaged up and limped into the players' lounge after the game to have a beer. Tony Murphy whispered in my ear. 'Watch what Kenny does when their players come in.'

I was intrigued. The Barnet players arrived in the bar to tuck into the customary sandwiches and a quick beer before their journey back to the smoke. The cocky b*****d who had nearly finished my career was laughing and full of himself as he got the beers in. To my delight, Kenny walked up to him and calmly said: 'I'm the old man . . . remember me?'

The Barnet player had a nervous look of surprise on his face and the room suddenly went deathly quiet. 'Look mate,' the trembling Cockney blabbered. 'The game's over now, let's forget what's been said.'

Kenny wouldn't let it go, though. He called him a cheat and a coward, and offered him outside. It made great viewing for me. This dirty b*****d had tried to break my leg – no doubt about it – and could easily have finished my career there and then. My captain had put him on the spot and he was now cowering in front of his own team-mates. His voice started to stutter and you could see the tears welling up in his eyes as the colour drained from his face.

Kenny made his point before rejoining his Northwich team-mates, while the Barnet players left our ground very quietly, with their tails between their legs.

I've always maintained Kenny was one of the best I've ever played with. He was the Bobby Moore of non-league football – no pace but read the game impeccably.

While I was recovering from that assault by the Barnet player, our new manager had been installed. It was John King, the 43-year-old ex-Tranmere Rovers boss who had also been a young player at Everton. It was a coup for Northwich to obtain the services of a well-respected manager of his calibre.

At this time, I was still relying on Tony Murphy to ferry me to and from home matches at Northwich and training on Tuesday and Thursday evenings. But if Tony had to work nights at Ford's, it meant I couldn't get to training.

John King's appointment in October 1981 brought stability to the team. After three creditable draws I was fit enough to be selected. I was named substitute for an away fixture at the mighty Altrincham. I remember warming up constantly in the second half but the new boss didn't put me on. I was fuming and feeling very frustrated. After another draw I knew I could hold the key to us getting a win, so I had to challenge the manager and let him know how I felt.

Straight after the game I approached him and told him I should be playing. John's words rocked me back on my heels a little: 'I've heard you can play a bit, son. But how can I play somebody who can't be bothered to turn up for training?'

He had a very valid point. I cheekily warned him that if I did get to training on that Thursday, he'd better start me on Saturday. He just said: 'We'll see what happens.'

Although I'd promised to attend training, I found out to my dismay that Tony Murphy was working nights that week. On Thursday evenings we trained on a floodlit shale pitch at the Guinness factory in Runcorn. I explained my problem to Dad but he just said that I had to make it to training one way or another.

So I decided to run all the way there.

I realised Runcorn was a fair way from our home, so I gave myself two hours in which to jog the full distance. It was November 5 and, therefore, not the best night of the year to be inhaling the smoky night air. I don't know if John King honestly expected to see me at training that night, once he knew Tony Murphy wouldn't be around to give me a lift, but I was determined not to let him down. I took it easy, jogging at a steady pace, and eventually arrived in Runcorn after one-and-three-quarter hours.

The dressing room was full when I arrived, with the manager stood in the centre. I was soaking with sweat. 'Well done, son,' he said. 'How did you get here?'

'I ran,' I replied.

I sat down to briefly rest my legs before training started. I managed to get through the two-hour session but felt so shattered afterwards there was no way I could run all the way back home – I was spent.

HAMMERED

Much to my relief, team-mate Graham Abel was willing to go out of his way and drive me all the way home to Prescot.

When we arrived back at my place, Graham clocked the distance in his car. It was 12 miles from door-to-door.

As I got out of his Ford Capri I told him that Johnny King had better start me on Saturday, or else I'd be off to another club.

Saturday arrived and Kingy was looking for his first win. We were playing A.P. Leamington, who were bottom of the league, and I was relieved to hear that I would be starting the game. We went 1-0 down but in the second half I found the net with the equaliser and then hit an unstoppable free-kick to seal the points.

After the game, the first he'd seen me play in, the manager took me to one side with some welcome words of encouragement: 'You did very well today. And running to training this week showed a great attitude. Don't lose the fire in your belly and hunger to succeed,' he said.

Kingy was well known for his quotations and he'd talk about his great admiration for the legendary boss Bill Shankly. 'Shanks' had favourite sayings he would use to inspire his Liverpool players to greater heights and so did Johnny King, a real character. He used to say: 'We are starting on a long boat trip and you all need to start rowing like f***.'

If you had a bad game, he'd stick with his nautical theme, point his finger at you and say: 'You were busy being sick over the side.' And he'd ask certain players who were off form: 'Have you lost your oar?' Another great quote came as we progressed further towards the FA Trophy final at Wembley in 1983. He'd keep saying: 'We're not far from Treasure Island!'

He was very infectious and enthusiastic about football. I look back and realise my decision to run 12 miles to training that bonfire night in '81 was a very important one. If I'd not bothered to jog through the dark, misty streets from Prescot to Runcorn, my football career could well have petered out or ended there and then.

In later years, after John returned to Tranmere as manager and dragged them from the foot of the fourth division to the brink of the

Premier League, he used me as an example of a young lad who ran 12 miles to training . . . just so that he could make the team for the next game.

King became an inspiration to me. A Londoner who grew up on Merseyside, he'd joined Everton as an apprentice and played 48 times for them in the late '50s. Like me, he was small and could therefore relate to me very easily. He encouraged me to train hard and push myself to the limit to compensate for my lack of inches. After each training session he took me aside and put me through hell with sit-ups and strength exercises, plus plenty of sprints.

His interest and confidence in me fuelled my own self-belief. Before one game he told me I was playing in the centre of midfield. His instructions were to treat the game like a boxing match. He described it as a head-to-head between me and the opposing midfield player. In the first couple of minutes, he said: 'Suss out his strengths and weaknesses and then dominate him.' I took this advice literally.

Kingy's words of wisdom were so true. Within the context of any match there are individual battles to be won: Centre-half against centre-forward; full-back versus winger, etc. I adopted his simple philosophy and carried it with me all the way to the Premier League.

The principles of sheer hard graft that I learned under John King's shrewd man-management at Northwich Victoria in the early '80s stood me in good stead throughout my playing career.

My first season at Northwich ended in heartache. Although we moved up to finish fourth in the APL, Enfield beat us in the semi-final of the FA Trophy and I was gutted to just miss out on the chance to play at Wembley. But another opportunity to fulfil that dream would come along much sooner than expected . . .

6. WEMBLEY WOE

BY the time the 1982-83 season came around, Jane Spruce, my girlfriend of nearly two years, had fallen pregnant. Although we had been together, off and on, since our school days, the pregnancy came as a big shock to us both. But it became a major positive in my life. The reality of bringing a child into the world gave me that extra impetus and desire to succeed.

The day we found out that she was definitely pregnant was one I'll never forget. I was working with George – Jane's father – helping him install central heating, while Jane was at home with her mother, Barbara, desperately awaiting the result of her pregnancy test. George was completely unaware that he was about to become a grandad and I knew he wouldn't be pleased by the news.

With Jane's test result due from her GP at any minute, I was terrified to go back to the house with George for dinner that night. When we arrived home, Jane still hadn't had confirmation, so she then rang the doctor's surgery while her mum and I stood waiting on the stairs with bated breath. George was out of earshot, in the kitchen making a cup of tea.

A few seconds later, Jane quietly put the phone down, turned to her mum and me and burst out crying. 'It's positive!' she cried. Jane and I ran up the stairs together and we both shed tears of joy.

But I was also very concerned. Neither of us seemed ready to bring a baby into the world but that wasn't the only problem on my mind. I told her I'd better go downstairs and break the news to her father but Barbara stopped me, saying it would be better coming from her.

I thought how awkward it would be going back to work with George. The next day he was working away under the floor-boards while I wondered what his reaction was going to be once his wife revealed our secret. His beloved daughter, who he idolised, was pregnant. I thought, 'George will probably bury *me* under those floor-boards if only he knew what I'd done to Jane!'

Barbara broke the news to her husband while I was training with Northwich Vics. When I got back to their place later that evening we all sat around the television. Jane had mentioned to me that her father had now been told of her pregnancy and I just sat there worrying and waiting for him to say something. But he never uttered a word to me that night.

The next morning, over breakfast, George asked me to pass him the sugar, before calmly adding the following ice-breaker: 'What have I told you, son, about losing your ball control!'

It was a relief to hear his joke and he went on to explain that while he wasn't happy about his daughter's pregnancy, he and Barbara would help us in any way possible.

Jane wanted to be married before the baby was born, so we set our wedding date for January 14, 1983, at Prescot registry office. The financial predicament I found myself in at such a young age was the catalyst for my success as a footballer. I had a wife and a child to look after and because we were skint, every game from then on became like a cup final for me. I realised my responsibilities and wanted a better life for my wife and child. There was even more of an edge to my game now.

George and Barbara were a great help. Jane's dad gave me his car – a Ford Cortina Mk11 – which I drove around for months before I'd even taken my driving test. I had no insurance, the car was a horrible gold colour and it was a death-trap. It would lurch violently left if you didn't have both hands on the steering wheel. How I passed my test I'll never know, because I'd had no driving lessons. I can only assume that the fact that my examiner was called Mike Ward did me a favour.

For all its flaws, though, George's old banger was a big help to me. It gave me independence and meant I no longer had to rely on my mate Tony Murphy for transport.

The team started to string together good results, especially in the cup competitions. We progressed through the early rounds of the FA Cup and landed a plum draw against Chester City at their

Sealand Road ground – my first competitive match against Football League opposition.

Determined to maintain Northwich's impressive cup pedigree, we went to Chester confident and came away with a creditable draw. The evening replay at Drill Field was nearly called off – the pitch was a bog and the rain fell relentlessly throughout the game. Johnny King decided to play me up front in the replay. I was feeling much stronger and definitely a little quicker as I scored two goals in an excellent 3-1 victory.

The second goal came from a ball over the top of their defence, which I latched on to, scampering across the ploughed field before burying a shot past their keeper. As I celebrated, I saw George and Jane standing by the corner flag, looking absolutely soaked. Jane was heavily pregnant, and I immediately dedicated those two goals to her and our unborn baby.

The next day I made the headlines on the back of the national papers. It read 'Dole Kid Ward Sinks Chester' and Dad was so proud that I was getting recognition again after being shown the door by Everton.

Unfortunately, our run in the FA Cup ended in the next round at Scunthorpe United, where we were unlucky to lose 2-1. It was after this defeat that John King told me that a number of league clubs were interested in me. But he immediately made it clear that he wouldn't let me go just for the sake of it. He wanted me to go to a decent club, one that would look after me and help me to progress. 'Keep the fire in your belly, Mark, and you'll be okay,' he'd say.

We were still in the FA Trophy and the lads were determined to put the disappointment of the previous season's semi-final defeat by Enfield behind them. We were due to play Kidderminster Harriers away in the first round on January 15 – the day after our wedding. Getting married the day before the game was not going to prevent me from playing, though. The way I saw it, the wedding day was an occasion for our families and friends to get drunk – I only had thoughts of playing the next day at Kidderminster.

I wish we could have been married in different circumstances. Jane

47

was heavily pregnant by now and she looked great on the big day. I've never regretted marrying her – it was the right thing to do.

The evening reception went well. George, who sang under the name of Earl Preston as lead vocalist with his group, the TTs (later to become the Realms), in the early '60s, got his old band together again and they helped to make a brilliant night of it with their medley of Beatles hits and other Merseybeat sounds. My father-in-law, George Spruce and his band were entertaining music lovers in Liverpool clubs such as The Cavern and earned a recording contract with Fontana before anyone had even heard of Lennon and McCartney. By early 1963, Earl Preston and the TTs were on the same bill as the Beatles, The Hollies, The Swinging Blue Jeans, The Dominoes and The Merseybeats.

Jane and I managed to get away early and head to the Shaftesbury Hotel in the city. We left the two families partying through the night back at George and Barbara's – and couldn't believe it afterwards to find out that there had been no fights!

Despite my determination to stay sober and fully focused on the cup-tie, John King was adamant he would pick me up himself from the hotel on the morning of the game. It was just a short journey through the Mersey tunnel from the Wirral where he lived. Kingy had become like a father-figure to me.

The 45-minute drive to Northwich, where our team bus was waiting to take us to Kidderminster, gave us the opportunity to have a good chat. John was well educated in the ways of football and talked common sense at all times. He had played for Everton and that was something that I, too, badly wanted to achieve.

In the dressing room before the first round tie at Kidderminster I got terrible stick from the lads about having got married and being 'under the thumb.' But the match went brilliantly for me. I scored twice in a 3-0 victory, with my strike partner Colin Chesters notching the other goal. Although my natural position was wide right, Kingy used me as both a striker and midfielder and the two different roles certainly enhanced my overall understanding of the game.

That opening round success sparked a superb run in our quest to reach Wembley. After further victories against Croydon, Bangor City (after a second replay) and a quarter-final win against Blyth Spartans, which also required a replay, we reached the semi-final again, this time against Dagenham. We were really wound up for the home-and-away tie and desperate not to experience the bitter disappointment of missing out on a trip to the Twin Towers for the second time in a year. We just edged the first leg at home – 3-2 – and although we knew the return clash at Dagenham was going to be tough, the Vics players were determined to get to fulfil our manager's dream of reaching 'Treasure Island'.

Dagenham were a good side and, once again, Kingy put me up front for a game played in front of a crowd of more than 3,000. I just wanted one chance to take us to Wembley and in the second half it came my way. I pounced on a through ball played over the top of the Daggers' defence. The pitch was hard and bobbly and as the ball bounced in front of me, it didn't fall kindly in my stride.

I'll admit it now, what I did next was cheating.

I used my hand to deliberately guide the ball forward into my path, before hitting an unstoppable right-foot shot that rocketed into the top corner of the net.

It wasn't blatant – nothing as obvious as Maradona's 'Hand of God' – but a few of the Dagenham players appealed and I fully expected the referee to disallow the goal. But my team-mates mobbed me, screaming 'We're on our way to Wembley!' And we were. My decisive, illegitimate goal was allowed to stand.

I was 20 years old and I'd already enjoyed a great year. I'd married my childhood sweetheart, somehow passed my driving test and I'd just found out that I'd been included in the England semi-pro squad. And, best of all, on March 30, 1983, I became a father when Jane gave birth to our beautiful daughter Melissa.

* * * *

I was determined to progress and make a full-time return to professional football, to resume where I'd left off at Everton. I just needed a manager to take a chance on me.

HAMMERED

With money tight at home, I pressurised Northwich to increase my wage to £60 a week and I also pushed the club to help me get a job. They came up trumps. One of Vics' directors, Alan Gleave, was sales director of the local Roberts Bakery, who were the club's main co-sponsors.

He created a role for me at the bakery as a checker, keeping tabs on all the bread trays that left the large site at Rudheath each morning. The bakery had been losing thousands of these trays each year but I found it an easy job.

I earned £120 a week at the bakery and, added to what I was getting as a player at Northwich, life became more manageable. I enjoyed getting up early to do a day's work and with our Wembley date looming, I became a bit of a local celebrity at the bakery.

The build-up to the big day – May 14, 1983 – was the most exciting time at the club since Vics reached the fourth round of the FA Cup in 1976-77, having beaten league sides Rochdale, Peterborough and Watford before going out to Oldham Athletic at Maine Road. We were rigged out with special suits for the grand occasion while the wives and girlfriends all got together to travel in their own bus to the game. There were constant rumours and reports linking me with Football League clubs before the end of the season – Crewe Alexandra and Scunthorpe United were mentioned in the press – but nothing distracted me from my burning ambition to be a Wembley winner.

In the tunnel before kick-off it was awesome, enough to make the hairs on the back of my neck stand up. I stood there, gazing up at the famous Twin Towers and kept telling myself that I wanted to be the best player on the pitch. My moment had arrived and I didn't intend to blow it.

Stan Storton, the Telford boss who had managed at Northwich in 1980-81, had done his homework. In the very first minute their left-back, Tony Turner, hit me hard and late with a disgraceful, over-the-top tackle that left my shin in a mess. A player would be banned *sine die* if he committed a tackle as violent as that today but it was clearly a deliberate ploy by Telford and Turner to put me out of the game. I cried out in anger at the realisation that I'd been reduced to a virtual passenger for the rest of the game.

I was gutted not just for myself, but for all my family and friends who had travelled south to support me. I just couldn't compete. We ended up losing the game 2-1 and I was bitterly disappointed. So much so that when the final whistle blew, I started to walk towards the tunnel. I remember an FA official trying to drag me back, saying: 'You can't just walk off, you've got to collect your medal.'

I just ignored him and kept on walking. I honestly didn't care about a loser's medal. I didn't want it.

When I reached the quiet solitude of the dressing room, I stripped off and got in one of the big individual baths to soak and mope. It seemed an age before my valiant team-mates, who had effectively played the whole game as 10 men, joined me back in the dressing room. I felt that I'd let them down.

Kenny Jones, Vic's all-time leading appearance record-holder, the man who had been quick to stick up for me when that nutter from Barnet tried to end my career, handed me my medal as I lay in the bath. I appreciated his gesture but I didn't want it and flung it to the other side of the dressing room.

Kenny went over to pick up my medal and handed it to me again. He said: 'If I can accept a medal, then so can you.'

His words made me come to my senses. I had so much respect for Kenny, both as a player and as a man. He ended up playing for the club 961 times, so who was I to petulantly toss my Wembley medal away like that, as if it meant nothing?

We drowned our sorrows late into the night after our Wembley woe. It would have been a fairytale finish to a great year for me if we'd won the FA Trophy but it wasn't the end of the world – either for me or Vics. Just 12 months later, the club returned to Wembley and after drawing 1-1 with Bangor City in the FA Trophy final, they won the replay at Stoke City's aptly named Victoria Ground. I was absolutely delighted for the players, supporters and everybody involved with this great, little club.

I don't have a great number of mementoes from my playing career but I do still have a copy of the *Northwich Guardian*'s souvenir cup final special and the club who gave me a route back into league football will always have a place in my heart.

HAMMERED

Just before the start of the 1983-84 season I received a phone call at home. It was the call I'd been waiting for – from a legendary centre-forward who I knew all about as a former Everton and England star. He was by then a young, up and coming Football League manager and he wanted to meet up for a chat in a Liverpool pub.

His name was Joe Royle, the boss of Oldham Athletic.

7. BAKER'S BOY LOSING DOUGH

OUR Billy was well into boxing and I'd work out with him and the other lads at the Whiston Higherside ABC Boxing Club in my efforts to be as fit as possible before the start of the 1983-84 season.

Their fitness regime was very gruelling and although I struggled to keep up with the others in the gym, I stuck at it because I knew it was definitely making me stronger. Billy kept himself very fit and I'd work on the pads and the bags in between some very strenuous exercises. But I'd particularly look forward to the road-run at the end of the session, knowing that none of the boxers could get near me when it came to running.

Boxing instilled discipline in Billy and, like many of the lads at the gym who also had a reputation for getting into trouble, the art of boxing no doubt helped to keep them on the straight and narrow.

Throughout our childhood we'd compete against each other. Being just over nine months older than Billy, I'd give him a head-start whenever we raced together. Dad would set Billy off from our house two minutes ahead of me. The usual course was over two and a half miles through the streets where we lived. We'd raced against each other many times and I'd always managed to reel my brother in before finishing back home.

But there was one memorable occasion when he got the better of me. I was tanking along, expecting Billy to appear in his usual place on a long stretch of road about half a mile from the finish. But, to my amazement, he was nowhere in sight. Had he gone faster than ever before or had I taken it too easy?

With so little distance left in which to catch him, I realised he'd done me for the first time. I approached our house convinced that I'd completed my fastest possible run, so how on earth had he beaten me?

Almost breathless, I entered the house and was stunned to find Billy sat with my Dad. 'What kept you?' my brother asked, with a smug grin on his face. Dad joined in, laughing and ribbing me for having finally lost out in a race against my brother.

I sat outside in the garden for a while feeling utterly devastated. Dad and Billy let me sulk for a good hour before admitting the truth. Just after Billy had left our street, he flagged down John Ashton, a lad we both knew who lived in the next road. He jumped into John's work's van and sped off, leaving me in hot pursuit of the Invisible Man.

Cruelly, they followed my progress around the streets and, with great timing, passed me in the nick of time to enable Billy to arrive back at home without having expended an ounce of effort.

I laughed when Billy owned up to his little scam and, deep down, I was happy because it confirmed that I hadn't been beaten fairly. I've always hated losing at anything and any defeat would leave me feeling depressed. My tenacity and will to win at all costs was going to be a massive ingredient in my future success as a footballer.

My earnings from the bakery in Northwich and part-time football for Northwich gave Jane and I the opportunity to buy our first home. We bought a two up, two down terraced house in Cronton Road, Whiston for what now seems the paltry sum of £15,500. She soon had the house looking spick and span and we were both very proud of it.

However, events were to change dramatically for both of us two weeks before the start of the new season. I was watching *Coronation Street* at home with Jane and Melissa when the phone rang.

'Hello, is that Mark?'

'Yes,' I answered.

'It's Joe Royle here, the manager of Oldham Athletic.'

My heart started pumping faster and I nearly dropped the phone. Joe went on to explain that he'd been monitoring my progress at Northwich and would like to discuss the possibility of signing me. We arranged to meet at The Baby Elephant pub in Woolton village at 6.00pm the very next day.

Feeling very elated, I gathered up my young wife and baby daughter and set off to tell our respective families about my possible life-changing phone call. We called first at Jane's parents and then I walked the short distance to The Watchmaker to tell Dad the news. He felt ecstatic and gave me a hug before drinking a toast.

That evening I spoke to John King, who confirmed that Oldham Athletic and their young manager Joe Royle would be ideal for me. He said he felt it was the right time for me to step up to the second tier of the Football League.

I couldn't sleep that night for thinking about my next day encounter with what could be my future manager. I'd already spoken to Roberts Bakery to agree the day off and my supervisor was very understanding and wished me all the best.

My drive to The Baby Elephant was nerve-racking. At the time I didn't think the rendezvous at a public house between a well-known football manager and a future signing was in any way unusual, but of course it wouldn't happen today. I made sure I arrived early and wanted to make a good impression on the former England centre-forward, who was a legend in the eyes of all Evertonians.

I bought myself a glass of Britvic orange juice and waited eagerly for Joe to arrive. The pub was very quiet at this time and seemed a good choice as a discreet meeting place – or so I thought.

The next minute, a group of six men sauntered in. I must have looked stupid, sat in a pub at 6.00 in the evening with an orange juice in front of me.

'Hey, Wardy, what the f*** are you doing in here?' I heard a voice shout. It was Gary Reid, a lad I knew well. He'd just finished work and was having a pint with his work-mates before heading home.

Woolton is a posh part of Liverpool and I didn't expect to see Reidy, or anybody else who knew me, in there. Before I could explain to him why I was looking uncomfortable supervising nothing stronger than an orange juice, Big Joe walked through the door, I stood up to greet him and then sat back down with six pairs of eyes fixed on the famous former Everton number nine. Three of Reidy's gang politely asked Joe for his autograph and he duly obliged. Reidy had obviously cottoned on to what was happening and shouted at Joe to 'sign him on!'

Explaining why he wanted me to sign for him at Oldham Athletic, Joe immediately put me at ease. He said that he and his scouts had been looking at me for some time. There was a hitch, though. The Oldham board of directors were not happy about him wanting to sign a non-league player for as much as £9,500. With those doubts about my ability to make the grade, Joe said the wage he could offer me would be a miserly £130 a week.

He seemed embarrassed by the financial offer. At first it didn't register with me because I was willing to sign for nothing. To play full-time professional football again had been my target ever since my release from Everton and here was Joe Royle offering me that golden opportunity.

I told him that it would mean having to take a £70 per week drop in wages to resume playing full-time. My combined earnings from the bakery and Northwich were £200 a week. A lot of players at the better non-league clubs were substantially better off if they were in full-time employment, sometimes earning far more than many full-time pros, so it was something for me to think about.

Joe guaranteed me that if – and it was a big 'if' – I progressed and played for the Oldham first team on a regular basis, then I could approach him for a pay rise. That was good enough for me and I told him I'd sign.

He looked pleased but, before he left, I made a statement that made him laugh. I promised him that I'd become his best player. He smiled and said he admired my confidence, shook my hand and told me he'd see me at Oldham's Boundary Park ground the next day, when we would complete the transfer formalities.

By this time, word had got round that Joe Royle was in The Baby Elephant. I passed the growing crowd clamouring for his autograph and wondered to myself if those same Everton fans would ever wait around to get my signature one day.

8. ROYLE APPROVAL

IT felt good to be part of a professional club again. I distinctly remember my first training session with Oldham Athletic. The 1983-84 season was just around the corner and my initial involvement as a Latics player was a practice match between 'The Probables' – those expected to play in the opening home game against Brighton & Hove Albion – and 'The Possibles'. I was put in the so-called weaker 'Possibles' team, although I was determined to quickly make my mark.

I was fearless. Playing with better players gave me even greater confidence and I knew from that first practice session that I was as good, if not better, than most of my new team-mates. That sounds arrogant, but I honestly found the transition from non-league to Football League Division Two quite easy.

In the days leading up to the first game of the new season I remember thinking that I'd be disappointed if Joe Royle – who had taken over from Jimmy Frizzell the previous year – didn't start me against newly-relegated Brighton, who had taken Manchester United to an FA Cup final replay just a few months earlier. I knew I was the best player he had available to play in my usual wide right-midfield position but would the manager take the chance to start his cheap, new non-league signing?

I needn't have worried. On the eve of the Brighton game Joe pulled me to one side after our last pre-season training session. He told me how I'd amazed him with my fitness levels and noted how comfortably I'd coped with the step up in class. 'You're in for tomorrow, son,' he said and wished me all the best.

I was convinced Joe had made the right decision. As far as I was concerned, it wasn't a gamble to start me on the right wing. I was full of confidence and couldn't wait to get back to Liverpool to tell Jane and Dad that I'd be making my league debut the following day.

HAMMERED

Making his Oldham Athletic bow alongside me on that afternoon of August 27, 1983 was the Manchester United and Scotland international Martin Buchan, an exceptional player and leader of men who was capped 34 times for his country. Joe had pulled off a transfer coup by persuading this cultured footballing centre-half to sign for the Latics on a free transfer from Old Trafford, having played more than 450 games for United over the previous 11 years.

Martin immediately made a big impression on all of us. He had this tremendous presence and whatever he said, about football or anything else, made sense. Even in training he looked immaculate and proved to be everything I'd read about him over the years. To play consistently well for Manchester United and represent his country with distinction for more than a decade was an achievement in itself, so it was a privilege for me to be making my league debut alongside a player of Martin's undoubted class.

Joe had put together a team with a fine blend of experience and youth. There was the excellent ex-Manchester City centre-half and captain Kenny Clements, enigmatic striker Roger Palmer, up and coming future Scottish international goalkeeper Andy Goram and local youngster Darron McDonough.

Among a crowd of 5,750 I brought along my own small entourage of Jane, Dad, brother Billy and father-in-law George. I was about eight weeks short of my 21st birthday and Dad had told me before the game not to be intimidated and to go out and enjoy the moment I'd been striving so hard for.

Every footballer remembers his league debut. It's a special game, an historical landmark in one's career. Some debuts are triumphant occasions to savour while others can be disastrous. I couldn't have planned mine any better.

It was a typically tight early season encounter, with players still finding their fitness, touch and trying to gain an understanding with their new team-mates. I saw plenty of the ball and was feeling pleased with my contribution as the game drifted towards a goalless draw.

We kept putting Brighton under severe pressure in the closing moments, though, and when Darron McDonough flicked on a long ball, I'd already started my run in to the penalty box. Brighton keeper Graham Moseley moved off his line and towards the ball but, out of the corner of his eye, he must have seen me diving horizontally to try and head it before he could get there. The ball seemed no more than six inches off the ground. Moseley was definitely favourite to get there before me and if he'd continued to advance off his line, there was going to be an almighty collision between us. Thankfully, he stopped and hesitated. What a mistake.

I met the ball full on my forehead, which sent it soaring into the top corner of the net. Picking myself up, I was immediately mobbed by team-mates. It was a truly wonderful feeling – unbelievable. The whistle blew before Brighton could even attempt a comeback.

A beaming Joe Royle was stood waiting for me at the side of the Boundary Park pitch. He knew in that dramatic final minute of the game that he'd made another very astute signing.

Radio Piccadilly interviewed me straight after my debut. And during the drive back to Liverpool I cringed as Jane, Dad, George and I listened to my babble on the airwaves, with me struggling to put into words how great it felt to score on my debut. I don't know if it's a Scouse thing or what, but in between every sentence I heard myself repeating the phrase 'you know'. I'd go: 'Well, you know, the ball was crossed from the left . . .' and . . . 'you know, I just dived and got my head to the ball.'

The Sunday papers made for satisfying reading, although I didn't allow myself to get carried away by that headline-making start and remained keen to listen, learn and work even harder to improve my game. I was hungry for more success and I just needed to secure my position in the team every week to achieve it. Dad kept telling me that there was more improvement to come.

One of the conditions of my transfer was an extra £25,000 to be paid to Northwich Victoria after I'd completed 25 games in the blue of Oldham and I was delighted that the good people at Drill Field didn't have to wait too long to benefit from the add-on clause. Although they were one of the most successful non-league teams in the country on the field, like almost all part-time clubs, they faced a constant struggle to balance the books. As their biggest asset at the time, my transfer at least did Northwich some financial good.

Having been in the side for a couple of months, Big Joe pulled me aside after training one day and said how delighted he was by my attitude and the start I'd made. He went on to say that the £9,500 Oldham initially paid for me was the best money he'd spent on a player. With that, I seized the opportunity to remind him of the wage rise he'd promised me at our first meeting in the pub. He fully agreed that I should be on more money, saying I'd done the business on the pitch and was already worth a lot more than the club had paid for me.

I'll always be grateful to Joe Royle for putting his faith in me. He defied the wishes of the Oldham board to sign me and gave me the chance to prove myself again as a pro. His judgement in signing me had been well and truly vindicated, even though I'd played only about 10 games when we agreed that my pay rise was in order.

I wanted £350 per week, and Joe was all in favour, but there was a stumbling block. He told me that chairman Ian Stott was willing to offer me only £250 per week. I was hurt and angry when I heard. I pointed out that based on the club's valuation, I'd be only £50 per week better off for having moved from Northwich to Oldham.

I was mad and, believing that you should always stand up for yourself and what you think is right, I told Joe that I needed to see the chairman. He organised a meeting with him for the following day but warned me not to expect any change from Stott. I hadn't been at Oldham long enough to get to know the chairman but I was determined to push all the boundaries to get the £220 per week increase that I felt I deserved.

Stott saw me in his office after training. He was very businesslike and straight to the point. He said: 'You've had a great start to your career here at Oldham but don't get carried away. I believe that £250 is a fair wage for you at this moment in time.'

Reminding him that I was the club's best player, I also pointed out that Oldham had paid a pittance for me and I was earning a meagre wage. I said that I'd already proven myself and warned him that if I didn't get the £350 I was seeking, I'd walk away from the club.

He seemed taken aback by my stance. 'You can't do that – you're under contract,' he said with apparent alarm in his voice.

It was a case of calling his bluff. He tried to intimidate me by saying that Oldham Athletic would retain my registration, which would effectively prevent me from joining another League club. I responded by saying that I'd just go and play Sunday morning football in a park with my mates back in Liverpool.

I left Ian Stott's office feeling very pleased with the solid stance I'd taken but, privately, I felt worried about the possible outcome of our strained contract talks. If I'd had an agent to look after me early on in my career I would have been on far higher wages than I was ever paid. Before players began employing agents to represent them in the late 80s, the clubs had them over a barrel.

I drove home to tell Jane what was said in my meeting with the chairman. She was worried that I'd provoked a situation that could endanger my career and our family's livelihood but, as it turned out, we had no cause for concern. I was about to go to bed that evening when the phone rang. It was Joe Royle – to say that the chairman had agreed to pay me what I'd wanted.

'Mark, whatever you said to him changed his mind,' said Joe, who added that he was pleased for me and thought I deserved every penny of the £350 per week.

Ian Stott knew I was becoming a big asset for the club. For the sake of another £100 a week, it was far better for all concerned to pay me the money I deserved, because he knew he would eventually realise a substantial return on the original investment.

* * * *

I'd settled in really well with all the other players at Oldham. And when Joe signed Mickey Quinn from Stockport County in January 1984, I had a ready-made mucker. Mick was from the tough district of Liverpool called Cantril Farm – or 'Cannibal Farm', as this '70s council estate is also known.

Every week Mick, Joe McBride, an ex-Everton youngster who joined us from Rotherham United, and I would share the driving duties from

HAMMERED

Liverpool to Oldham and back. Joe had a brand new Volkswagen Golf convertible, Mickey had a big, white Ford Granada and I had . . . 'The Pram'. It was Mick who christened my Ford Escort Mk II – a real dog of a car, it has to be said – The Pram because we were always having to push it after it had broken down.

I thrived on training and loved every minute of it, even Tuesdays – running day. As we usually had Wednesdays off, Joe Royle and Billy Urmson, the first team coach, would make sure they got their pound of sweat from us all, sending us on a long-distance run up the hill in Oldham, followed by endless sprints. At first I really struggled and would spew up my breakfast every Tuesday after pushing myself to the limit. Joe would stand over me and say: 'What have you had for breakfast this morning, son? Come on, let's see it . . .'

My travel arrangements to Oldham soon put a strain on my relationship with Jane. By getting a lift with either Joe McBride or Mickey Quinn, it meant I was at the mercy of them and their social itinerary. If they fancied a pint in Oldham after training, then I had to go with them or get the train home.

A few of the players would nearly always meet at the top of Boundary Park Road for an excellent pub lunch in the White Hart. We were a right little firm of drinkers – Mickey, Joe, Andy Goram, Darron McDonough and myself. We all liked a bet too, especially Mick and Andy.

It's well documented that gambling is an inherent footballer's disease. It comes with the territory. We'd study the *Sporting Life* as soon as we met up in the dressing room each morning before training began and decide our selections over steak and kidney pie and chips in The White Hart afterwards. Perhaps it was no surprise when, years later, Mickey – who later enjoyed cult hero status as one of Newcastle United's famous Number Nines – appeared on TV's *Celebrity Fit Club* and wrote a book titled *Who Ate All The Pies!*

We'd bet in the region of £20-£40 a day. This was the time when I believe gambling took a hold on Andy Goram, who, even so, still went on to have a brilliant career with Rangers and Scotland.

As honest as he is, it was well known that Andy was a big punter. On the other hand, after his long and distinguished playing career ended,

Mickey used his brain and extensive knowledge of racehorses to forge a second career. He became a successful horse racing trainer, producing more than 40 winners from his stables at Newmarket, as well as being a respected horse and football radio pundit for TalkSPORT. Like me, Mickey has done time in jail but I really admire this great character for what he has achieved.

Looking back, though, at the way we put away unhealthy food, drank pints of lager and gambled on the horses each day, such an undisciplined lifestyle would never be tolerated by any football club today. But in those days, none of us stopped to think that the way we conducted ourselves was wrong or damaging to our careers. And the clubs themselves did little or nothing to discourage players from indulging in their various vices.

Whenever we played away, the fridge on board the Oldham team bus was fully stocked with beer. If we'd been playing a match in, say, London or the south, by the time we got off the bus back at Boundary Park later that evening, I would hardly be able to stand up. How the three of us then managed to drive back home to Liverpool on a regular basis, I'll never know. But this carefree routine became the norm.

Not that Jane would ever get used to it. She wasn't happy about me coming home late and stinking of beer. My lame excuse, that I had no choice because I was a passenger in one of the other lad's cars, didn't wash with her.

Darron McDonough would often try and keep us out in Oldham. A local lad made good, he knew all the best drinking haunts in town. But Darron was forever getting into scraps. It was a regular occurrence for him to come in for training on Monday morning sporting a black eye. Joe Royle would say to him: 'Lost one again?' But Darron could handle himself in a scrap, and he'd quickly answer the manager back: 'You should see the state of the other fella!'

There was a violent 80s cult movie out on video at the time that we played regularly on the coach to away games. It was called *Class of 1984*, about a punk gang inflicting terror on the teachers and pupils of a lawless inner-city high school in America. After watching it, Joe Royle started calling our little group 'The Class of 84'.

HAMMERED

Much of my time at Oldham was spent in the company of fellow Scouser Mickey Quinn. We hit it off straight away and he had a wicked sense of humour. Mick's dad, 'Old Mick' as we knew him, had a pub in Cannibal Farm called the Tithe Barn. I would regularly visit there with Mick to see his father. On Mondays – or 'Mad Monday' as it was known – the place was packed full. Many of the customers were there to spend a large chunk of their giro, while those who were lucky enough to have a job would be off work that day to recover from their weekend binge.

Many a time Mickey and I would turn up intending to have just one or two quiet shandies. But once we stepped foot inside the Tithe Barn, we invariably stayed until the early hours of the next morning. With its karaoke and disco, Old Mick ran a great pub and his lager was always spot on. We called the Tithe Barn the 'Bermuda Triangle'. Once inside the place, you went missing for hours.

These days Mick runs the popular Black Angus pub in Cannibal Farm. I took former Everton favourite Duncan Ferguson there one night in the mid-90s to introduce him to Old Mick and Mickey's brother, Mark Quinn. I was player/coach at Birmingham City at the time and I realised the big fella needed some good people around him. They looked after Big Duncan and I'm pleased to say that he remains a good friend of the Quinns to this day.

We did get into some scrapes at Oldham, though. One night after a game, Mick and I were in the local Brannigans nightclub with Darron McDonough. I ended up on Mickey's shoulders, being carted around the dance floor. Suddenly he slipped and I landed on top of him. He said instantly: 'My ankle's f****d'.

I even had to drive him home in his big, white Granada, which I called 'The Ambulance'. I dropped him off and he was s******g himself because he knew he wouldn't be fit for Oldham's game on the following Tuesday night. Mick was our star striker and banging in the goals for fun. How was he going to explain his injury to Joe Royle? He couldn't very well tell him the truth: 'Wardy was on my shoulders in Brannigans and I slipped'.

The best excuse he could come up with was that he was out walking the dog and slipped off the kerb.

Mick and I were both very competitive and it came to a head one day in training. A young apprentice gave me a right kicking down the shin and Mick started laughing. I got my revenge as usual. I went in hard on the youngster and kicked both the ball and him into the air.

Mick thought I was out of order and we squared up to each other. Before we knew it, we were both rolling around in the mud. It's surprising how your emotions can sometimes boil over in a practice game and lead you to scrap with your best mate at the club. Mickey was a big, powerful man and under normal circumstances I'd be a fool to take him on, but thankfully our little skirmish was broken up before any blood was spilt.

Trudging dejectedly back to the dressing room after it had all cooled down, I suddenly remembered that I'd travelled into training that morning in The Ambulance. I showered and heard all the lads stirring it up in the dressing room. Darron offered to drop me off at the train station, while Andy Goram said he'd bring in some boxing gloves so that we could have the second round of our bout the following day. The train looked like my best option but, just as I grabbed my bag and thought about heading for the station, Mick tapped me on the shoulder, stuck out his hand and said: 'Let's go for a pint, Wardy.'

We left the ground and got p****d, never mentioning our silly little fracas again.

I've always said that players don't make friends in football because of the nature of the business. Acquaintances, yes – and many of them, because you go from club to club. But I can honestly say that Mickey Quinn and I were real buddies.

Our gambling on the horses was not really a means of making money – of course, we all lost over a period of time – but it became part and parcel of everyday life. Much more than having a punt in the local bookies, we all loved an afternoon at Haydock Park racecourse. Once we had a real race against time to get there for the first race. Joe Royle had got word of our intentions and had deliberately prolonged the training session even more than usual. When it was finally over, the lads concerned raced off the pitch, dived into the shower and rushed to The Ambulance.

I jumped in the back while Darron got in the passenger seat. But before Mick could reverse his car, I leapt out to go back into the dressing room to retrieve the bag I'd forgotten, leaving the rear door of the car open behind me. Even so, Mick still decided he would turn the car around to save precious time. He was in the process of reversing the big Granada just as I stepped back outside onto the pavement, only to witness the metal crunching sound of the door being crushed against a concrete lamp post.

Mickey shot out of the driver's seat while I apologised to him for leaving the door open. He told me to shut up and get in the back seat. But the door so badly buckled that it was impossible to close it. With all the strength he could muster, an angry Mick kicked the damaged door into submission until it was flush with the rest of the car. It still wouldn't shut properly, though, so I was instructed to hold on to the door handle tight inside while seated in the back.

Mick drove like a raving lunatic, flying down the M62 and breaking all sorts of speed records to try and make it to Haydock in time for the first race. I used all the strength I had to hold on to the door, hoping it wouldn't fly open on the motorway. Mick kept saying he had a 'certainty' in the first and that if it won, it would pay for the damage and a new door.

Arriving at the racecourse in record time, we were confronted by large queues to the car parks. 'Wardy, we're going to try and blag our way into the jockeys' car park,' announced Mick. 'If anybody asks, you're a jockey.'

Darron burst out laughing at the thought of me trying to pass myself off as the Tony McCoy of the '80s but I had no choice but to agree to the scam as Mick was stopped at the entrance by the first car park attendant. Typically, Mick reeled off the patter.

'Sorry, Guv, we're in a mad rush.

'I've got a jockey in the back. We've had a slight accident on the way and he's riding in the first race.'

And off we went into the jockeys' car park. I remember Mickey having £100 on the horse he fancied at odds of 5/1. It won pulling a train and not only did it pay for his car door to be fixed, it set us up for yet another great day of fun at Haydock Park.

* * * *

Although well established in the first team in my wide right position, I was still learning the game all the time. The older pros, especially Martin Buchan and Kenny Clements, looked after the younger players and would tell us to calm down if they thought we were getting out of hand. I had a lot of respect for them both.

Captain of Manchester United's 1977 FA Cup-winning side against Liverpool and veteran of Scotland's 1974 and '78 World Cup finals adventures, Martin set the highest standards in every sense. I remember him interrupting one half-time team-talk to administer a dressing down to Jon Bowden, our young central midfield player. With Joe Royle in full flow, Martin stuck up his hand and asked the manager if he could interrupt him to say something.

Martin had noticed Jon spitting on the dressing room floor. He looked across and asked him: 'If you were at home, would you spit on the floor?' Jon seemed surprised by the nature and timing of this question and admitted that, of course, he wouldn't do it at home.

'Then don't do it in here then,' a furious Martin told him. 'We have to walk across this floor and we don't want to stand in your filthy mess.'

I thought it was great of Martin to address this disgusting habit. That's what he was like – a man of few words but whenever he did open his mouth, he spoke intelligently and for the right reasons.

Sadly, Martin struggled with a bad thigh injury and decided to hang up his boots later that season. Before going on to briefly manage Burnley, he invited all the lads to join him for farewell drinks at his local wine bar in Manchester. I arrived with Mickey, Joe McBride, Andy Goram and Darron McDonough but all the other lads eventually turned up too.

To our amazement, we were greeted by Martin sat on a stool holding a guitar. He could play it too. The highlight of a wonderful evening was a duet between Martin, on guitar, and Mickey, on vocals, singing the Del Shannon hit *Runaway*. It was such a memorable performance that everyone in the bar was cheering at the end.

* * * *

By the end of season 1984-85, I'd managed to play in every competitive game in my two seasons with Oldham – 84 league and 12 cup matches. There were rumours that bigger clubs wanted to sign me but I was enjoying life with the Latics and also looking forward to the pre-season break and spending time in Spain with Jane and Melissa.

Once again, though, Joe Royle would surprise me with another phone call out of the blue before the start of the 1985-86 season.

9. HAPPY HAMMER

IT was early evening on Tuesday, August 13, 1985 and Joe Royle was phoning me again. He asked if I was sitting down because he had some great news to tell me. He said that John Lyall, the West Ham United manager, would be at my house within the hour to pick me up.

He went on to add that the Oldham Athletic board of directors had agreed a fee of £250,000 for my transfer to the Hammers.

I was speechless for a few moments and then my heart began to race with excitement. His call had come out of the blue.

Joe asked if I was okay and then said that he trusted John Lyall to look after me and that first division West Ham would be great for me. He mentioned their tremendous history and referred to them as a family club with tradition and values.

I turned to Jane and told her to start packing. She was overwhelmed at first: 'What about Melissa?' she asked, saying that she didn't want to move to London. Her tears started and as I tried to calm her down, I got her dad George on the phone and he was ecstatic for us. He agreed that this move would be a life-changing experience for us both and reassured his daughter that both he and Jane's mum would collect Melissa and look after her until the signing was completed.

I couldn't believe that a renowned top flight manager was going out of his way to personally pick me up and drive me back to London with him. Joe Royle stressed to me that John Lyall wanted me to sign the next day, so I could make my debut on the Saturday.

Before we had time to finish packing there was a knock on the door of our house. Jane was as nervous as me at meeting my future manager for the first time and she was still crying. I opened the door to be greeted by John and his chief scout Eddie Baily. I'm a great believer in first impressions and John and Eddie both made an instant impact on us both as men with great presence.

HAMMERED

Jane was still wiping her eyes dry as John told me to put the kettle on. I instantly left for the kitchen to start making tea for our two guests. By the time I returned to the living room, Jane was much happier, laughing even, and in deep conversation with John and Eddie. The whole atmosphere became much more relaxed.

John started telling me how many times Eddie had been to watch me play and why they had travelled all the way up from Essex. He wanted me to make my debut for the Hammers in the opening game of the season at Birmingham that coming Saturday.

He was absolutely brilliant. He told me that his car should be okay parked in the street because he had just given a scally a pound to look after it. We all laughed – but he wasn't joking. As we left the house to begin our journey south, there stood by John's gold Jaguar was a snotty-nosed kid. John ruffled his hair as he walked past him and said: 'Thanks, son.'

I've always maintained that John's gentlemanly manner and the way he treated Jane and I from the start had a massive bearing upon my success at West Ham. He was a man of great honour and integrity, the sort you automatically wanted to run through brick walls for.

I soon learnt that you could go and talk to John if ever you had a problem, no matter what it was. He ran the club from top to bottom. He oozed authority but the fact that he wanted to be addressed as 'John', and not 'Boss' or 'Gaffer', summed him up as a person. He quickly became a father-figure to me and always commanded my utmost respect.

John and Eddie kept us entertained with their stories on the drive to London. They informed us in detail of West Ham's history and the different characters on the playing staff.

Eddie told me of the games he had seen me play. One, in particular, was a recent pre-season friendly for Oldham against Runcorn. He said he was impressed with my attitude and tenacity and even though I scored a couple of goals, it was my all round game that took his eye. It was only last year that I learned from John's son, Murray, that I was the only player his father ever signed without actually having seen play before the deal was completed, which is some compliment to Eddie as well as me.

I knew I was in the presence of true professionals, although at the time I didn't know about Eddie's credentials. He'd been a tremendous inside-forward in his day, a star of Tottenham's championship side of 1951 and an England international before returning to White Hart Lane as Bill Nicholson's right-hand man. He knew his stuff.

Jane and I were dropped off at the Bell House Hotel in Epping. Joining an east London club, we had imagined that we'd end up being abandoned in the middle of a concrete jungle, but the opposite was true. Within a few hours, we were in beautiful rural Essex, surrounded by forestry and green fields – a world away from the little cobbled street we'd just left behind. After John and Eddie had made sure that we'd checked in at the hotel okay, the Hammers boss left by saying he'd pick me up in the morning and take me to Upton Park to sign my contract.

That first evening in the hotel was unreal. Everything had happened in the space of a couple of hours. One minute I was at home watching *Coronation Street* and an hour later I was on my way to London with the West Ham manager and one of the shrewdest tactical brains in the game. I had to pinch myself and couldn't sleep that night. The events of the day and the anticipation of what was to come were too much for me.

Jane was coming round to the fact that we'd be spending at least the next couple of years of our lives in London, or Essex to be more precise, and I think John's approach had calmed and reassured her. We made phone calls back home to Liverpool, where our families and friends wished us both all the luck in the world.

I started to think of the transfer fee – £250,000 (£225,000 up front and a further £25,000 after I'd played 25 games) was a lot of money for a 22-year-old youngster who had played for just two seasons in Division Two. It was only two years previously that the board at Oldham were questioning Joe Royle's decision to pay £9,500 for me. I was being bought as a direct replacement for Paul Allen, who had left for Spurs in a £400,000 deal that summer, so I knew it was going to be a massive challenge for me but one I relished.

After breakfast in the Bell House, John arrived bang on time to pick me up. We were going first to Upton Park to sign the contract and then on to the club's training HQ at Chadwell Heath to meet the players. When we arrived at the ground John told me he was signing another player that day. It was Frank McAvennie, from Scottish club St Mirren. I'd never heard of him, and he'd probably never heard of me, but you couldn't miss the lad with the ginger hair, dyed blond.

Frank was already waiting outside John's office when we were introduced. We hit it off instantly and although Frank's broad Glaswegian accent was a struggle to comprehend at first, we were soon talking the same language – football. Like myself, he was excited about playing at the top level of English football for the first time and the little known Jock and the Scouser would be the only new faces brought to West Ham before the start of the 1985-86 season. Frank and I would become good mates on and off the pitch but the West Ham faithful didn't have a clue who John Lyall's new signings were and neither did most of our team-mates.

I was called into John's office and simply signed the contract he pushed in front of me. He mentioned that if I produced the goods on the pitch, then I would be looked after financially. I had very little experience in signing contracts, although Frank mentioned he had an advisor. Very few players employed agents to represent them at the time but it didn't concern me anyway. I trusted John to look after me and I signed without hesitation. Money was not important at that time – I just wanted to play and become successful.

My wage had crept up to £500 per week with bonuses. The bonus became a big talking point during that season after the players held a meeting to consider two options on offer to us.

We could either accept a fixed £50 per league point or link our bonuses to home attendance figures. If we did well, then crowds would increase and the players would get a cut of the gate depending on the size of the crowd.

There was a vote by the players and Tony Cottee, Frank McAvennie and myself favoured the £50 per point system. The older brigade, including Phil Parkes, Tony Gale and Alvin Martin, wanted to opt for the crowd bonus. But the points incentive system was the one that we agreed on for that season.

It seemed a wise choice as the fans, probably underwhelmed by the club's lack of major summer signings, were slow to turn out at Upton Park in the early weeks of the season. The games against QPR (15,530), Luton Town (14,004), Leicester City (as low as 12,125) and Nottingham Forest (14,540) were poorly attended compared to the second half of the season, when crowds virtually doubled. As that memorable season unfolded and we set about attempting to win the championship for the first time in the club's history, the senior Hammers wouldn't let the three of us who opposed that idea forget our costly decision to force through a bonus scheme linked to attendances!

Chadwell Heath was a very impressive training ground – a world apart from the facilities we had at Oldham. John took me into his office and ordered a young apprentice to go out on to the training pitch and bring back the club captain, English international centre-back Alvin Martin.

A few minutes later Alvin appeared, drenched in sweat, as John made the introductions. Alvin shook my hand and wished me all the best. Being a fellow Scouser from Bootle, the docks area of Liverpool, Alvin immediately took me under his wing and we became firm friends. Alvin and his wife Maggie became very important in helping Jane and I settle in London. Once a week we were invited over to the Martins' Gidea Park home for a meal and a beer. Maggie would cook a delicious steak Diane and it was good for Jane to have some female company.

Alvin gave me sound advice and he'd always stressed that West Ham fans wouldn't tolerate a player who didn't always give 100 per cent. Over the years the fans had destroyed players' careers with their abuse. I took everything he told me on board and I knew the fans would take to me. From what Alvin was saying, I felt confident the fans would appreciate my wholehearted approach to every game.

As you ran out at Upton Park, the opposite standing area was known as the Chicken Run. The fans were stood very close to the pitch and it was here that the most verbal supporters would congregate and give out ruthless stick to the opposition, or even one of their own if they thought he deserved it. I must say they never gave me a hard time and I loved playing for them.

I was looking forward to my first training session as a Hammer but I felt nervous. For the first time in my life, I felt out of my depth during that first session with much more experienced and senior players than myself. I didn't hold back and certainly got stuck in, but I was like a fish out of water. I found the pace, accuracy and precision of the passing unbelievable. The quality was something I'd not expected.

Obviously I knew I was going to be playing with far better players than ever before but this was mesmerising. The two centre-halves, Alvin Martin and Tony Gale, had the touch and vision of a skilful forward. I didn't get a kick. It was as if I'd been playing on another planet for Oldham. Every one of the lads moved the ball around with speed and their first touch was impeccable. Alan Devonshire, in particular, was outstanding. I realised I was going to have to improve and adapt very quickly if I was to get a run in the side.

After training I sat with the lads having lunch in the canteen and tried to suss out the dressing room characters. Straight away I identified the joker, the one who dished out the biggest stick to his team-mates. Tony Gale was nicknamed 'Reggie' after the notorious East End gangster Reggie Kray – not for being a hard case, but because of his brutal way with words that could cut his victims in half. But he was great company and always livened up the atmosphere of the place no matter where you were.

Frank McAvennie was initially put with me in The Bell at Epping and we hit it off instantly. On the other hand, Jane and Frank's girlfriend, Anita Blue, didn't get on. It didn't stop Frank and I becoming close mates, though. We roomed together on away trips and that was an experience in itself.

Frank's favourite pastime was to try and charm a waitress or hotel chamber maid into spending the night with him – and he was very successful at it. On one occasion he was chatting up the girl who was waiting on our table. She explained that her boyfriend would be picking her up when she finished her shift, so I told Frank to forget it and we left for our room. He wasn't easily put off, though.

Some of the players would take a mild sleeping tablet to help them sleep better the night before a match. I took my 'sleeper' as soon as I got back to the room and about an hour later I was drifting in and out of sleep when I heard Frank on the phone ordering sandwiches from room service. The young girl he'd been trying to chat up brought his order to the room and, despite the effects of the sedative, I vaguely remembered the blonde waitress creeping into bed next to Frank.

The next thing, I was fast asleep but when I opened my eyes in the morning, I was greeted with a mop of blonde hair falling over the side of Frank's bed. Nothing unusual in that – I assumed it belonged to my randy team-mate – but as I looked more closely, I noticed a pair of tits sticking upright in the air! I jumped out of bed, used the bathroom and told Frank I was going down for breakfast. Before I left the room, I suggested he got rid of his companion before first team coach Mick McGiven came knocking at the door.

Eagle-eyed Mick was one of John Lyall's trusted lieutenants and didn't miss a trick. I sat alone downstairs eating and thinking of Frank enjoying his 'breakfast' in bed. Mind you, to be fair to him, he scored on the pitch, too, that afternoon having played another blinder both on and off the field!

My debut for West Ham was against Birmingham City at St Andrews. It was a quiet start for me and we lost the game 1-0. I wasn't happy about my contribution and couldn't wait for my home debut against QPR on the Tuesday night. Frank and I were both eager to make a big impression on our new fans.

Frank had been bought for £340,000 as an attacking midfielder but striker Paul Goddard had picked up a nasty shoulder injury at Birmingham, so John Lyall decided to put Frank up front with Tony Cottee. It was a masterstroke that transformed our season. We out-played QPR on the night – 3-1 – and Frank scored twice, with Alan Dickens – a replacement for the injured Goddard – getting the third from my flighted cross.

I enjoyed the derby atmosphere under the lights and even though the attendance was low, there was something special about playing at Upton Park. I felt more confident after my display against QPR and, little did we know at the time, but the crowds would get bigger week by week during this record-breaking season.

Alan Devonshire was consistently outstanding on the left side of midfield, Frank and Tony Cottee had developed a great understanding and defenders couldn't cope with their pace. Alvin and 'Galey' were organised and disciplined at the back. They lacked a bit of pace but that didn't matter because they both read the game so well, were never caught out of position or by a ball played over the top and our midfield quartet would all drop deep to help the back four.

It suited our style perfectly because we hit teams on the break, especially away from home, with slick passing and movement. We played short, neat passes started from the back by our footballing centre-halves. Or Phil Parkes – one of the finest keepers in England – would throw the ball directly to the feet of either 'Dev' or myself. Or, alternatively, we'd collect it from our full-back – in my case Ray Stewart and in Dev's either Steve Walford or George Parris.

Alan Dickens was one of the most stylish, young midfielders in the country but the side had great balance, too. In the heart of midfield, it was down to our ball-winner, either Neil Orr or Geoff Pike, to win possession and feed the more creative players around them.

They reckon I was one of the first wing-backs in the English game before the phrase had even been invented but I never shirked responsibility and was happy to get up and down the right flank. If I wasn't attacking and looking to put in crosses for Frank and Tony, I'd be back defending in front of Ray. It was a real pleasure to be part of that side.

Ronnie Boyce, John's other coaching assistant, kept me back after training to work on my crossing. He would get a young apprentice to play up against me and I would practice taking him on and whipping low crosses into the near-post area. 'Boycey' had been a great player and loyal servant at West Ham for many years and he could still kick a ball. He was still good technically and showed me how it needed to be done.

With neither Frank nor Tony among the biggest target men, it was no good humping high balls into the box, so I practiced whipping crosses into the danger areas.

Cottee was exceptional in the penalty area, a deadly finisher and goal-poacher. He was so single-minded, even selfish at times, in his quest for goals but his impressive record speaks for itself.

Frank was more of an all round team player who would run his socks off for the team and look to come short and link the play. The two strikers complemented each other superbly, forging a formidable partnership that produced 46 league goals.

I only managed three goals myself, the most pleasurable coming in a 2-1 home win (Cottee got the other) at home against Manchester United in early February. It should have been four, though, because my disallowed strike in the League Cup defeat at Old Trafford should have stood. We were awarded an indirect free-kick but I let fly from about 25 yards and we were all sure United keeper Gary Bailey finger-tipped the ball on its way into the net. I'd scored from a similar distance at Oxford a few weeks earlier and was gutted that this one was ruled out.

The Sunday afternoon home win over United, played in front of the ITV cameras, was sweet revenge for that controversial cup exit earlier in the season. I was determined to make my mark in every way and apart from scoring our first after a neat set-up from Dev, I also got myself booked for slamming Kevin Moran into the Chicken Run wall.

* * * *

Living at the Bell was fun at first, an exciting new experience, but hotel life gets you down after a while. Frank had moved to a hotel in Brentwood and Jane had been struggling to settle, so she was constantly going back and forth to Liverpool with Melissa. What made it even more upsetting for her was that the house we'd left behind at Whiston was burgled and ransacked on the very night we'd travelled down in John Lyall's car. Local thieves must have read about my impending move in the *Liverpool Post* or *Echo*, realised the house would be empty for a few days and just went in and caused a big mess that father-in-law George had to clear up for us. I never went back to that house but Jane did on one of her trips home and it wasn't nice for her to discover the damage that had been caused to our former home.

To his credit, John Lyall would personally take Jane and I out after training to visit numerous estate agents in some of the best areas of Essex. What manager would do that for a new player these days?

After weeks living out of a hotel, it was becoming important to find somewhere more permanent and we eventually bought a nice three-bedroom, semi-detached house in Roundmead Avenue, Loughton, on the edge of Epping Forest, ideally located within easy reach of both Chadwell Heath and the club's main ground at Upton Park.

One day I went in The Standard pub in Loughton, put my name down for a game of pool and waited my turn. It had amazed me that the locals preferred to keep themselves to themselves and never bothered to talk to me. One lad recognised me, though, and before I knew it I had four pints lined up on the bar in front of me. It was a nice, friendly gesture on his part but it annoyed me to think that I was only accepted in the pub because I was a West Ham player, whereas if I'd been an unknown Scouser working locally as a joiner or brickie, then I would have been ignored.

I left feeling disgusted and walked over to the big pub in the village called The Crown, where I was greeted from behind the bar by a large figure of a man. This gentle giant talked with me for about half an hour and was really friendly and entertaining. It was Eddie Johnson, a well-known figure in the East End of London. I enjoyed his company and legendary tales about the Kray twins who he grew up with. I also used to go to the Lotus Club in Forest Gate, which was run by Eddie's brother Kenny.

Eddie introduced me to his wife Shirley and they would join Jane and myself on occasional nights out in London. Jane enjoyed trips to the West End, especially the shops.

Eddie and Shirley became very good friends of ours. Apart from being great company when we went out as couples, they would also kindly look after Melissa if Jane and I needed time out on our own.

It was around this time that I met Mick Tobyn, who remains my best mate to this day. Mick lived right beside our training ground and his two young sons, Gary and Danny, would be in the players' car park every day collecting autographs. It was before an away game at Coventry that I noticed the boys as I got off the team coach. I asked them if they had tickets and that's when Mick introduced himself to me. I gave them some complimentaries and invited all three of them to join me afterwards in the players' lounge.

I enjoyed Mick's company and invited him to be my guest at the next home game. I liked looking after the boys and Mick, who are true West Ham supporters. Some 24 years on, Mick and I still see each other as much as we can. He has been a true friend and I've been treated as one of his family ever since we met.

It took some time for Jane to settle down, though, and John Lyall soon became aware of the situation and made it his business to sort it out. He was alarmed one Friday when Mick McGiven brought it to his attention that I'd lost half a stone in weight in the space of seven days.

The players were all weighed by Mick, who would stand alongside the scales clutching his clip-board and pen, after training every Friday. Some of the bigger lads who had to work a bit harder to keep the pounds off, like Galey and Parkesy, were sometimes a little reluctant to step on the scales, but I was never far off 10st throughout my four and a half years with West Ham.

But on this particular Friday, I'd dipped by around seven pounds and he obviously mentioned this to the manager because John immediately called me into his office to find out what the problem was.

Jane had gone back to Liverpool for the week with Melissa to see her parents again and I hadn't eaten as much as normal while she was away. It wasn't as if I went without food out of neglect or because I couldn't be bothered to cook. Actually, I'm not bad in the kitchen. Eating just didn't appeal to me. I can easily go a day or two with hardly anything and, besides, I always liked to feel physically hungry before a game.

However, John demanded to know why I'd lost so much weight and when I explained that Jane had gone back to Merseyside for a week, he wasn't at all happy. 'Get her on the phone now – she's coming back,' he insisted.

HAMMERED

She was adamant that she wanted to return to Liverpool permanently at that stage but John was having none of it. I told him that Jane couldn't settle and it was putting a strain on our marriage. 'Right,' he said, 'I'll be at your house tonight at six o'clock.'

I opened the door to John, who strolled in and targeted my wife straight away: 'Forget the idea of moving back to Liverpool, lady,' he told her in no uncertain terms. 'I spent a lot of money on this man and to replace him would cost the club a fortune.'

Over a cup of tea Jane explained how she felt and how difficult it was for her living some 200-odd miles from home. John was very astute. He somehow managed to convince Jane that our future lay here – full stop. Just before he left he came out with the clincher – I was to receive a £100 per week wage increase. That put a smile on her face . . . 'more shoes', I thought!

An extra £100 per week wasn't a massive increase, especially as John insisted that I also had to extend my contract by another year. He had done a good night's work for all concerned in our home that evening.

The last thing John wanted was for any of his players to be distracted by worries off the field and his man-management skills were second to none. Despite Jane's homesickness, I was a very happy Hammer and revelled in my first season with the club. It had been a long, hard campaign but I couldn't wait for each game to come around.

Our final home match of that unforgettable season was against relegation-bound Ipswich Town. It was our ninth game in just 28 days during a breathless April in which we'd won seven of our previous eight games, and for the first time all season there were more than 31,000 fans packed inside Upton Park. The senior players who had favoured a bonus scheme based on crowd figures were cursing again but we were now within touching distance of the title and we all wanted to be part of West Ham history.

It didn't look good when Ipswich took an early lead but Alan Dickens equalised and then, with three minutes left, I earned the controversial penalty from which Ray Stewart scored the winner.

I've often been asked, did I fall or was I pushed when I darted between Town defenders Ian Cranson and Nigel Gleghorn and came crashing down by the byline at the North Bank end. It wasn't my style to cheat but let's just say that I did what I had to do.

All that mattered is that the ref awarded the penalty and Ray, as usual, stepped up and coolly put it away. The dramatic 2-1 win sparked wild scenes of delight on the Upton Park terraces and on the pitch after the game. We'd kept alive our title hopes. It meant the championship wouldn't be decided until the last Saturday of the season.

We thought our 3-2 victory at West Bromwich Albion the following Saturday would be enough to bring the league championship to West Ham for the first time in the club's history but it wasn't to be. Liverpool's 1-0 win at Chelsea clinched it for the Reds, which meant our last game – a 3-1 defeat at Everton – was meaningless, especially as UEFA had banned English clubs from entering European competition for five seasons following the Heysel tragedy a year earlier. How I would love to have gone 'home' to Goodison that Monday night still fighting for the title.

Still, to finish third in the old first division, four points behind Liverpool and two adrift of Everton, was no mean feat and the Hammers have never managed to finish as high in the top flight since then. If we hadn't made such a disappointing start to the season, failing to win any of our first seven league matches, then I'm convinced we would have done it.

Ever-present for my third successive season, I'd surprised myself by playing in all 42 league games plus the 10 cup ties – an ever-present record matched only by Tony Gale and Phil Parkes. I was lucky to be involved at a great club run by an equally great manager.

10. HARD MEN

MY personal battles against some of the hardest left-backs English football has ever seen were right up my street. I relished every minute of them.

I faced a number of quality left-backs in my time at West Ham, including Arsenal's 86-times capped England man Kenny Sansom, Nigel Winterburn (Wimbledon and Arsenal), Terry Phelan (Wimbledon), Derek Statham (West Brom), Tony Dorigo (Aston Villa and Chelsea), Paul Power (Everton), Jim Beglin and Barry Venison (both Liverpool) and Arthur Albiston (Manchester United).

But Mark Dennis (Southampton & QPR), Pat Van Den Hauwe (Everton) and Stuart Pearce (Nottingham Forest) are the trio I recall as the genuine hard men of my era when I was still an out-and-out right-winger.

Dennis pushed me flush on the nose, right in front of the dug-out, at The Dell and stood over me saying: 'You're not gonna get a kick tonight, you little c***.'

I knew of the former Birmingham City left-back's reputation and we had a good contest afterwards. It was bullying but opponents like Dennis could never intimidate me. If anything, players like him just sparked me into wanting to dominate my direct opponent even more.

Neither Van Den Hauwe nor Pearce ever resorted to verbal abuse or used wind-up tactics against me. Most of the time those who had plenty to say rarely carried out their threats in any case. But Van Den Hauwe and Pearce didn't need to be lairy in that way – they were already both physically intimidating enough.

West Ham fans like to remind me of my physical clashes with the tall, rugged Chelsea and Scotland left-back, Doug Rougvie. I loved my scraps with him and one night I stuck my fingers up his nose as we both tumbled to ground in front of the Chicken Run. To be honest, I felt sorry for him because it was me who was doing the bullying! Frank McAvennie wound me up before the game about getting stuck into Rougvie and that's what I did.

I'm not proud of everything I've done on the football field. I'll admit, I once took a bite out of Terry Butcher's back on the night his struggling Ipswich team came to Upton Park when West Ham were going for the league title. We both fell to the ground in a challenge and as the former England captain got to his feet, I bit him high up on the back. Well, I wouldn't have been able to reach him once he'd fully got to his feet! He went mad at me, called me all the names under the sun, but then we just got on with the game.

Afterwards, with Ipswich virtually condemned to relegation, Butcher vented his fury by kicking in the referee's dressing room door.

But, by and large, there was a lot more give and take between players back then. Chelsea's David Speedie was a little hard nut and I remember catching him in the groin after he came out worst in our 50/50 clash at Upton Park. My boot was raised high and I poleaxed him. But then I justified it in my mind by thinking that he'd have done the same to me.

A few weeks later, I happened to be on a night out in Stringfellows nightclub and bumped into a few of the Chelsea lads, including Speedie. 'Oi you, you little c***', he said after spotting me at the bar. He came over and playfully 'butted' the side of my head. I had a little, friendly dig back at him but within seconds Speedie was offering to buy me a drink. 'You're just like me,' he said.

Players of my era could get away with so much more than they can in the modern game, with 25 cameras scattered all over the stadium. Even if the ref and his assistants don't spot you doing something you shouldn't today, then the Sky cameras will.

Pat Van Den Hauwe would have probably faced a life ban from the game if Sky had been around when we played against each other! I remember him as Everton's lunatic left-back, a nasty bit of work who would just kick out and assault you off the ball. In the last game of the 1985-86 season we visited Goodison for the game that would decide second place in the championship race after Liverpool had clinched the title two days earlier.

We were outclassed by Everton on the night but that didn't deter 'Psycho Pat' from leaving his mark on me. With only minutes of this meaningless game remaining, Everton were cruising to an easy 3-1 win. The ball was on the opposite side of the pitch and Van Den Hauwe came in from the side and booted me high up in the groin area.

Everton skipper Peter Reid witnessed his team-mate's thuggish act and as I lay on the floor, 'Reidy' was trying to help me up. He was going mad at the loony left-back. I was no angel but I'm convinced Van Den Hauwe, who started at Birmingham and went on to play for Tottenham and Millwall, was not either.

Stuart Pearce deservedly gets my vote as the best full-back I ever played against. He was hard but fair. He'd try and intimidate you with his shorts rolled up showing off those massive thighs and when he tackled you it was all or nothing – the ball, you and everything that stood in his way.

His nickname 'Psycho' was undeserved, though, because he was class on the ball and just had an overwhelming desire to win. Pearce paid me one of the biggest ever compliments in his autobiography *Psycho*, published in 2000. He wrote: 'I am often asked who is the most difficult player I have ever faced over the years and people are usually surprised when I reply Mark Ward.'

Pearce was nearing the end of his playing days with West Ham in 1999, at the time his story was published, before going into management and coaching with Forest and then Manchester City. He went on to be a key member of Fabio Capello's England staff. Stuart went on: 'Even West Ham supporters seem surprised that I have picked out one of their less lauded Hammers rather than Marco Van Basten, for instance.

'Mark Ward was a direct little player who liked to run at you with the ball at his feet. It is probably through him that I have had more bad games at Upton Park than at many other places. I was up against him when I was substituted for one of the three times in my Forest career.'

Stuart Pearce played 570 league games for Coventry City, Forest, Newcastle United, West Ham and Manchester City. He was capped 78 times at senior level by England, many as captain since 1992. That compliment, from a player and a man of his immense stature in the game, meant a lot to me. I can assure him that our respect is mutual.

11. LONDON LIFE

THE turning point for Jane to settle in London was when I splashed out £1,800 and bought her a big, black Irish mare from Harvey Smith's son Robert, who had stables at Quendon in north Essex. Jane had owned a pony as a kid and always wanted another horse, one that looked like Black Beauty. We had 'Bridie' stabled nearby on a private estate in Epping Forest and her day to day involvement at the stables made life easier.

It was good to finally feel more settled as a family again when a negative article about me appeared in *The Sun* in October 1986, clearly suggesting I was missing Liverpool more than I actually was.

Journalist Steve Howard came to the training ground to interview me for what was intended to be a piece angled towards my claims for international recognition. John Lyall wasn't one for pushing his players publicly but early in my second season with the Hammers there was talk of me making Bobby Robson's England squad. John was great at handling the press and he agreed for Howard to come down to Chadwell Heath.

I did the interview and, naively, I let my guard down and mentioned how unsettled my wife had been since our move south. I thought nothing more about it until I saw the piece in the paper the next day under the headline 'Homesick Hammer!'

When John read it, he was furious and called me into his office demanding an explanation. He had just sold Paul Goddard to Newcastle United and the thought of the fans reading about another player wanting away from Upton Park was unacceptable to him. I'd never seen him so angry.

I tried to explain that I hadn't meant it to come out the way it read and that the quotes from me about missing our family and friends in Liverpool really concerned Jane rather than myself. I was very happy to be at West Ham. My off the cuff comments had been taken out of context and once I'd told John what had happened, he picked up the phone and called Howard's office to vent his fury. I only heard one side of the conversation between the journalist and my unhappy boss but John ended the call with the words 'Don't ever step foot inside West Ham again.'

I had to pinch myself at times. Life had changed so significantly for Jane and I. London life was so different to what we'd left behind in Liverpool. To give you a clearer insight into just how much it had changed, you need only look at the difference in property prices. Only a few months before my transfer to West Ham, after Oldham had increased my money and I'd signed a new contract, Jane and I bought a two up two-down in Whiston that cost £15,500.

The first house we bought following my move to the Hammers, in Roundmead Way, cost £73,000. We sold that about 18 months later for almost double the price – £140,000 – and moved into a lovely, four-bedroom detached in Rowans Way, Loughton. That one cost £250,000 – but please, don't anyone tell me what it's worth today, even in the midst of the latest slump in house prices!

I look back and believe that Jane would have been the original football WAG if only the phrase had been invented in the mid-80s. She was very fashion-conscious and loved shopping for clothes and shoes. Now she had her own horse, too. I tell you, she would have given the WAGs of today a run for their money!

Melissa had settled into her school and life couldn't have been better. My team-mates had all helped me in that first record-breaking season and I enjoyed every moment at the club. Socially, I didn't go out that much. London seemed such a huge place and the lads lived in all different parts of the capital. I was closest to Alvin Martin, my fellow Scouser, and enjoyed his company.

The players' Christmas parties were held at the Phoenix Apollo restaurant in Stratford. Panay and Gill, the two Greek lads who owned the place, looked after us big-time. It was a famous eatery that attracted plenty of TV stars and showbiz celebrities. All the most popular Page 3 girls of the day – Samantha Fox, Suzanne Mizzi and

Jenny Blyth – were regulars. Jenny was to become Frank McAvennie's bird and I knew they were destined for each other as soon as I saw her push her tits into his face after a game at Upton Park. Frank didn't need a second invitation and it was only a matter of time before they were shacked up together.

It was a good job I was happily married when I signed for West Ham. If I'd been single like Frank, I think I'd have found it hard to concentrate on the football with all the night life and women available.

Some of the players would go to the races and the dogs and it was at Walthamstow greyhound stadium where I presented a trophy to the winning owner of the last heat of the night. Each race that night was named after a West Ham player. It was a very boozy evening and by the time the last race came round, I was bladdered. The Mark Ward Stakes could have been won by a Jack Russell for all I knew!

The rest of the lads laughed their b******s off as I staggered over the sand to the centre of the track to present the trophy to the winning owner. That was just the start. Then it was off to Charlie Chans, the nightclub beneath the main grandstand, for more ale.

It was during my nights out with the lads that I was introduced to the lawyer Henri Brandman. He had a mate called Eamonn Connolly who was the property and racing manager for the 'porn baron' David Sullivan. I would regularly go to Newmarket, Sandown, Windsor and all the other racetracks in the south-east. I loved a bet and it was great to be invited in to the parade ring and meet the jockeys and other famous people. David Sullivan rarely went to the small race meetings, so when I could I would tag along with Eamonn. Jane loved the races, too. It was an opportunity for her to indulge her favourite hobby of dressing up.

One memorable boozy night out at Royal Ascot nearly ended disastrously for me, though, and it was my wife who nearly wrecked my career, if not my life.

After a great day at Ascot with Mick Tobyn and his girl Kathy, the four of us decided to have a meal at Winnigans, the nearby pub-restaurant owned by Alan Ball. We were all very drunk and for some reason Jane took offence to something I said. She stormed out of the pub and I quickly followed to see what she was up to. In seconds, she was behind the wheel of our BMW and had started the engine. I stood in front of the car and told her to get out and behave herself.

Without warning, she pressed the accelerator and before I could react I was thrown up and over the car and landed on my backside. She realised what she had done and put on the brakes, with my head resting against a rear tyre.

I heard Kathy screaming at what she had just witnessed. She thought I was dead. Amazingly, Jane put her foot down again and the tyre brushed my head as it took off on the gravel car park. She clipped the wall of the pub before blasting down the road.

Kathy and Mick came to my aid. I had no seat left in my trousers and my white shirt had a thick black rubber mark where the tyre had caught me. I couldn't believe it and Mick was furious. Jane and I were staying locally at a hotel and the three of us went off in Mick's car to try and find her.

She had gone back to the hotel, locked the door to our room and wouldn't let me in. I had no option but to go back with Mick and Kathy to their place at Chadwell Heath and spend the night there. Jane and I made up in the morning, though.

Our days at the races were plentiful and they nearly always ended up with a massive p**s-up. Thankfully, though, this was the one and only time I was nearly run over by my irate wife!

I've been asked why, in common with many footballers, I liked to gamble. I can put it down to two things. Firstly, having to run to the bookies as a young kid to put on my dad's bets. And secondly, footballers have so much spare time to themselves after training each day that they need some form of excitement to occupy them. Horseracing – and gambling on the gee-gees – often fills that void.

I admit, my gambling got out of hand at times. Jane knew I enjoyed a bet but she didn't know how much I was staking. It all came to a head for me in March 1989, when she decided to have a few days back home with her parents – during Cheltenham Festival week. Much against my better judgement, I withdrew £5,000 from our joint bank account to have a good wager at Cheltenham, one of the highlights of the national hunt season. I thought it would be easy to double my money and put the original £5,000 back into the account without Jane ever knowing.

Things didn't exactly go to plan. After the first day I was £1,000 down and my losses doubled to two grand the following day. My money dwindled away until I had £1,500 left. It was Gold Cup day and I was in deep trouble. Desert Orchid, the magnificent grey, was 7-2 for the race. Jane was due back from Liverpool and I needed to recoup the money I'd lost.

So I had a grand on at 7-2, hoping to win £3,500. With the £500 I still had and the return of my original stake, it would leave me straight.

I nervously placed the bet and although I wasn't confident, 'Dessie' and jockey Simon Sherwood battled up the famous hill on heavy ground to overhaul Yahoo. He won his most famous race by a length-and-a-half – and saved my a*** in the process.

I quickly deposited the £5,000 back into our account and realised how lucky I was. It taught me a lesson . . . for a while. I was beginning to realise that I liked to live on the edge but it was unfair on Jane.

As well as getting a buzz from betting on horses, I soon discovered the thrill of riding one too. I started spending time with Jane at the stables and learnt to ride her horse, Bridie. In fact, I loved every minute of riding a massive beast that could be so unpredictable. I'd trot off on a Sunday along the tiny tracks in Epping Forest to the all-weather track and gallop the horse. I was even jumping over big poles in the indoor ménage and regularly falling off!

I was called into John Lyall's office after training one day to explain my reckless equine antics. How he found out, I'll never know, but I assured him it was Jane's horse and I'd never sat on the animal. 'If you come in here injured from a fall, I'll have you,' he warned me.

Alan Devonshire was known as 'Honest Dev' because he was our bookie. If any of the West Ham lads wanted to place a bet on anything, he'd look at the odds and, if he was happy to lay the bet, would give us a point more than what was generally on offer at the high street bookies.

One world class flat racer he liked to lay was the legendary Dancing

HAMMERED

Brave. All the lads backed it when it won the 2000 Guineas in 1986 and then, shortly afterwards, Dev laid it again to lose in the Derby. It finished a very close second (behind Sharastani), when it clearly should have won, so he was jubilant.

But Dev laid it at Royal Ascot and again in the Prix de l'Arc de Triomphe at Longchamp and history tells us that it romped those two races in '86 with Pat Eddery on board. I think Dev was happy when Dancing Brave went out to stud. It had cost him a small fortune.

I have to admit that I felt blessed to be part of a fantastic dressing room at West Ham. Billy Bonds was the player who set the benchmark for us all even though he missed all of my first season at the club due to a serious toe injury. He rarely spoke but when he did he always talked a lot of sense and all the players had enormous respect for him.

I remember Bill playing centre-midfield against Newcastle United at home in May 1987 and he was up against a talented, young Paul Gascoigne. We drew 1-1 – I scored from a free-kick – but the game was remembered for this young man's performance against the old warhorse Bonzo. Billy was 40, Gazza 18.

Gazza was untouchable and to try and emphasise his class he taunted Billy by calling him 'Grandad'. I remember giving him six of my studs down his leg for disrespecting the Upton Park legend. But being the man that he is, Billy never retaliated. After the game he commented that his young Geordie opponent was going to be a fantastic talent – and he wasn't wrong.

Talking of wind-up merchants, in September 1987 I was sent off for the first time in the Football League – at Wimbledon's Plough Lane ground. I came to respect Dennis Wise as a born winner, but that day against the 'Crazy Gang' he got away with conning both me and the referee.

With about half an hour of the game gone and Wisey having just given Wimbledon the lead, we both went in hard against each other and put our heads together as we rose from the soggy pitch. Being the crafty little cockney that he is, Wisey decided to throw himself to the ground as if I'd butted him.

All hell let loose. Dennis was such a convincing actor, even his own players thought I'd butted him – and so did referee Alf Buksh, who

92

rushed over to show me the red card. I went mad and there was a free for all involving Vinnie Jones, big John Fashanu, Lawrie Sanchez and the rest. I didn't want to leave the pitch . . . especially after I looked down at Wisey, who had put the Dons ahead, and saw him winking at me with a smug grin on his face.

His hand was outstretched on the turf as I finally started to walk, so I deliberately trod on it. The referee was too busy separating Alvin and Fashanu and trying to calm other skirmishes to notice what I'd done. Tony Cottee earned us a 1-1 draw with a second-half header and it was a great result because it was so hard to get anything against the hard-working, uncompromising footballers of Wimbledon.

The trouble didn't end at the final whistle, though. After we'd all showered, somebody told Alvin that there may be some 'afters' in the players' lounge. The big fella came up to me and told me to walk behind him on entering the tiny players' room.

As the 'Crazy Gang' caught sight of us, they surged towards us with Dennis, his hand bandaged, screaming insults. There was no backing down but it was more a case of bravado and threats than actual fists. I remained behind Alvin, not taking any chances. He never shied away from a fight and I felt safe behind my captain.

Alvin knew how to sort out the opposition and also how to deal with anyone causing trouble within our own ranks.

Paul Ince was a cocky young kid and I liked him straight away. He was very talented and had a certain arrogance about him. He was very confident and I like that in a player. In training one day, the legendary Liam Brady was up against 'Incey'. Liam had arrived from Italy in March '87 and it was such an honour to play with this midfield master with a magic wand of a left foot.

Incey took the ball off Liam and rattled in a goal from 20 yards before turning round to Liam and boasting: 'You *used* to be the top man, but I am now.'

All the lads were gobsmacked that this young kid was so full of himself. Later, when he signed for Manchester United, I had to laugh at the 'Guv'nor' label Paul decided to bestow upon himself. He was nowhere near the hard man he portrayed himself to be.

HAMMERED

Once, after an argument over a game of cards on the team bus, Paul came to me with a bloody lip. 'Wardy, David Kelly has just punched me in the mouth. What should I do?' I was shocked, as Kelly was the last man you would think of punching anybody. I told Paul he should have given him a dig back.

Alvin put him in his place the old-fashioned way. We were getting beaten on the plastic pitch at Luton Town in November 1988 and Alvin barked at Incey to 'keep it simple.' To which the petulant, young midfielder retaliated with: 'F*** off, you Scouse c***.' I heard him say it and thought, 'You've overstepped the mark there, Paul'.

The whistle blew for half-time and, 3-0 down, we trudged off for an ear-bashing from John Lyall. Paul was just in front of me walking up the tunnel at Kenilworth Road when a big hand pushed me to one side. Alvin grabbed Incey and held him up against the wall. Unbelievably, he then head-butted Incey right in the face and let him fall to the floor. 'Don't ever speak to me like that again,' Alvin told him.

Paul picked himself up and we all sat waiting for John to give his half time team-talk. Incey was crying and John asked what had gone on. Alvin said: 'Don't worry, John, it's sorted,' and John went on to roast us about our poor performance. I'm sure John really knew what had happened but conveniently chose to let his captain deal with the situation in the way that he did.

Alvin scored our only goal in the second half that day but we still lost 4-1 as relegation loomed.

I just hope Paul remembers his own attitude when he was young and can become the successful manager he hopes to be.

The other young talent with an arrogant streak in him during my time at West Ham was Julian Dicks, who John had signed from Birmingham City in March '88. As he was our left-back, I was often up against him in training but this proved a big mistake.

Our physical battles got so out of hand that John decided we always had to be on the same team. He even made us room together on away trips, to ensure we both got on well for the good of the team.

Julian was a fantastic player with an unbelievable left foot and he was as hard as nails. We soon learnt to enjoy each other's company and we had a common interest – winning. He would make me laugh. He would eat packets of crisps on the team bus before the game and drink cans of Coke whilst burping his head off. His unorthodox diet and pre-match build-up didn't stop him getting 'man of the match' most weeks, though.

Unlike Paul Ince, Julian went on to become a Hammers legend. If 'Dicksy' had had an extra yard of pace, he'd have been even better than Stuart Pearce.

I only ever played against Julian once and that was in the Merseyside derby. Julian had signed for Liverpool in September 1993 and he was marking me on his debut for the Reds at Goodison. We shook hands before the game and I was sure it was going to be a good contest, as we knew each other's game inside out.

The extra pace I had enabled me to get the better of him that day with two ex-Hammers – myself and Tony Cottee – scoring in a 2-0 Everton victory.

It was May 12, 1988 when I received the news I had dreaded. Dad had suffered a heart-attack and died in his sleep. John was very sympathetic and told me to have as much time as I needed to go home and be with my family.

It was a massive shock even though we all knew my father hadn't been too well. He was only 52 years of age – still so young – and I still miss him to this day. He never gave up on me becoming a professional, even when Everton let me go at 18.

He was a character and his old mates still speak highly of him to this day. I was always very proud of my dad for being the man he was, and I always will be. I'm certain that if he hadn't died so young, I would not have ended up in prison. I'd have been too scared to disappoint him.

12. LOW MACARI

THE reason I left West Ham at the end of 1989 can best be summed up in two words: Lou Macari.

My reasons for wanting to leave the Hammers have never been told. I was very happy playing for West Ham and loved living in Essex. Even though we had been relegated from the top flight in May 1989, I never thought I'd play for any other club.

Then the shock news reached me that John Lyall had been sacked just days after the club had dropped into Division Two.

I was devastated. I tried phoning him immediately but it was a while before I got through at his home. I remember holding back the tears as I spoke to him. I had to tell John how sorry I was to learn of the board's decision to sack him after 34 years' service as man and boy at the club that became his life. John was his old self and, typically, he put others before himself, telling me not to worry and to concentrate on looking after myself, Jane and Melissa.

When I reflect on the way the West Ham directors treated John, it was disgraceful. He should have been offered a job overseeing the club – a Director of Football type role.

But John was a powerful man who dominated every aspect of the club. He'd been there that long, had the respect of all his players and maybe he would have been a thorn in the side of the people who knew nothing about the game.

All the talk was that the club were looking for a manager outside the West Ham unit and that's exactly what they did when they recruited Lou Macari from Swindon Town in the summer of '89.

I got to meet the next manager of West Ham quite by accident, in the bookies where I lived in Loughton. My old mate Mickey Quinn had signed for Portsmouth from Oldham Athletic. Mick has always been racing mad and had bought a horse called Town Patrol.

He'd tell me over the phone how good this horse was. I think I must have had shares in the beast, because I'd backed it every time and it had never won a race. He rang telling me this was the day for the horse to 'go in'. Not again, I thought, but what the hell . . . I had to have another go at trying to recoup the pounds I'd previously lost on the nag.

I shot round to the bookies just before the off to see what price I could get on the horse. As I pushed the door of the bookies open, who should cross my path but Lou Macari. Our eyes met and he recognised me instantly. He was very friendly and introduced himself. As we stood in the doorway he started to explain that he'd just been interviewed for the manager's job at West Ham and, if he got it, he was looking to live in Loughton.

While he continued talking to me, the race involving Mickey's horse was off and running. Macari shook my hand and told me he'd see me again pretty soon.

My attention went straight to the big screen, where I realised the race was in progress. To my horror, Mickey's horse surged through the final furlong and won by a length at 7-1!

I still had the £50 stake clutched in my hand that I couldn't put on because of my unexpected meeting with Macari. I would have won £350. I was made up for Mickey, though. He has since gone on to become a successful racehorse trainer but, like I've always said, first impressions mean a lot to me and I wasn't impressed by Macari in the bookies that day.

One week later he got the nod and was appointed the new manager of West Ham United. I had already informed my team-mates of my chance meeting with Macari and I remember one of the lads chirping up that he was probably having a few grand on himself to get the Upton Park job.

The general opinion among the dressing room was that we didn't want Macari as our new manager. Billy Bonds was the natural successor to John Lyall. How can you possibly give somebody a job who has wagered £6,000 to win £4,000 on his own team to lose a match, as Macari did in his time at Swindon?

I had watched Lou Macari's teams and knew that their direct approach would not suit the more sophisticated ball-players of West Ham – the Alan Devonshires and Liam Bradys.

The next time I saw him was at the training ground. We were all sat waiting for him in one of the dressing rooms to be introduced as our new gaffer. Macari walked nervously into the room. He had a habit of touching his face whenever he spoke and his first speech to the lads lasted just over a minute.

We were waiting for our new manager to address us in a positive manner, to give us some direction and encouragement for the forthcoming season. He told us things would 'have to change around the club' for us to bounce back into the big-time once again. And that was it.

He left the dressing room with the lads comparing the nervous little man with no personality to our previous manager John Lyall. I already knew he couldn't lace John's boots – as a manager or a man.

As captain, Alvin Martin tried to convince the rest of the squad that we should at least give Macari a chance but his demeanour and attitude towards his players would prove his downfall.

The amazing thing is that Lou Macari was a tremendous footballer, who became a big star at both Celtic and Manchester United in the '70s. Yet the way he wanted his teams to play football was the total opposite to the way he'd played the game under the great Jock Stein at Parkhead and Tommy Docherty at Old Trafford. It didn't make sense.

For instance, I was dumfounded the day, in training, when he told me that I could never receive the ball from our keeper Phil Parkes. Parkesy was brilliant at throwing the ball out quickly to wide positions – either left to Alan Devonshire or right to me. He was a major source of me receiving the ball early and on the run. To order Parkesy to kick everything long, with our defenders all pushed up to the halfway line, was completely alien to us. How could cultured players like Dev, Liam Brady, Tony Gale, Alvin Martin and the others adapt to this ugly style of football?

Lou was still very fit and would take training himself in the morning. He'd run off at a good pace and bark at the players to keep up with him.

He really didn't have a clue about how to coach the talent at his disposal. Julian Dicks would kick the f*** out of Lou whenever he joined in the training games. It was embarrassing to watch a fellow pro humiliate the manager by kicking lumps out of him.

Watching Dicksy scythe down Lou reminded me of the time I hurt John Lyall once in a training accident. I was chasing down a player in an explosive five-a-side. John was refereeing the game and unwisely turned his back on the play to give somebody a ticking off. The player side-stepped John but I went crashing into the back of him at full force, lifting him off his feet.

He picked himself up and hobbled out of the gym, leaving me totally embarrassed at having hurt the manager.

I went to see John after training but Rob Jenkins, our physio, told me he'd already gone to Upton Park for a meeting – and that he was still feeling very sore. The next morning I arrived for training early, as usual, and looked across to the table where John and his coaches Ronnie Boyce and Mick McGiven sat planning their training schedule over a cup of tea.

To my horror, John had a massive leg brace and plaster covering the whole of his leg that was propped up on a chair. I walked over to the table all red-faced and apologetic. In a serious tone, John told me the knee that had finished his playing career in the early 60s was damaged beyond repair. And he added that his wife Yvonne was going to have to drive him around for weeks until he was healed. I was gutted.

I walked slowly to the dressing room kicking myself for my stupidity and the inconvenience John would have to endure because of my clumsiness. Five minutes passed and I was sat alone thinking about what I had done. Then the door opened and John walked in, right as rain, laughing his head off. 'Got you, you little bugger!' he said. 'Your face was a picture this morning when you walked in.'

The rest of his staff were all stood behind him laughing at my expense. It was a brilliant set-up – they had me hook, line and sinker.

Years later, John told me that when I hit him from behind, it felt as if he'd been hit by a wild buffalo.

I never caught Macari in the way I did John, but there were times when I wish I had. For the first time in my career I felt very unhappy. The restrictions and the way the manager wanted us to play was affecting me.

It all happened 20 minutes before kick-off of a game at Upton Park. I was out of favour with Lou and so was Alan Devonshire. We were both sat in the players' lounge talking football and watching the horse racing when a young apprentice approached me and told me the manager wanted to see me in the boot room.

I wondered what the little p***k wanted, because we'd really fallen out and I couldn't stand the sight of him. He was waiting for me in the boot room and thrust a wad of notes into my hand, telling me to back a horse called Sayyure in the 3.10 at Newton Abbot.

I was shocked and speechless that Macari had just given me £400. What other football manager would even consider placing a bet on a horse race 20 minutes before his team were about to go out and play? Where was his focus? Not fully on the team or the game, obviously.

I had 30 minutes before the 'off' in which to go outside, find a bookie and place the bet. I walked back into the players' lounge to find Dev, who was as shocked as me at what I'd been asked to do so close to the start of a match, but he quickly grabbed the paper to look at the race involving Macari's horse. Its SP was 5-2 second favourite. Dev turned to me and said that he'd lay it for me, which came as a relief because I didn't fancy running through the crowds to put the bet on.

Dev would lose a grand if the horse won at odds of 5-2 but I thought it would be great if he could take the manager's £400.

The game kicked off and Dev left his seat behind the dug-out after 10 minutes to find out whether the horse had won. While he was gone, I was praying it hadn't.

Within a few minutes, Dev came back with a big smile on his face. The horse had lost. Not even in the first three. 'Get in!' we said.

That was the final straw. I didn't want to play for West Ham United again. Not while Macari was in charge. I loved the club but bringing him in was a big mistake. He didn't deserve to be the manager of such a great club. I had to leave – and quick.

Every day I took a written transfer request into Macari but he didn't even open the letter. He just ripped the envelope in half and put it in the bin. I wanted to chin him. And I believe that's what he wanted me to do.

Lou brought former £1m player Justin Fashanu to the club. Fashanu made his Hammers debut in a league game against Blackburn Rovers at Ewood Park at the end of November '89. I was allowed to attend a funeral back in Liverpool and was to meet the team later at the hotel on the Friday night. I arrived at the Moat House in Blackburn a couple of hours after the team bus had arrived. I told the receptionist my name and that I was with the West Ham United team.

The receptionist passed me my key for the room and said: 'Room 320, Mr Ward . . . and you're rooming with Mr Fashanu.'

I nearly dropped the key. 'No love, you've got that wrong. I room with Mr Dicks.'

She showed me a piece of paper and there, on the written list, it read: 'Ward and Fashanu – room 320'. I s*** myself.

I left the key on the reception desk and started to pace up and down looking for help. Awful thoughts came into my head. Being asleep in the bed next to Justin? No f*****g way! I was panicking now, and started to look for somebody to talk to. Where the f*** was Alvin? He would sort it out.

Just at that moment I heard lots of sniggering. I turned the corner and there, p*****g themselves laughing, were Alvin, Galey and Dicksy. It was a good set-up and I was so relieved to hear that big Justin was rooming on his own that night.

In May 1998, long after publicly admitting he was gay, Fashanu was found hanging in a lock-up garage in London's East End. He'd committed suicide.

* * * *

To help me get away from Macari I decided to appoint an agent to handle things on my behalf. David Kelly got me the number for Dennis Roach, who became one of the best known football agents in the '80s. He told me that John Toshack, who was managing Real Sociedad in Spain, was very interested in signing me.

My problem was Macari, who was reluctant to let me go. He didn't want cash for me, he wanted to trade me for players. I was losing patience, so I had to do something drastic. We were playing away to Aston Villa in a midweek League Cup tie on October 25 and on the morning of the game I told Jane I wasn't going to meet the squad to travel to the West Midlands. Instead, I'd go in and train with Billy Bonds and his youth team players.

I'd already told Macari numerous times that I didn't want to play for him but he was still putting me in the squad. It was getting personal.

I arrived at Chadwell Heath and Bonzo was surprised to see me. I told him what I was doing, so Billy told me to get changed and join in. Why hadn't the club given Billy the job? I'd never have left with him in charge.

Because of my failure to meet up with the squad, I knew I'd be in big trouble – and I was right. Macari got straight on to the PFA to complain about me. I was halfway through my training session at Chadwell Heath when I was summoned to the phone. It was Gordon Taylor, the top man at the PFA. He was brilliant, very calm and assuring. He heard my side of the story and told me that if he could agree with Lou that I would be put on the transfer list, then I would leave and attend the game at Villa Park that night.

I went home, picked Jane up and headed to Villa Park to present myself to the manager. I met Macari outside the dressing room and he told me he wanted to talk outside the ground. Jane was stood waiting to see if I was playing. He stood in front of us both and started to tell me how much he disliked me and the way I was going about trying to leave the club.

Before I could get a word in, Jane gave him a torrent of abuse. She told him what she thought of him and asked why he'd made us travel all this way when he wasn't going to play me? I didn't need to say anything. My wife said it all. I just wanted to give him a dig.

HAMMERED

Macari had a big problem. He'd agreed with Gordon Taylor that I would be put on the transfer list if I got to the game, ready to play. I kept my part of the deal but Macari had not cleared this decision with his board of directors.

It was getting very messy and a meeting at the PFA headquarters was arranged. After discussions I was told the news that I was on the transfer list. That's all I asked for. I knew it wouldn't be long before I was at another club.

Macari didn't want money for me he wanted players or a player in exchange. West Ham had put a valuation of £1m on my head. He was making it difficult for me.

I really fancied going to Spain and linking up with the Liverpool legend John Toshack. What I didn't know at this time is that Liverpool boss Kenny Dalglish had bid £1m for me. Macari had turned this down because he wanted Jan Molby and Mike Hooper in exchange. And that was a no-go from the start as far as the Anfield hierarchy were concerned.

I didn't discover Liverpool's offer for me until a few years later, when I met Roy Evans, the former Reds manager, in a bar in the city. He told me how close I'd been to becoming a Liverpool player.

Just as I was dreaming about a move to Spain's *La Liga*, the phone rang late at night. It was after 11.00pm on Boxing Day. I answered and a Scouse voice said: 'Hello Wardy, it's Peter Reid. I've got somebody who wants to speak to you.' The phone was passed over and a voice said to me. 'Mark, it's Howard Kendall. I've got permission to talk to you about a move to Man City. Can you come to Maine Road tomorrow to have a chat with me? I need a team full of Scousers to keep this lot up!'

I told him of my interest in going to Spain but Howard told me that he'd just come back after managing Athletic Bilbao and it was not all it was cracked up to be. Howard had taken over a poor Manchester City team languishing at the bottom of the first division. I found out from Dennis Roach that Macari wanted City's Ian Bishop and Trevor Morley in exchange for me.

I drove Jane up to Manchester the very next day to meet Howard

Kendall and his No.2 Peter Reid. Howard is a legend on Merseyside following his success as a player and manager at Everton. I never got the opportunity to play for him before I was shown the door at Goodison as a kid and was looking forward to meeting him.

When we arrived at Maine Road the day after Boxing Day the ground was deserted. The only two City employees at the club were Howard and Peter. We were taken to the boardroom, where sandwiches were waiting for us. Howard joked that he and 'Reidy' had been up early making the butties.

Howard turned to Jane and asked her what she would like to drink. 'Cointreau, lime and soda,' my wife replied. 'Make that two of them, Reidy lad, I've never tried that before,' said Howard, typifying the very relaxed atmosphere. I instantly felt comfortable among these two great football people of Merseyside. We talked about everything for a couple of hours and I agreed to sign for Howard and become a Man City player, subject to agreeing personal terms.

But with two other players involved, the transfer was never going to be straightforward. The deal had to be right for them, too. I took Jane to Liverpool to see her family and then travelled back to London to face Macari.

Two days later I was travelling back to the north-west on the train with him and agent Jerome Anderson, who was representing one of the City players. Dennis Roach was flying in to be at Maine Road for the completion of the deal. The journey on the train to Manchester was uncomfortable. I sat opposite Lou and we never spoke a word. I didn't like the man and it was only because of him that I was leaving West Ham.

Dennis had my deal done and dusted within two hours of negotiations with Howard, while Ian Bishop and Trevor Morley were still trying to agree terms. 'F*** this,' Howard said as he led me into the Maine Road restaurant for a meal and a drink. We'd finished our steak but the transfer still hadn't been agreed four hours later.

Howard wanted to know what was holding up the deal. He was told that Morley wanted his wife's horse to be included as part of his re-location expenses. 'F*****g hell!' an exasperated Howard said. 'I can sort this out. Mark's missus has got a horse in London and Morley's missus has got one up here. So it's simple . . . just get them to swap horses!'

There was obviously no way the two women would agree to it but I had to laugh at my new manager's simple solution to a bizarre stumbling block.

Finally, City's charmless chairman Peter Swales arrived at our table to tell us that the deal was done with the words 'about bloody time'. He trudged off and never even shook my hand or welcomed me to his club.

It was then that Macari came over to Howard to wish him all the best, before turning to me and saying: 'I hope I never see you again.'

'Charming,' Howard said, as Lou left Maine Road – he wasn't impressed with him either.

I sat in Howard's office with him, Peter Reid and Mr Man City, Tony Book. The whisky was flowing but I just wanted to get back to Liverpool to see Jane and Melissa who were waiting for me at the in-laws. It was 10.30pm and Howard turned to me and said that I was to drive him to my in-laws, where he'd drop me off and complete the rest of the journey alone to his home at Formby.

It seemed very strange to find myself driving the manager's car, with him in the passenger seat, having just signed for my new club but I felt so at ease with Howard. As we pulled up outside Jane's parents' house, he asked if it was okay to come inside and meet my family.

When Jane's dad, George, opened the door he eagerly invited Howard in. The small living room was jam-packed but George and his wife Barbara made enough room for Howard to sit down. 'Would you like a drink?' Barbara asked.

And there Howard sat for just on an hour, as if he was one of the family. A plate of turkey curry later, he jumped up, shook my hand and told me not to be late for training the next morning.

After he'd left I sat with Jane and her family and they were flabbergasted that a manager like Howard Kendall could be so down to earth and such great company. I realised I would be working with a special man and couldn't wait to get started.

I was proved right about Lou Macari. He lasted only seven months in the job at West Ham. I was becoming a good judge of managers – and what it takes to be one.

13. ANYONE FOR TENNIS?

MY first day's training with Manchester City was just like the good old days at West Ham under John Lyall – we did everything with the ball.

I couldn't believe Howard's enthusiasm. He was jogging around the centre-circle like a young apprentice so eager to get started. Yet only hours earlier we'd been drinking and eating turkey curry at my in-laws.

Howard's return to English football was no surprise. He was – and still is – the most successful manager in Everton's history and when he left them in 1987 they had just been crowned champions for the second time under his management.

He had inherited a Man City team full of potential but languishing at the bottom of the first division table when he returned from Spain, where he'd spent a year managing Athletic Bilbao and getting them into Europe.

Potentially the future looked great for City because they had some very good youngsters who had come through the ranks but they had taken some batterings prior to Howard's appointment. A 6-0 thrashing by Derby County on November 11 signalled the end for manager Mel Machin.

Howard, who took over in mid-December after Tony Book's three-game spell as caretaker-manager, had to bring in players he knew well and who he could rely on to do the job quickly and get City out of the mire. It wasn't a popular move among City fans that most of his signings were of Everton blue blood but Howard knew what he was getting in the likes of his leader Peter Reid, Adrian Heath, Alan Harper and Wayne Clarke. They were all terrific players with a wealth of experience.

The quality of the young lads at City was exceptional: Paul Lake,

HAMMERED

David White, Steve Redmond, Andy Hinchcliffe and Ian Brightwell were all first-teamers and Howard soon established a good blend.

Keeping them in the top flight, following promotion the previous May, was going to be a tall order but relegation was never even mentioned under Howard.

My debut for City was against Millwall at Maine Road on December 30, when I partnered Peter Reid in the centre of midfield. Howard told me to play to the right of centre and try to feed the flying machine, David White, with the ball as much as possible.

Walking out for the warm-up with Reidy, I heard shouts from some unhappy supporters. They weren't at all pleased about their favourite players Ian Bishop, who had scored in their sensational 5-1 home win over Manchester United at the start of the season, and Trevor Morley, whose goal clinched promotion at Bradford the previous May, being swapped for me. They were two very good and popular players in their own right and I knew I had to perform to win over the disgruntled City fans.

Howard immediately showed confidence in me by putting me in the thick of it alongside Reidy. Up against me in midfield that day was the notorious Millwall hard-man Terry Hurlock. He had a ruthless reputation and always looked the part with his wild, straggly hair and stocky build. Hurlock tried to intimidate me in the first few minutes of the game but it didn't work. Reidy told me to switch from left to right, and vice-versa, whenever it suited me and he'd look after Hurlock.

Whenever those two warriors clashed it was a match to savour. But Peter had too much class for Hurlock and his quick feet and short passing game had the Millwall marauder in a daze. I'd played mainly on the right wing for West Ham in the previous four and a half years but I enjoyed the battle fought out in the centre of midfield and it was an experience playing with Reid, a proper general.

More important than my satisfying debut was our 2-0 victory, with David White underlining his unbelievable pace in scoring both goals.

Even in that first week I could see the young players benefiting from the more experienced men around them.

I'd only been at the club a couple of weeks when I learnt that Howard had apparently arranged for us to play a friendly game in Tenerife. There was a break in the fixture list, so we were off to the sun. But, much to my amazement, when we arrived we were told there was no game.

This little excursion was a glorified p**s-up, or a team-bonding exercise if you'd prefer! A time for the squad to forge the team spirit that was essential if we were to continue to pull clear of the three relegation places as 1990 dawned.

I wasn't the biggest of drinkers at the time but there were plenty of opportunities to practise. Being very competitive by nature, I started to drink with the lads but it took all my powers to last the distance and there were times when I ended up getting in a terrible state. I did it to be part of the team and I enjoyed the great banter along the way.

I came to realise that Howard was brilliant at testing players' attitudes away from the training ground and the relaxed atmosphere at the bar was his target zone, the place where he knew he could get inside a player's head. He was very clever at it and even though you knew he'd been drinking, he always remained lucid, alert and wouldn't forget a thing.

He would bring up situations and provoke debates and arguments. He'd ask players outright for their views on all range of topics, but mostly it was football on the agenda.

A good example of this came late one evening when Reidy, Heath, Harper, Clarke and myself – his five mid-season recruits with past Everton connections – visited the pub opposite our hotel for a nightcap. We knew Howard and his coaching staff would be there, too. We were all well drunk by this time and there was the usual banter before Howard started to dig me out.

He shouted over to me that he'd seen me playing tennis that afternoon and that I was useless. He wasn't wrong. Paul Lake, the up and coming star whose career would be sadly ended by injury the following year, had smacked my a*** on court, big-time. Paul was a tremendous athlete and I couldn't get a point off him.

The manager must have been sat watching my humiliation, because

111

he kept on chipping away at me, baiting me for a response. I came back at him that I'd beat him in a game of tennis – which is exactly the response he'd been waiting for.

'Right,' he said, 'I'll play you tomorrow at 10 o'clock in the morning for a hundred quid.'

By this time all the coaching staff and the lads were in on the confrontation, and then Howard added the proviso: 'If you don't turn up, you forfeit the hundred quid.'

Tony Book – 'Mr Manchester City' and Howard's Maine Road assistant – came up behind me and whispered in my ear: 'You'd better get to bed, Mark, as the gaffer is a good tennis player.'

The coaching staff and the lads were placing bets with each other on who would win. I finished my drink and as I strode confidently out of the pub, I looked over my shoulder to see Howard still going strong on the wine. I honestly thought it would be him not turning up, as it had already gone three in the morning.

I went straight to bed and awoke with the worst hangover ever and feeling absolutely dreadful. Recalling the challenge with Howard, I checked my watch and it was already 9.50am. 'F***! Only 10 minutes to spare . . . '

Steve Redmond, my room-mate, told me to run down the corridor and see if Howard was still in his room. I threw on my shorts, slipped on a pair of flip-flops and raced to Howard's room, praying he was still fast asleep and feeling as bad as me.

To my horror, when I looked in to his room, the maid was making the bed and there was no sign of Howard!

I sprinted back to my room, switched my flip-flops for trainers, grabbed my T-shirt and ran down to the reception area. I hadn't had a wash or had time to brush my teeth. And my hangover was getting worse by the second with all the running around.

As I raced through the hotel I spotted Howard sat at the bar smoking a cigar and reading the paper. As I walked towards him he said: 'Right, son, what do you want to drink?'

I noticed he had a bottle of champagne on ice and half had already gone. 'A bottle of water,' I croaked through my dry throat. He passed me the water and told me that he knew that I would turn up for the game of tennis because I was a winner and that was why he'd bought me. 'Let's go and play,' he said.

Howard beat me that morning two sets to one and I was absolutely gutted. His game-plan was that he would loft the ball high into the air and wait for me to make errors by trying to smash the ball for a winner. My shots either went into the net or well wide of the target.

After he'd secured match-point, he shook my hand and told me we were going for a drink at the pool bar. I felt very dehydrated and certainly not up for any more alcohol. But after some encouragement from Howard, I had two San Miguels and felt as right as rain.

The lads and coaching staff started to rise following the previous night's drinking session and they all wanted to know the outcome of the tennis match. Howard took great delight in telling everyone how he'd beaten me 2-1 and I got plenty of stick off the lads as they handed over their pesetas to the coaching staff.

As the day progressed around the bar and pool, Howard kept asking me for his £100 winnings. Tony Book once again whispered in my ear: 'Play him tomorrow at two in the afternoon for double or quits. He'll have had about eight pints by then.' So I challenged him to a return match at two o'clock the following afternoon – double or quits, £200 or nothing, just as Tony had suggested.

The next afternoon at 2pm we both walked out on to the sunken clay tennis court at the hotel. Above us the crowd gathered to watch the re-match – as well as all the City players and staff, the viewing gallery had been boosted by the presence of waiters and hotel staff.

I felt very under pressure. I'd prepared well by having an early night and ate breakfast with the gaffer, who, to my knowledge, had been out all night and had been on the ale again since breakfast.

Howard's tactics were just the same as they had been the previous day – lobbing the ball high and waiting for me to make mistakes – but I just took my time and managed to beat him two sets to one. But only just – he battled for every point and made a nonsense of our age difference.

He shook my hand afterwards and we were clapped off the court. I realised quickly that 43-year-old Howard was different from other managers I'd worked with. He had his own way. By goading me into challenging him, he knew that I'd turn up for the tennis match even though I was feeling dog-rough. Like he said, I was a winner and that was the kind of player he needed at City.

A good 1-1 draw at Old Trafford against United in the Manchester derby in early February, with Ian Brightwell scoring a cracker, was a result that gave us even more confidence for the rest of the season.

In April we managed to win 2-1 at title-chasing Aston Villa with Reidy and myself – two Huyton lads – scoring. It was City's first away league win of the season. Four consecutive victories in our last six matches, and only one defeat in our last 11 games, meant we had avoided relegation by five points. Considering the perilous position we were in when Howard Kendall took charge, the final league position of 14th was a magnificent achievement by all at the club, especially the gaffer.

He had taken over a roller-coaster club, a team destined for the second division, and it was only his mid-winter signings that kept City in the top tier of English football that season. Reid, Heath and Harper were inspirational and given all the emerging young talent at the club, things were looking up for next season.

14. THE MIGHTY QUINN

ONE of Howard Kendall's best signings for Manchester City was the capture of the tall Republic of Ireland striker Niall Quinn.

Niall wasn't the finished article when he arrived from Arsenal before the transfer deadline in March 1990. He had been an in and out performer at Highbury and had never been given a decent run in the first team.

When I was at West Ham the legendary Irish international Liam Brady kept on telling me that John Lyall should snap up big 'Quinny'. Well, Howard did just that. He saw potential in a centre-forward who, with work to improve his touch and regular first team football, possessed enormous talent.

All the training at City revolved around Niall, improving his touch and awareness. Howard would still join in training sessions himself and although he couldn't run, his first touch was still immaculate. If we were working on corners or free-kicks, he'd show us exactly how he wanted the ball delivered into the right spot by whipping it in himself.

Head tennis and small-sided games in compact areas were regular features of training. You could visibly see Quinny improve week by week and he was such a great lad, too.

One Wednesday afternoon in April '91 we were rooming together at our hotel a few hours before our match against Leeds United at Elland Road. Quinny was lying down with his long legs dangling over the end of the bed that was totally inadequate for a man of his height.

He knew I liked a bet and the Channel 4 racing had just started on the television. He told me that he had an account with a bookmaker in London and asked if I wanted to go halves with him on some bets that afternoon.

I agreed, and with that he picked up the phone and rang the bookies.

HAMMERED

'Hello, it's Niall, can I have £200 on the nose on the favourite in the 2.10 at Newmarket.'

'F*****g hell', I thought, 'he doesn't mess around'. If the horse lost, then I'd be down £100. It lost.

'Right, let's get our dough back in the next race,' I suggested.

We had the same bet of £200 on the next favourite. This one also lost.

I was already £200 down in just over half an hour. Our amazing run of losses continued all afternoon until the racing on the telly had finished. When the maths was done I totted up I owed Quinny over a grand. I told him, jokingly, it was the last time I'd room with him.

He just laughed and asked if we should have the last £700 left in his account on one horse to get us out of trouble. We were in the process of having a shower and getting our shirts and ties on to meet the team in the hotel's reception area to travel to the game. Niall opened up his 'Bible', *The Sporting Life*, and told me to pick the winner to save our bacon. There was a National Hunt flat race at Stratford with over 30 runners. I turned to Quinny: 'How the f*** do I pick the winner with the size of this field?'

'The bigger the field, the bigger the certainty,' he replied. So I started to study form. We'd been backing favourites all day and I wasn't going to change our method. The favourite in this one was trained by Martin Pipe, the best jump racing trainer, and the horse was called Edelweiss. It was priced at 7-2, so if we had Quinny's last £700 on the nose, we we'd get back £3,150 to put us £150 in front.

'Go on, Quinny . . . Edelweiss,' I said, nearly cutting my throat as I shaved. He struck the bet and we stood staring at Teletext waiting anxiously for the result.

Niall said there was a number we could dial up to listen to the commentary live from the racecourse. He got the number from the *Sporting Life* and dialled it quickly.

The commentary went something like this: 'Edelweiss leads the field heading down the back straight and goes on by two lengths'. We both started jumping up and down and then put our ears back to the receiver, which was upside down on the bed, so we could hear every word of the commentary.

116

The commentator went on to say that with two furlongs to go, Edelweiss was storming clear and the rest of the field was in another county.

We slammed the phone down and ran down to reception to meet the rest of the City team. We both sat next to each other on the team coach singing 'Edelweiss', the popular song from the hit musical *The Sound of Music*.

Howard Kendall, Peter Reid and the rest of the squad couldn't work out why we were singing that old classic. But the turbulent, nerve-wracking events of the afternoon's racing didn't stop us both playing our part in a 2-1 win – and yes, Quinny scored again.

There was a lesson to be learnt, though. It's too easy to get an account with a bookmaker, especially if you are a professional footballer with too much money and time on your hands. I know so many who have lost hundreds of thousands of pounds, and the amounts squandered are much higher in this day and age.

I've lost too much money myself over the years gambling on horses – I rarely bet on football – but, thankfully, I've never had a phone account, or I'd dread to think how much more I'd have squandered. It worked out okay for Niall and me that day in Leeds but if Edelweiss hadn't won, I'd have blown £1,500 – a lot of money to me then and even more so today.

Niall Quinn was the best target man I ever played with and one of the nicest men you could ever wish to meet. He went on to own successful horses and it's great to see him back in football as chairman of Sunderland, where he is a cult hero.

* * * *

Jane, Melissa and I had been living in the Hillcrest Hotel at Cronton, near Widnes, for six months waiting for the sale of our house in Loughton to go through. We eventually sold the property for a big loss. The recession, soaring interest rates of up to 13 per cent and the stock market crash in the late '80s knocked the stuffing out of the housing market and we left Essex having not made a penny on the sale of our home. It was just unfortunate timing for us.

HAMMERED

A good start to the 1990-91 season – only two defeats in our first 16 league matches – gave everybody at Maine Road optimism for a successful campaign but big changes at the top were in the air. In mid-November it was announced out of the blue that Howard Kendall was leaving City to go back to Everton.

A lot of people were surprised because of the quality of the side he was assembling – full-back Neil Pointon, although not a Scouser himself, strengthened the Everton connection at City when he moved across from Goodison that summer. But Howard is an Evertonian through and through and he was only being honest when he explained that he could only leave Maine Road for one club – and that was Everton, where he'd made himself a legend as both player and manager in the '70s and '80s. I was shocked by the announcement, or rather its timing, but not too surprised.

The natural successor to Howard at City was Peter Reid, who – on his mentor's recommendation – became the club's first ever player-manager. It was a great opportunity for Peter, who, at 34, was nearing the end of his playing days, to prove that he had good management credentials.

We had a tough trip to Anfield in one of Reidy's first games in charge and were losing 1-0 when we were awarded a penalty. I'd already taken three penalties that season and scored each time but facing Bruce Grobbelaar at Anfield was a pressure kick. Reidy grabbed hold of me and told me to make sure I hit the target. I was always confident of hitting the target anyway and realised how important this kick was if we were to claw our way back into the game. I struck it with such power it flew past Grobbelaar and we were level.

Liverpool went ahead again and with minutes to go we got a corner. I ran and collected the ball and knew if I put it in the right area, the big fella Quinny would get to it. We had practiced corners and free-kicks religiously using Quinny and I delivered the cross perfectly, right on to the penalty spot, where Niall rose majestically and powered an unstoppable header into the top corner.

The 2-2 draw at Anfield was a great result for City and especially our new manager. Although we were gutted that Howard had left to return to Everton, Reidy was going to be a fine replacement in his own right.

He gave the lads two weeks' grace to stop calling him 'Reidy' because he wanted us to refer to him as either 'Gaffer' or 'Boss'. I kept on calling him Reidy way beyond his fortnight deadline and he'd tell me he was going to fine me. We did have a fall-out and it cost me £500.

We were playing Derby County at home shortly before the end of the season. Our keeper Tony Coton had been sent off with City leading 2-1. There was only one person to go in goal and that was big Niall. He'd already scored, along with David White, and we had 20 minutes to hang on with Quinny in goal.

During the course of the season Niall and I had a competition in training. If I scored five penalties out of five against him, he'd give me a tenner. He had to save only one for me to give him a tenner. Nine of my 11 league goals in 1990-91 came from the penalty spot but in our private competition, Quinny and I were about even with each other over the course of the season.

Peter Reid was on the bench this day and was barking out instructions from the dug-out. With 10 minutes to go Derby were awarded a penalty and Dean Saunders stepped up to face big Quinny. I stood on the edge of the box and remember telling a Derby player that Niall would save it.

Saunders strode up and hit a perfect penalty into the bottom right-hand corner. I knew if Niall dived the right way, he'd save it – and he did. He tipped Saunders' shot around the post and the City faithful erupted in celebration of the big man.

With a nervous few minutes to hold on to our 2-1 lead, Reidy was ordering me to 'just sit tight in midfield'. I tried to nick a ball but misjudged it and Derby nearly scored.

The manager swore at me and I told him to 'f*** off!' I should never have said it – it was disrespectful and out of order. Within a minute, Reidy had my number up and brought himself on for me. He put out his hand for me to shake it but, feeling angry and hard done by, I just walked straight past him.

I trudged off up the tunnel and, on my way, stupidly kicked the plastic water bucket that was adjacent the opposing dug-out. I kicked it with such force that my foot went straight through the bucket, spraying water everywhere. The copper who stood by the players' tunnel was soaked and so, too, was the unfortunate Tony Coton.

I was oblivious to the mess I'd caused as I was too busy embarrassingly trying to release my foot from the bucket, which had become jammed around my boot. But I knew I was in big trouble.

I showered and headed for the players' bar as quickly as I could. As I left the ground, I was dreading going in to face Reidy at training the following week. The only consolation was that we'd held on for a hard-fought victory, with Niall scoring and then saving a penalty.

First thing Monday morning, I was summoned to the manager's office and as soon as I walked in Reidy told me to wipe the smirk from my face. He told me that he'd had to apologise to the policeman in charge on matchday and was fining me two weeks' wages.

Big Sam Ellis, Reidy's assistant, fought my corner and said he thought the manager's punishment was a bit severe, as I'd done well for the team. 'Okay then, you little b*****d – I want £500 off you and I'll put it in the players' pool for the end-of-season p***-up!'

I left his office feeling that I'd got away with murder. I never even paid the £500 fine and whenever I've seen Peter since, he has always reminded me what I still owe him.

With six victories in our last eight matches, and the impressive Quinny top-scoring with 21 league goals, Manchester City ended 1990-91 in fifth place – their highest final league position in 13 years and the first time they had finished above United in that period.

At the end of the season I went to London, along with team-mates Adrian Heath, Alan Harper and Wayne Clarke, to represent City at the PFA annual awards. Sat at a table with the Everton players was a good friend of Howard Kendall's, a mad blue named Tommy Griffiths, who called me over to join him and the other Evertonians. Tommy took me to one side and told me that I'd be an Everton player before next season. 'How do you know?' I asked him. 'Believe me, Mark, you'll be an Everton player,' he repeated.

Tommy sounded so confident of my impending transfer that I confided in Adrian Heath, asking him what he thought. He said that as 'Griff' was Howard's trusted mate, he wouldn't say what he did if it wasn't true. I had to put it to the back of my mind, though. I knew it would be a dream come true to play for Everton but I didn't realise how close I really was to signing for my beloved Blues.

15. THE GREATEST FEELING

I WAS lying on the beach in Portugal that summer thinking all the time about the conversation I'd had with Howard Kendall's mate Tommy Griff. How true was his belief that I was going to be an Everton player again? I wanted it more than anything but pre-season training was just around the corner and I was still at Manchester City.

After our amazing fifth-place finish, there was a lot of excitement around Maine Road. Reidy had organised a pre-season tour to Ireland – a country I've always loved to visit. We were due to play Cork City and were based at Jury's Hotel. After our game, which we won 2-1 in front of a big crowd all wanting to see the Republic of Ireland star Niall Quinn, Reidy gave us the next day off.

I was up early and the lads had all arranged to meet in a little pub across the bridge from the hotel – for the start of our pub crawl around Cork. I hadn't been to this delightful city before but soon realised it was a beautiful place. I left the hotel to find a newsagent, where I bought the *Sporting Life* so that we could pick out our bets for the day. I sat down in the cosy little pub looking forward to a pleasurable day of drinking and gambling.

A couple more of the team had joined me and I was just about to take my first sip of the pint of Guinness that had been plonked down in front of me when I saw big Sam Ellis walking towards me. My initial thought was that Reidy had sent him along to stay with the lads so we didn't get into any trouble. How wrong I was.

'Mark, the gaffer wants to see you,' Sam said, but I wasn't falling for it. 'I don't think so, Sam,' I responded. 'I'm not walking all the way back to the hotel – you're winding me up.'

'I'm telling you, son, he's waiting for you in his room – he needs to see you urgently.'

I still wasn't having it. I thought Peter Reid's No.2 was just trying to make me look a knob-head, walking back to the hotel just to satisfy a stupid prank. He stood there waiting, towering over me. I remained seated and wouldn't budge.

'Don't you believe me?' Sam went on. He then picked up my perfect pint of the beautiful black liquid and, to my amazement, downed it in one. He slammed the empty glass down on the bar and said in a distinctly more forceful tone: 'Get your a*** back to the hotel now, little fella.'

I knew this time he was serious, so I reluctantly left the lads behind at the pub. I started to wonder if I'd done anything wrong or, worse, whether there was bad news from home.

As I approached the little bridge Alan Harper was heading my way. I started to remonstrate with him, complaining that Sam Ellis had told me I had to see Reidy, and how Sam had just downed my pint in one.

Alan Harper told me he'd just seen the gaffer and that there was some good news awaiting me. He left to meet up with the lads in the pub while I went back to the hotel to see what Reidy wanted.

He opened his door with a towel wrapped around him, having just got out of the shower. 'Come in and sit down, you little b*****d,' he said. 'Right, listen to me . . . get yourself on the next plane back to Liverpool. Your 'dad' wants to sign you again – I've just got off the phone to Howard. You and Alan Harper are going to Everton!'

I jumped up, unable to believe what I was hearing. Reidy was rabbiting on about the £500 I still owed him for my petulance at the end of the game against Derby County three months earlier but I wasn't listening. As I bolted for the door, he shouted: 'Hey, you still owe me that monkey.' I just laughed and sprinted to my room to ring Jane and the family to tell them the unbelievable news.

I ran back to the pub to meet the lads, who had all heard the news from Alan Harper that he and I would be leaving City to join Everton. I was feeling on top of the world and couldn't wait to step on the plane and return to Liverpool.

Try as we did, we couldn't get a flight until the next morning, so there was only one thing to do. We got absolutely bladdered and had a great send-off in the company of our team-mates.

It was a good way of saying goodbye. I'd only been at City for 18 months and I'd enjoyed every minute. The fans were fantastic and I believe I played my part in helping the club re-establish itself in the top flight.

But Everton – *my* club – had come back for me and it was the best news I could ever hear. Alan and I arrived in Liverpool the next morning and I was so excited. It was a £1million deal – Tommy Griff had been right all along.

Alan and I met Howard in the Hillcrest Hotel, just around the corner from my new house in Julian Way, Cronton. There was no need for Howard to persuade either of us to sign for Everton. We went straight to the bar where we drank and ate in the restaurant. After a good five hours in Howard's hospitable company, the only thing I learnt from him was that he was going to play me on the left side of midfield. I told him I'd play anywhere for Everton – it didn't matter. I was going to give blood for the club I love.

The next day I met Les Helm, the Everton physio, at Goodison Park. Les had been in the army with my dad years before. He was very much old school and I warmed to him straight away. He took me to a clinic in Rodney Street for a thorough medical before signing later that day. The medical was very rigorous, with all my joints, bones and major organs checked by leading consultants.

It seemed like an age before we were given the all-clear – and then Les came to tell me that there might be a problem. One of the consultants had detected a small defect in my back. He told me it was known as Spondylosis – a small curvature of the spine. Apparently, it was a birth defect.

I was shocked and very worried. My dream move back to Everton could be ruined because of this medical discovery. I was panicking but Les remained very calm. He tried to reassure me by pointing out that I'd played more than 300 first class games with this condition, so it shouldn't prevent me from playing another 300.

My fitness record and games missed through injury was very impressive. I told Les that I'd played three full seasons in succession without missing a game for either Oldham or West Ham. And I'd missed only two of a possible 57 matches for Man City in the previous season-and-a-half.

Les spoke to Howard Kendall on the phone and my fears eased when the manager responded emphatically by saying that, defect or no defect, I was signing for Everton.

It was with a feeling of great relief that I was rushed to Goodison, where I hastily put pen to paper before facing the media. It had taken me just over 10 years to make my way back to the club where I'd started as a 16-year-old kid in 1981. After a good deal of heartbreak and a tremendous amount of hard work, I was back where I belonged. Goodison was, and will always be, my spiritual home.

Howard told me that Colin Harvey, his assistant, was totally behind his decision to bring me back to Everton. Colin had been in charge of the reserves when I was released under Gordon Lee, although I no longer blamed anybody for Everton's decision to release me at the age of 18. It was a long, hard journey to get back to the club I loved but it was worth it. I wasn't ready for top-class football when they let me go in '81 but now I was certain that I was good enough to pull on the famous blue shirt.

I couldn't wait for my debut away at Nottingham Forest on the Saturday but my sights were also set firmly on my home debut – against reigning champions Arsenal on Tuesday, August 20. The Forest game ended in a disappointing 2-1 defeat but everyone was looking forward to Arsenal coming to Goodison. It would be a major test for us.

Howard explained to me before I signed that I'd be playing out of position, on the left of midfield, because he had, in his words, 'a world-class winger' in Robert Warzycha on the right flank. The Polish international had burst onto the Everton scene with his electric pace and attacking play following his £500,000 signing from Gornik Zabrze the previous March. But it didn't bother me where I played. Right, left or centre – it was all the same to me.

The build-up to my home debut became almost too overwhelming. I'd picked up a little knock on my knee against Forest on the Saturday and didn't go in for treatment on the Sunday because I didn't want to jeopardise my place in the starting eleven against the Gunners.

Nothing, and I mean nothing, was going to stop me running out at Goodison on that Tuesday evening.

Even though I'd be playing out of position, Howard said that he didn't expect me to run down the left wing and cross balls with my weaker left foot. He told me to come inside when I could, to link up with the forwards – fellow new signing Peter Beardsley and Tony Cottee, my former West Ham team-mate – and to try shots from distance. I've always been able to hit a ball with pace and, given the opportunity, I relished striking long-range efforts.

In the dressing room before kick-off everybody was wishing each other all the best. As I pulled on the '11' shirt – the number I'd worn throughout my second season with Man City – I looked around me at some of the great players I was about to take to the pitch with: goalkeeper Neville Southall, skipper Dave Watson, Kevin Ratcliffe, Kevin Sheedy, Beardsley and Cottee, plus Martin Keown, John Ebbrell, Alan Harper and Warzycha.

I contemplated how far I'd come in my career . . . all that hard work running 12 miles to training at Northwich when I couldn't get a lift ... spewing up in training at Oldham in order to become as fit as the rest of the squad . . . the learning process under John Lyall at West Ham. Now I felt at home. The only thing missing that night was Dad. How proud he would have been to see his son make his home first team debut for *his* Everton. Still, all my family and mates were at Goodison on what turned out to be a truly memorable occasion for me.

As the two teams gathered in the tunnel, I heard the start of the *Z-Cars* music. An amazing surge of adrenalin shot through my veins and all the hairs on my body stood to attention. It was a feeling I'll never forget. My heart was pumping and I was becoming very emotional. All the years of dreaming of running out at Goodison with an Everton shirt on my back and now it was actually happening. It was unreal.

I ran on to the perfect lush turf and took in all the atmosphere that the Goodison crowd is so famous for. I was determined to make this a game that I'd never forget.

I was up against the Arsenal and England right-back Lee Dixon – a very strong and able defender. I knew I wouldn't get much joy out of him on the outside, so I was planning to run inside to link up with Beardsley and Cottee – just as Howard suggested – and, if given enough space, unleash one of my bullet shots.

As the game progressed I wasn't getting any change out of Dixon, so I started to probe inside more and more. Midway through the first half I picked up a ball from Harper and ran inside. A gap opened between two midfield players and I took the ball as far as I could, hoping to let fly with a shot from distance. Before being closed down by Tony Adams or David O'Leary – I can't remember which central defender – I looked up and hit a shot from fully 25 yards. I scored most of my goals from distance and, usually, you know instinctively if it's going to be a goal as soon as the ball leaves your boot.

I felt this particular shot lacked the power to beat the great David Seaman. Even so, I followed the path of the ball, hoping in anticipation, and just at the last second it curled away from the big hand of the England No.1 and flew into the top corner of the goal. 'I've scored! I've scored!' I couldn't believe it. I ran back to the halfway line, where my team-mates congratulated me, saying what a great goal I'd scored. It was too good to be true. The shot wasn't the best but it had just beaten the England goalkeeper.

I was brimming with confidence now and wanted the ball at every opportunity. As I walked off the pitch at half-time the applause from the Goodison faithful was deafening. The little niggling injury in my knee hadn't bothered me and I was fully charged up and didn't want the game to finish.

I thought about Dad and how he would have reacted when my shot hit the back of the net. I still believe to this day that he was there for me in spirit that night, blowing the ball past Seaman to give me my first Everton goal on my home debut. My greatest-ever game.

Later, I was to play and score in a Merseyside derby and collect a man-of-the-match award as well as a winners' medal at Wembley. But, for me, this game is the one I'll always remember most until the day I die.

But the dream didn't end there. Late on in the second half I hit a free-kick and it whizzed past the wall and beat Seaman for the second time.

Cottee put the seal on a 3-1 victory and it couldn't have gone any better.

Howard brought me off with five minutes to go – Pat Nevin was my replacement – and the ovation I got from the 31,200 inside Goodison was very special. It meant everything to me – it still does. This is, without doubt, my biggest and happiest memory in football.

16. TROUBLE WITH MO

I COULDN'T wait to get up in the morning and arrive at Bellefield for training. In fact I'd usually be there just after Neville Southall. Big Nev was always the first in and the last to leave training.

We'd have coffee and toast and be in the gym playing head tennis well before any of the other players arrived.

For a goalkeeper, Nev had an unbelievable touch on the ball. He always wanted to play out on field in training and if you were on his team in a game you had a good chance of winning because he was an excellent target man.

It was his tackling that scared Howard Kendall. If Nev got a bit too aggressive, the manager would put him back in goal. It was so difficult to get the ball off the big fella. As a goalkeeper there was nobody better. I've always said he's the best I've played with, which is saying something when you consider that includes outstanding keepers such as Phil Parkes, Andy Goram and Tony Coton.

Watching the great 92-times capped, Wales international No.1 train with the other keepers at the club, you realised just how good he was – head and shoulders above them. A one-off. If he didn't like you, he wouldn't pretend and be false. He wouldn't talk to you – full-stop.

He wanted everybody to give the same 100 per cent effort he always gave and if you didn't do that, he'd turn on you. Nev was a true pro.

One thing he hated more than people who didn't put in everything was to be chipped in training. In shooting practice, the lads would line up with a ball waiting to test the big fella with a shot from outside the box. 'Go on, Wardy,' Ian Snodin said, 'chip Nev – it will do his head in.'

On this particular day I laid the ball into Howard and he knocked it to the side for me to strike a shot at goal. As I approached the ball, I chipped it over Nev's head and it nestled in the net. All the lads started laughing and whistling. But not Southall.

HAMMERED

He came charging towards me like a raging bull – and I was off. After three laps of the training ground I got brave and decided to take my punishment. All the lads and Howard had been watching the chase and the manager was shouting to Nev to go easy on me, as there was a game on Saturday.

Not that Nev took any notice of him. He grabbed me with his massive hands and pummelled me from head to toe. He picked me up, then threw me back onto the turf and his parting shot was to jump on me with his studs scraping the skin off my back.

As I soaked in the bath at home that night, trying to relieve the aches and pains from Nev's assault, Jane asked if I'd been fighting after seeing the cuts and bruises on my body. 'No,' I said, 'Nev did this to me – but he was only playing about!'

I never chipped him again and neither did any of the other lads. I learnt the hard way that you couldn't take liberties with Neville Southall.

Alan Harper and I weren't Howard Kendall's only signings in the summer of '91. Howard pulled off a major coup by capturing Peter Beardsley from Liverpool for £1m – and what a player he was. It was amazing that Reds' boss Graeme Souness should let him go to their city rivals but it was certainly Everton's gain and Liverpool's loss. Outstanding for club and country, Peter was a pleasure to play with and such a nice fella, too.

In November '91 Howard signed Scottish international centre-forward Maurice Johnston from Glasgow Rangers for £1.5m. Mo introduced himself to me the first day in training, saying how his pal Frank McAvennie had told him all about the 'wee man', and we instantly became good mates.

McAvennie and Johnston were like two peas in a pod. They were Scottish international forwards from Glasgow, with red-hair dyed blond, and both had played for Celtic. On the social side, they loved nothing better than shagging birds and having a little drink or six. And like McAvennie in my West Ham days, I ended up rooming with Maurice on away trips. Oh, and the most important similarity was that they both liked scoring goals.

By this time, though, Maurice was way past his best, and I remember telling him so just a few weeks in to his brief Everton career. Even so, we became firm mates and he was good company.

Our final league position of 12th was disappointing but Howard was still trying to put his own squad together. I was quite happy with my overall performance and I must have been consistent because I played in 37 out of the 42 league games in that 1991-92 campaign.

At the end of the season a tour had been arranged in the exotic location of Mauritius, where we were going to play friendlies against their national team and Aston Villa. The squad left Bellefield bound for Heathrow but, with cans of lager flowing fast from the moment we left Merseyside, I was feeling drunk by the time we reached the Keele services on the M6 in Staffordshire.

When we arrived at Heathrow airport, most of the squad were drunk – all except Peter Beardsley, who is teetotal. We still had a 12-hour flight to take in – Business Class and free booze all the way! It was going to be an interesting journey, because Aston Villa – managed by the flamboyant Ron Atkinson – were on the same plane.

In fact, the Villa players were there to greet us when we arrived in the VIP lounge at Heathrow. After hours of boozing on the bus, we must have looked like Raggy A*** Rovers compared to them but the one big difference between the teams in that lounge was that the Villa lads had their wives and girlfriends in tow.

Howard got his bedraggled squad together for a team meeting. He said: 'Yes, lads, you can see that some of the Villa players have their wives and girlfriends with them. But it's been a rule of mine that no women should come on any of our away trips. Okay?' And that was that. We started to socialise with the Villa lads, who said that bringing along their partners was optional. The Villa party would be staying at a different hotel anyway, so it wasn't a problem to us.

The alcohol was flowing freely again as soon as we took off. The plane was spilt between the Everton and Villa lads with some among our first division rivals Villa sat holding hands with the WAGs of the day.

For part of the journey I was seated in between Peter Beardsley and Villa's Paul McGrath. Peter was great company even though he didn't drink. He was always there on our nights out, looking out for the lads, and it was actually him who challenged me to drink a glass of champagne quicker than the Irishman McGrath, who had a reputation as a big drinker at the time.

He was also great company and we were getting on great but I knew I was up against it. Peter poured the vintage champers into the crystal glasses and said 'go'. I felt the bubbly liquid rush down my throat and was struggling to empty the glass in one. Before I was even half way down my glass, McGrath was getting a refill. Beardsley was laughing, goading me that I was out of my depth.

I got hammered but it was McGrath who ended up passing out. Now that's what I call a result . . . I always hated being on the losing side!

Paul and I were briefly interrupted during our personal drinking duel by Peter Beagrie spewing vomit all over the back of our seats. He was in a terrible state. Our squad had been drinking for hours, so it was hardly a surprise that one of us would be throwing up before landing.

Howard had been sat holding court with his squad while Big Ron was upstairs in First Class with his missus and the directors of both clubs. Atkinson decided to relieve his obvious boredom with a visit to see how his players were getting on. Still looking immaculate in his suit some 10 hours into the flight, he strode up the aisle of the plane and approached Howard whose shirt was open and stained with red wine. An interesting discussion ensued between two of the most famous managers in English football.

The Everton boss started to ask Big Ron how much he wanted for Paul McGrath. But as Atkinson knelt on the seat in the row in front of our boss to have a chat, he unfortunately placed his knee on a damp towel that was covering the remains of Beagrie's sick!

He shot up, grabbing a napkin to wipe away the mess, before telling a fully relaxed Howard to control his players and returning upstairs to the sanctuary of his wife.

There was no expense spared on the trip to Mauritius. On arrival at our hotel we were introduced to our own butlers and we had lavish rooms all to ourselves. Everybody just wanted to get some sleep, even though it was mid-afternoon, but Howard told everyone to dump their gear in their rooms and to meet at the pool bar as soon as possible. Neil Moore, one of the young lads in the squad, was instructed to bring along his ghetto-blaster to provide some musical entertainment around the pool.

We all started to congregate around the pool bar and I noticed the hotel was full of honeymooning couples. 'God help them,' I thought.

'Mooro' turned up looking a bit sheepish with his music box but Howard immediately put him at ease: 'Right son, turn it on, let's see what you're made of.' Young Neil pressed 'play' and the deafening sound of Little Richard's 'I Feel Good' shattered the tranquil air. The couples around the pool shot bolt upright, startled by the noise, only to see a group of drunken footballers dancing and diving into the pool.

I felt so sorry for the newlyweds in our hotel. But one thing was made clear by Howard – nobody was to disrespect the hotel staff or other residents. He wouldn't stand for any of that nonsense.

We were on the Indian Ocean paradise isle for a full two weeks and the game against Aston Villa was played in front of a 20,000-plus crowd. The kick-off had to be delayed by an hour because there were so many trying to get in. We lost the game but I put that down to the fact that the Villa squad hadn't drunk as much as we did!

These trips abroad – we also visited Switzerland, Spain and Ireland – were all about team-bonding and creating a unity and spirit among the players and management. The ideal tour venue for me was Dublin. On one trip I asked Howard if he could arrange a day at the races for the lads who wanted to go. 'No problem,' he said and the gaffer organised a day out at The Curragh, in nearby County Kildare.

After two or three days on the black velvet, three Scousers – captain Dave Watson, Alan Harper and me – were the only ones with the staying power to take up the free booze on offer in the champagne bar at Ireland's premier flat racecourse. My good friend Dave Taylor, a big Evertonian, had flown over for a couple of days and accompanied the three of us.

It wasn't long before we'd backed a few winners and made new friends in the bar. The bubbly was flowing and by the end of the race meeting the bucket, which was in the shape of a top hat, had been on all of our heads while we merrily sang songs to keep all and sundry entertained.

The Moët & Chandon champagne bucket was on my head just as Alan Harper walked past to go to the bar. He jokingly hit the top of the bucket with his fist but I wish he hadn't. The 'top hat' dug into the bridge of my nose, causing blood to spurt from a deep wound and turn my white shirt red. I was that drunk, I never felt a thing, but 'Waggy' lifted the bucket off my head and took me to the toilet to try and stop the bleeding.

We left the racecourse in the company of a rock band, who took us to a little pub for a bowl of clam chowder before we headed back to our hotel.

Contrary to Dr Watson's diagnosis that it was 'just a scratch', the wound across my nose was still seeping blood and it obviously needed stitching. To make things worse, my eyes had started to swell up. It looked as though I'd taken a bad beating and had been fighting. I had to make sure I wasn't seen by Howard.

Sod's law, wasn't it? Just as we walked through reception, who should be strolling out of the bar but the gaffer. He couldn't have timed it better. He looked straight at me and said: 'I don't want to know, you'd better not have been fighting – that's the last time I organise anything for you.'

'I haven't been fighting. I had this champagne bucket on my head and . . .'

Before I could finish explaining, he cut me short and told me to get upstairs and clean myself up before anybody else saw me. Waggy and Alan tried to tell the full story and plead my innocence but Howard had a right cob on and left not believing his captain.

I also upset Howard following several eventful nights out with Maurice Johnston. Mo and I would go out socially after games and on a Monday, if we didn't have a mid-week match, he'd encourage me to go for a 'wee shandy' that would inevitably lead to a lager-top, then progress to a full pint and, before we knew it, we'd been out all day and most of the night.

One memorable escapade happened while visiting a German training camp in the pre-season of 1992-93. We had some big-name clubs to play in the two weeks we were there and having trained very hard, Howard decided to give the squad two days off.

Maurice and I were out late on our second day of steady drinking and heading back to the hotel at the training camp. We were about 10 miles from base when we realised we were way past our curfew with a tough game against Borussia Moenchengladbach coming up the next day. There was just one watering hole left before our hotel, so we decided to have one more drink before getting back.

This bar was empty but for about four frauleins all sat at the bar. We were well hammered by now and after getting my beer I slumped into a big leather couch. Maurice started dancing in the small area by a stage and I was egging him on as he started to take off his shirt. This amused the women and with their encouragement, he was down to his undies in seconds. I was telling him to go 'the full monty'.

At this point I rushed to the toilet, at bursting point after all the lager I'd consumed. As I stepped back into the bar, I was stopped dead in my tracks. There, stood at the bar, were Howard Kendall, Jim Greenwood, Everton's chief executive, and the chairman, Dr David Marsh.

And stood among them was Mo – in his underpants!

It didn't look good on the two of us. We were supposed to be back at the hotel, tucked up in our beds, like all the other players.

I couldn't leave my mate to take all the stick, so I walked to the bar to face the music. Howard greeted me with: 'I knew you'd be with him – what do you want to drink? And you, Maurice, go and put some clothes on.'

Talk about sobering up quickly. I tried to hide how p****d I really was by saying as little as possible. Howard told us to finish our drinks and 'f*** off back to the hotel as quickly as possible.'

He then he added: 'I haven't seen you two today – and you haven't seen us either. Okay?'

With that we scarpered out of the bar and got into a taxi. But the action didn't end there. We got back to our room and all the other lads were asleep. But instead of crashing out after our massive bender, Maurice started a fight.

He could get very aggressive when he'd had too much to drink and we squared up to each other. I caught him and as he fell to ground, his head crashed against the wooden bed. Blood gushed from his head and I bolted from the room in search of our captain.

Waggy was asleep but I woke him to say that Maurice was carrying on. He first advised me to 'knock him out' but then got up out of bed to calm the situation, and eventually we all got to sleep at the end of a long and eventful night.

After breakfast, the squad congregated at the front of the hotel for the start of training. Howard strolled over and as he walked past Maurice, he asked 'Present from the little fella?'

Mo's bruised face had a big cut and looked even worse with his eyes closed. Maurice was always apologetic to me and after awaking that morning he wanted to know why his face was in such a state.

There were never any hard feelings between us. The ironic thing was, while I struggled to play the full 90 minutes against Moenchengladbach, Maurice had the luxury of nursing his hangover from the subs' bench, laughing his b******s off at me!

Another altercation I had with him came in January 1993, after a long day out at a Southport restaurant owned by Evertonian Joe Farley. Joe was a mate of my father-in-law, George, and had been at mine and Jane's wedding. He was a tough, well known figure in Liverpool and also a black belt in karate.

Ian Snodin, Graeme Sharp, Mo and I left training to meet Joe at his restaurant. There were a few other lads there and we enjoyed great food and the wine was flowing.

Then Maurice, not unusually, started to be a bit disrespectful to everyone around him and he picked on me in particular. I just knew he wouldn't stop and as arguing with him was a waste of time, I asked him outside with me. We both got up to sort it out but before we reached the door of the restaurant, big Joe grabbed us by the scruff of the neck and said: 'If there's any fighting to be done here, it will be me knocking the f*** out of both of you. So behave yourselves.'

That was good enough for me but not Maurice. He was still angry and kept blabbering on. Joe instructed Mo's mate, Dave Sheron, to take him home and, much to everyone's relief, that's what he did.

Sharpy then thought it would be a good idea to go and see Peter Beardsley at his local pub, The Fisherman's Rest, in nearby Birkdale. It was a Wednesday – quiz night – and teetotal Peter's only night out of the week.

What happened when we arrived at the pub is still a bit of a mystery to me. The pub was busy and I noticed Peter sat at the bar. As we made our way to greet him, a Liverpool fan made a disparaging remark about Everton. And in a split second, Sharpy, myself and Snods were scrapping with a couple of lads. It was over before it started and Peter quickly got us all away from the pub and into his car.

We thought nothing of the little fracas – no-one got hurt – and were laughing about it on the way to our next port of call. At training the next morning, we were all talking about the strange events of the previous evening – Maurice being sent to bed and the little skirmish at The Fisherman's Rest. Everybody had arrived at training except Maurice. I presumed he felt too rough to make it in.

But, just as we were about to start the session, he poked his head into the dressing room – and what a head it was. He was deformed! His whole face had swollen like a balloon and his mouth was lopsided. He was in so much pain that he could hardly speak.

Colin Harvey entered the dressing room, looked at Mo and me and said: 'The gaffer wants you two in his office straight away.'

Howard had heard about the fight in the pub by the next morning. He had plenty of local friends and contacts and you could never keep anything from him. One of the Sunday tabloids ran with the big headline: 'Everton Star in Pub Brawl', accompanied by a picture of yours truly and reported that I'd been barred from The Fisherman's Rest for my unruly behaviour.

Maurice quickly explained what had happened to his face. He was often put to bed stinking drunk but this time it turned out that he'd woken up in the night and tripped over a shoe at the top of the stairs. He fell the whole way down the gallery staircase, hitting his face on the wall at the bottom. He said he hit it so hard, the plaster came off the wall.

I felt like saying 'serves you right for being a p***k' but I felt sorry for him – he was a right mess. We stood there in front of Howard like a couple of naughty schoolboys.

'I've heard what happened last night in the Fisherman's Rest. You're both being fined two weeks' wages. I've had enough of you both. You're going to hospital this minute,' he said to Maurice and then told me to get down stairs and ready for training.

I tried in vain to explain what happened to Howard, saying: 'Maurice wasn't with me in the pub last night, gaffer.'

I've never seen Howard so angry. 'Well, how the f*** has he got a face like that?'

I turned to look at Maurice, the Elephant Man, and I had nothing else to add. It looked all over as if he'd been in a brawl. Howard added that he admired my loyalty before telling me to get out of his sight.

There was no denying that Maurice had a broken face. His cheekbone was smashed and he couldn't play for six weeks. Years later, I told Howard again that Maurice hadn't been with us that night the fight broke out at the pub but he still wouldn't believe me.

Howard hated any of his players or staff speaking out of turn to the press or disrespecting the club in any way. Tony Cottee had been going through a lean patch in front of goal towards the end of 1992 and a piece in a Sunday newspaper headlined that the Everton squad wasn't good enough and the midfield lacked creativity. Tony insisted afterwards that his criticism was really directed at the manager, for not picking the right players, not his team-mates. Whether he was misquoted or not, Howard was livid.

On the Monday morning before training, he gathered everyone together and announced that Tony would be taking the whole squad and staff out for a Chinese meal that night . . . all paid for by him. As far as Howard was concerned, Tony had betrayed his team-mates and he wouldn't tolerate it.

Every player had to attend the Chinese – no excuses – and I was made up that we were all going to enjoy another night out. The table went the whole length of the restaurant. I remember looking down to the opposite end of the table, where Tony was sat, and his face was as long as the table! The food bill came to £1,000 and he was so p****d off that I don't think he ate a thing.

He wasn't the only one who had to treat his team-mates that night, though. I can't recall what misdemeanour I'd committed this time, but I had to pay for the champagne.

17. FIGHTING BACK

THE inaugural FA Premier League campaign started well with a 3-0 win over the 1992-93 champions-elect Manchester United at Old Trafford. That was our first away fixture and there was talk of us finishing in the top six but my season was brought to an abrupt and very painful end after just eight matches.

We were playing at Blackburn Rovers in an evening game on September 15. It was early in the first half and I remember the ball being played in to me and letting it run across my body, so I could pass it on to Barry Horne with the outside of my right foot.

The tackle from Mark Atkins was late and brutal. My foot was planted on the turf as the reckless Rovers midfielder lunged at me with both feet, hitting me from the side.

The pain was instant and I just lay motionless, too scared to move. I knew instantly that my right ankle was f****d. I laugh to myself now when I see players – usually foreigners – rolling around pretending they are hurt. Let me tell you, when you break bones you don't roll around as if you've been shot by a sniper – you are in too much pain to even move.

I was carried off on a stretcher and Howard, realising it was serious, came down from the stands and onto the pitch to see how bad my injury was. I was rushed to Blackburn Royal Infirmary accompanied by Dr Ian Irvine, the Everton club doctor. He was giving me gas and air, trying his best to ease the agony by telling me it was 'better than sex!'

X-rays confirmed a fracture to the fibula and tibia just above the ankle. After much consultation, it was agreed that club surgeon Dr Johnson would perform the operation the next day at the Arrowe Park Hospital on The Wirral.

If the pain was intense immediately after the tackle, it was nothing compared to how bad I felt after surgery. I awoke with a plaster cast stretching from my ankle up to my knee. The pain was like nothing else. It was if the ankle was trying to explode out of the plaster.

My a*** was like a dart-board after all the morphine the nurses had given me to try and ease the pain. As soon as Everton physio Les Helm came to visit me, he demanded that the hospital medics removed the plaster and when they did I felt instant relief. I still hurt but at least it was manageable now.

Les and I had a good talk and he told me the extent of the damage. The surgeon had to insert two metal plates, held together by eight screws, to knit the bones back together.

He told me it was going to be a long, hard journey back to fitness and warned me that I'd have to learn to walk again, never mind think about running or kicking a ball.

I was very down, being injured was a new thing to me. I'd had a great injury-free run over the years but now my luck had run out.

I started to feel a lot of anger and resentment towards Mark Atkins. It was a terrible, late tackle and I knew he meant to hurt me – if not quite to the extent that he did. Only he can say.

Atkins' actions hadn't stopped Everton leaving Ewood Park with a 3-2 away victory – but I was hell bent on revenge.

My rehabilitation with Les Helm was going to be crucial to my comeback attempt but we got off to a bad start due to the difficulty I had coming to terms with the seriousness of the injury and what was going to prove the longest lay-off I'd ever experience.

Les wanted me in the swimming pool to get some movement back in the ankle, so we arranged to meet at the Liverpool Moat House hotel, which has its own pool. I'd been drinking on the Saturday and failed to turn up, as arranged, at the Moat House the next morning. Big mistake.

Les b*******d me, big-time, when I saw him on the Monday and then refused to talk to me for a whole week. He then stressed the fact that only I could put the necessary work in to get myself back playing again. He was spot on, of course, and I promised him I wouldn't let him down again and that I'd become the model injured player.

The swelling and scar tissue resulting from surgery was a big problem at first. When I looked at the state of my ankle, I had doubted whether I'd ever play football again. But Les worked hard every day to break down the scar tissue. We became close and I found out he'd been in the same army regiment as my father. Les was old school but he knew his stuff and proved very entertaining. I never had a day off, spending every day in the gym and continuing to have treatment.

I set myself a target of making it back in time for the start of the 1993-94 season. Every week that went by I was feeling stronger. I'd done weight-lifting before and enjoyed it but now it became almost an obsession with me and I was pushing my body to extremes.

Dave Ash, the training ground janitor, also helped me a lot. He was fit as a fiddle, a martial arts expert and part-time bouncer who looked after the Everton lads whenever we needed a favour.

I was told that the two plates and screws had to be removed before I could start jogging and kicking a ball but nothing stopped me trying to bench-press more and more weights as the days and weeks went by. I got to a stage where Dave Ash put 230 pounds on the bar in the gym at Bellefield and I was going for a new personal best in one lift. It was a big weight, especially for somebody who weighed only 140 pounds.

I let the bar hit my chest and pushed the weight gradually up to lock out my arms. I did it – a new personal best. I got up quickly and the effort it took to push the weight caused me to collapse. Good job Dave was there to stop me hitting the floor and possibly doing myself further damage.

By this time I felt unbelievably strong and after the operation to remove the metal from my ankle, I was ahead of schedule to resume playing.

After three Premiership wins on the bounce in January '93, February was to be a terrible month for the team with four defeats. I couldn't wait to get back and push to regain my first team place.

By now I was sprinting and doing light ball work. I still had a slight limp and the lads jokingly called me 'The Gimp'.

After a draw against Oldham Athletic at Goodison on the February 27, which ended a run of four consecutive defeats, the midweek home match against Blackburn Rovers was another we had to win. I'd trained with the first team squad on the Friday before the Oldham game and after my second day back on the Monday, I felt good – even though my touch was a bit rusty after such a long time on the sidelines.

Following training on the Tuesday morning I was summoned to Howard's office. We were playing Blackburn that evening and he said: 'Do you fancy it tonight?'

I nearly fell off the chair. Before I could react, Howard added: 'You're the fittest man at the club and we badly need a lift. I want to start you tonight if you're up for it.'

I'd only been training with the first team for two days. It was just short of six months since I suffered that horrific injury at Blackburn.

I told Howard I was in and very much looking forward to it. I knew, deep down, that there would be nobody fitter then me walking on to the Goodison turf that night. If my touch was still a little off, I'd make up for it with my work-rate. I was going to do my job and help the team secure a much needed victory. And that's what we did.

Considering how long I'd been out, I felt amazingly fit, which was testimony to the masterful job performed by the surgeon, the patience and dedication of Les Helm and the help I had from Dave Ash as well as my own determination. I got through my comeback game on pure adrenalin and we had come from behind to virtually seal a 2-1 victory when, with five minutes remaining, Blackburn made a substitution.

Mark Atkins, the player who had nearly ended my career, was coming on. I'll admit, my head was ready to explode and I wanted revenge on him.

Ian Snodin gave me a look and said 'leave it to me.' I just wanted a 50-50 – me and Atkins – and I was going to cut him in two. I wanted retribution for the pain and anguish he had caused me, without even offering the courtesy of an apology. It was payback time.

But before I got another touch of the ball, I could see my No. 7 being held up. I trudged off the pitch, straight past Howard and got into the bath. Minutes later the dressing room was filled with the buzz of a well-deserved victory.

I was hauled out of the bath by Colin Harvey and sat down with the rest of the lads. Howard looked straight at me and asked me why I thought he'd taken me off. I responded by admitting: 'I'd have cut Atkins in half if you hadn't.'

Howard couldn't take a chance by leaving me on for the final five minutes because he knew what I was capable of doing.

He went on to say in front of all the others that I'd shown what can be achieved in the face of a serious injury if the player concerned dedicates himself to working hard.

It got better for me on the Saturday at Coventry, where, in front of the live Sky TV cameras, who were seen for the first time at all top flight grounds that season, I scored a spectacular volley to clinch a 1-0 victory.

My right ankle was never the same again, though. It now lacks the same degree of movement I had in my left ankle before my worst-ever injury.

But, looking back to the spring of 1993, I was just so relieved to be playing after realising how close I could have been to ending my career. I was still only 30 and had a lot of football left in me. With the care and support of my club, a dedicated physio and a will to win, I had managed the impossible. When I look back over my career, I rate this as my biggest achievement. My desire to play in the blue shirt was the main reason for me getting back so incredibly soon after such a horrific injury.

18. SHOOTING THE POPE

FOOTBALLERS and secrets go hand in hand. On a sporting level, that's often a necessity. Many professional sports people truly believe the old adage that what happens in the dressing room, stays there. It works perfectly until such time as a player or manager needs some self-serving publicity – a transfer, a backhander or simply a favour.

It is perfectly legitimate for people to spill the beans on trivia such as who spends the longest time in the shower and other rubbish like that. Arguments and fights carry a different agenda and in any case they happen all the time. It's part and parcel of the game and you can't let every cough and splutter be aired for public consumption. Away from the pitch, the wrong kind of publicity can cause serious damage to clubs and individual players. In exceptional circumstances, it can even end a person's career.

That is one reason I'm glad that, although I once shot a man, it never made it into the papers. It is also why I was relieved that an unrelated saga around the same time, in which I became embroiled in a six-month feud with a notorious gangster, was never exposed to the glare of publicity.

That particular episode started with a hoodlum pinching my chair in a nightclub restaurant and ended only when the man involved – a major Liverpool crime figure with accusations of murder on his charge sheet – decided not to pursue his vendetta. He had been trying to blackmail me and Everton knew all about it.

Both incidents – the 'Shooting of the Pope' and the gangster saga – happened within the space of a few months at the end of 1992, and both had a common venue as a starting point – The Continental nightclub, or 'The Conty', as we all knew it. Both incidents were also more related to the social scene rather than football issues.

Christmas time as a professional footballer is vitally important.

HAMMERED

There are a lot of league points to play for and the balance of a team's whole season can go either way depending on results. Christmas with the family is not the norm. Training, travelling and playing matches are a player's priorities.

Jane loved Christmas and everything that went with it, and I suppose I never really showed much seasonal spirit. On every Christmas Day for about 15 years I was training. As long as everyone close to me had their presents and could enjoy themselves at home, I was happy, but it was the football that was paying for all the nice presents at that time of year, so football always came first for me. Jane would give me ear ache about it at first but she got used to the pitfalls of being married to a footballer and got on with Christmas without me.

The one non-football aspect of the festive season that I always looked forward to was the players' annual Christmas party. No matter which club I was at, the agenda and the conclusion was the same: booze, birds and mayhem, all with the aim of fostering a good team spirit. I went to some memorable bashes over the years, the best nights coming with the players of West Ham and Everton.

One stands out above all the others, and not just because it was full of the usual hilarity. It turned into something altogether much more surreal.

Let's go back to the Everton Xmas party of 1992. Our Christmas gatherings were always held at The Conty, in the city centre, the frequently favoured venue of Everton and Liverpool players at any time of the year. The main attraction was simple: the best looking women were always to be found there. They were darlings. On any given Tuesday night, you'd be hard pressed to find more gorgeous women anywhere else in the country.

A lot of the girls seemed to be there for one reason only – to ensnare a footballer. To be fair, a lot of the time the players didn't take much catching. Why would they? Whenever I took some mates to the Conty, we were always well looked after by the bouncers and staff. There was a restaurant upstairs and Franco, the manager, always made room for and welcomed the Everton and Liverpool players.

Our Christmas parties were always fancy dress affairs. If you didn't arrive in a costume, you didn't get in. It had been that way for years. I remember my brother Billy dressing up as a naughty nun one year. From the front he was perfect, he looked just like a nun, or at least a transvestite nun.

But viewed from the back, there was no costume at all – just the sight of his black knickers and suspenders. The lads spent ages groping him. After a few drinks and with his patience wearing thinner by the minute, he turned to me and said: 'If anyone else feels my a*** again, Mark, I'm going to chin them.'

It was a ludicrous scene, with nearly 200 men all dressed in ridiculous costumes. One year our captain, Dave 'Waggy' Watson, brought along his clan all dressed as Hawaiian girls. There wore grass skirts, flip-flops and a lovely pair of coconuts each. Well, two hairy coconuts anyway. Looking at Waggy, my first thought was, 'Are those skirts flammable?' Only one way to find out . . .

I borrowed a cigarette lighter, sneaked up behind him, and put the flame to the skirt. What they were made of, I don't know, but his skirt ignited pretty spectacularly. One whoosh and his a*** was ablaze. That gave us both a bit of a fright but after putting out the flames, Waggy chased me around the reception area with no back to his skirt and his singed bum on display to all!

The tickets for the Christmas party cost £25 per head and were allocated to the players in early December, so we had time to distribute them to our relatives and friends. They were like gold dust. The usual mob I took included brother Billy and his sparring partner Kevin Kennedy, plus my two old school mates, Kevin Hayes and Peter McGuinness.

It was good value, because that got you entry into the nightclub, a buffet, a stripper, and a free bar until about 11pm. From 9.30 on the night, the management would allow free entry to a select group of attractive women who'd been handpicked and provided with tickets in the weeks running up to the event. Wives and girlfriends were banned. That wasn't unusual at Everton players' functions at the time, nor on any trips arranged by Howard Kendall.

The Christmas party culture is another part of the game that seems to have changed over the past decade. Every year you hear of another club, especially in the Premier League, who have decided to ban the party or whose players have decided voluntarily to skip it. It's all go-karting and double tonic waters now.

Actually, I'm sure the antics still go on, but players these days know they simply cannot get away with any bad behaviour, particularly big-name players at top clubs who are constantly under the media microscope.

Our Everton parties were well organised in every respect. It was vital that absolutely no dickheads – apart from us – should be allowed in to potentially cause any trouble. We didn't have mobile phones with their built-in cameras in those days, while normal cameras were frowned upon. Yet it's still amazing how few incidents ever leaked to the press.

The party proper would be in the evening but we'd all congregate at the Moat House hotel, across the road from The Conty, for a pre-party session. Between 2pm and 3pm, a steady stream of Everton players and their mates would arrive dressed up as Batman, Spiderman, Popeye, nuns, ra-ra girls or whatever. We'd spend four or five hours drinking there before making our way to the club.

At this stage, any new players who had never attended a Christmas party before would have to take to the dance floor and sing in front of everyone. This would always be a test of character. At my first Everton party I practiced for ages beforehand and then sang *Summertime*, the George Gershwin classic, which is still my party-piece.

After the sing-song ended at about 10pm, it was time for the stripper, and it was at this point in 1992 that our party took its first bizarre turn. As the stripper started her act, Billy Kenny, one of the youngest members of the squad, also started to undress. To the amazement of everyone present, he kept on going until he was totally naked, and then he started dancing in front of this girl with his wedding tackle in his hands, trying desperately to get some response from it, but to no avail whatsoever.

It's no exaggeration to say that Billy was the best up and coming footballer in Liverpool at that time, and causing a massive buzz way beyond Merseyside. He was the next big thing, a wonderkid and sure-fire certainty to make it to the top.

Billy had joined Everton as a boy, made it to the first-team squad when he was 17, and by the time of that party he was 19-years-old and apparently on the verge of a major breakthrough in the game. I got on well with him and rated him highly as a talented midfielder who was good on the ball. He was a funny lad, always making people laugh and a typical Scouser.

What we didn't know at the time was that he was also well down the road to self-destruction, ruining his career through cocaine. I have no idea how he got into drugs, but it's not hard to see how it might have happened.

He was a young lad, thrust into the limelight and suddenly being talked about as a wonderful talent before he'd actually made it. He had a few quid in his pocket, he was in an environment where he would work hard and show a certain amount of dedication and commitment, but hard partying was also on offer. Most of us stuck to booze as our drug of choice.

But there were other temptations all around Billy – and he leapt at them. It was a bad situation, which got totally out of hand before anyone realised what was happening to him. He was a mess and probably beyond the help of any of his team-mates before we were aware that his drug abuse was destroying him.

One Monday morning, sometime not long after that party, I arrived at training early as usual to have my cup of tea with Neville Southall, who was already there. Nev was upstairs brewing a cuppa when I walked into the dressing room. What I saw rocked me back on my heels. There was Billy Kenny, sat stark naked in the corner with his feet up on the bench, clearly disorientated and grasping his erection.

He looked a pathetic sight, as if he was totally lost in every sense. He only uttered one sentence: 'Wardy, I'm all f****d up.'

I was too shocked to reply. I couldn't think of anything to say. I immediately legged it back up the stairs to fetch Nev. Together, we dragged Billy across the dressing room and launched him, head-first, into the cold plunge tub. We stood over him until his hard-on had subsided and he looked as though he was calming down a bit.

Then we put him under the shower, dried him off and helped him to put his kit on. How he got through the training that morning I'll never know. It wasn't long before his drug problems became common knowledge among the staff and his demise at Everton kicked in.

I met up with Billy again a few years back and was delighted to see that he'd got his life back on track and appeared to have put his personal problems behind him.

It was a few hours after Billy's naked dance with the stripper at the party of '92 that things really got out of hand. I'd had a lot to drink but sometimes things happen that have a sobering effect very quickly and this was one of them.

During the course of the evening my fellow midfielder John Ebbrell kept on sneaking up to me and slyly punching me before running off. I was dressed as Dennis The Menace. In drinking terms, 'Ebbo' was considered a bit of a softie, and I suppose he thought that taking a few playful punches at me was his best chance of winding me up. It must have been getting towards one in the morning when he punched me for the last time – quite hard actually – in the side of the head.

As Ebbo ran off, my brother Billy said to me: 'He's out of order, Mark. Go and sort him out.' I was quite drunk by that time, having been on it since two o'clock that afternoon, so I'd been knocking back the booze for nearly 11 hours solid. As I turned to go after Ebbo, I crashed into this huge bloke, dressed as a cowboy, who was standing nearby.

I later found out the John Wayne look-a-like was Dave Watson's next-door neighbour. He was enormous and his costume was accurate right down to the holster and gun – a replica, obviously, fitted up to work as a water pistol or cap-gun.

That's what I assumed, anyway, as I yanked it out of the holster and staggered away looking for Popeye – aka John Ebbrell. There were three different bar areas in The Conty and I assumed he'd be skulking in the corner of one of them.

But there was no sign of him in the first bar, nor the second. I walked into the third and still no Ebbo. But Neville Southall was propping up the bar and deep in conversation with Barry Horne, who was dressed as The Pope. His costume was the full works.

'You seen Ebbo?' I asked Barry. 'No, why?' he responded. I waved the gun in front of him and Nev and said: 'Because he's going to get some of this . . . '

We all fell about laughing. Barry must also have assumed it was going to fire only water. 'Why don't you shoot The Pope?' he then suggested in all innocence.

I can't quite recall whether he raised his arms slightly or not, but we were in very close proximity, a foot or two apart at most. At that moment I'd forgotten all about Ebbo. I raised the gun, aimed it straight at the centre of The Pope's chest and pulled the trigger.

The noise was staggering, unbelievable. And as this bang reverberated around the bar, we were all stunned to see a massive flash of fire shoot from the barrel and Barry, who took a direct hit, was flung backwards.

It was a real gun! There'd been a bullet in the chamber. I'd shot one of my team-mates at point-blank range in the chest. The saving mercy – and thank God for it – was that the bullet was a blank, designed to crumple and ignite on impact rather than explode.

Still, Barry was knocked back, and he was on fire. His robes were burning and it was only the rapid intervention of one of our mates, Roy Wright, that stopped an even more serious situation unfolding. He chucked a pint over Barry to put out the flames.

The shock and amazement I felt as we watched Barry's chest being extinguished is hard to describe. Everyone else who saw what happened was equally stunned. I don't think anyone even managed to say anything at all about it until the following morning – it was that unreal.

I got into training early as usual. Needless to say, we were all badly hungover and all the talk among the players was about the shooting of the Pope.

Barry hadn't come in. I was starting to get worried when he finally arrived, about 20 minutes late. He had his papal tunic in his hands.

He threw it on the floor at my feet, looked me straight in the eye and said: 'F*****g hell, Wardy, I thought you'd killed me last night. I was only joking when I said you should shoot The Pope!'

That broke the ice and the lads fell about laughing their nuts off. There was a massive hole in Barry's costume. That one certainly wasn't going back to the shop. He then pulled his T-shirt up to reveal a huge bruise on his chest, caused by the impact of the bullet.

And just as he was displaying his wounds, Ebbo walked into the dressing room, oblivious to what had happened the night before. When he heard that I'd actually been looking for him, he realised he'd had a lucky escape.

Thinking about it later, I realised that if I'd caught up with John, the whole thing could have ended with dire consequences. Knowing how I was at that time – impulsive, diving into situations without thinking, doing stuff first and putting my brain into action later – I would probably have wrestled him to the ground, held the gun to his ear or temple, and pulled the trigger. I would have expected to give him a fright with an earful of water or a loud 'BANG!' from the cap.

But I might actually have scarred him for life or blinded him.

Apparently, as I'd dashed away from 'John Wayne' after nicking his weapon, he'd shouted after me not to shoot the gun under any circumstances. I hadn't heard him.

What would the public have made of that incident if it had ever been reported in the tabloids?

19. THREATENING BEHAVIOUR

THE shooting incident involving Barry Horne didn't make the newspapers and neither did a much more sinister encounter – my run-in with a notorious Liverpool crime figure, which was triggered by a night out at The Conty that had turned ugly earlier on in that same season.

Everton had been playing away at Queens Park Rangers on Saturday, October 26, 1991 and a few of the players had planned a session to welcome one of the new young lads, Matt Jackson, who had recently joined us from Luton Town, once our coach arrived back in Liverpool that night.

After a few drinks to kick-off with in the Labour Club and The Watchmaker pub, the players, accompanied by my mate Peter McGuinness, arrived at The Conty quite late. But that wasn't a problem, because the reliable Franco got us a table, sat us all down – I put my jacket on the back of my chair – and took our orders. I left 'Waggy' and the lads waiting for the food while I nipped downstairs to the loo.

When I got back a few minutes later, my team-mates were all tucking into their ribs and chips but I immediately noticed that my chair had gone. A guy sat with his friends on the table next to us had moved it and was sat on it.

I went over to him and politely tried to explain that he'd mistakenly taken my seat. 'Excuse me, mate, you're in my chair,' is all I said. He just ignored me, so I immediately sensed trouble. I repeated what I'd said and then he stood up and, in the same movement, butted me in the side of the head. As I hadn't had a drink at the time, I'd half anticipated his aggressive movement, pulled away and as he lunged towards me I grabbed his head.

I couldn't believe I'd been head-butted for simply asking for my chair, which still had my jacket, containing my wallet and other personal belongings, hanging from the back of it. It was a set-up – the guy probably knew we were Everton players and just decided to be clever. But, with his head in my hands, I unleashed four or five punches and blood was spilt.

What I didn't know at the time was that this guy, in his fifties, was one of the most notorious gangsters in Liverpool, a hard-core villain. I'm not going to name him here – I'll call him The Blackmailer – but let's just say that he's been accused of many serious crimes, including armed robberies, and was later to stand trial for the fatal shooting in his own house of another well known Liverpool gangster. He was subsequently acquitted of that one, although – and as he later admitted – the police maintained that he was guilty.

He was a dangerous man who you didn't want to cross but here I was punching him in the face. I obviously had no idea who he was at the time or the extent of his connections. But I found out within seconds.

One of his sidekicks that night was another well-known figure in the city, a former boxer who clearly hadn't lost his touch. When it all kicked off, he punched me from the side, on my jaw, and knocked me out cold.

I was dragged into the kitchen of the restaurant and came round a few moments later. All I remember is waking up to see Dave Watson stood above me and then the two of us being ushered towards the exit door by a couple of bouncers.

All the staff at The Conty knew full well who The Blackmailer was, they knew his associates and they knew it was in no-one's best interests to continue any kind of physical confrontation on their premises.

As we left, Waggy spotted my assailant in the car park. I was still unaware who he was at this point and I wanted to know what all the fuss had been about and why I'd been attacked in the first place. As I approached him to ask these questions, I was stopped in my tracks. Standing barely five feet away from us in the car park of The Conty, The Blackmailer suddenly produced a long knife from his inside jacket pocket and said: 'Do you want some of this?' I nearly s*** myself when I saw the shiny, silver blade.

Above: Liverpool's Ray Clemence and John Toshack at Huyton Labour Club presenting the Whiston Juniors end-of-season awards. Kevin Hayes – The Egg – is receiving his trophy from 'Clem', with me – aged 12 – to his left.

Below: A South Liverpool charity game in the early '60s. Billy Ward – my dad – is third from the right in the back, with Evertonian Eddie Kavanagh to his right. In front of Dad is Liverpool legend Billy Liddell.

Left: Me playing with West Ham against Chelsea in 1988.

Right: At West Ham in 1987.

Top: With West Ham in a 1986 match against Everton.

Left: Me and the late, great West Ham manager John Lyall.

Below: Me and West Ham playing Manchester United in 1986.

Above: The squad photo, taken by Geoff Statham. Left to right are (back row): Brian Morley, Tony Murphy, Dave Ryan, John Anderson, Dave Fretwell. Centre: manager John King, Paul Reid, Colin Chesters, Phil Jones, Graham Abel, Steve Craven, George Connolly. Front: Jeff Forshaw, Paul Bennett, Ken Jones (captain), Phil Wilson and me.

Below: My debut goal for Oldham.

Above: It's Wardy the builder!

Below: A family christening with Mum and my brothers and sisters.

Above: Oldham's manager Joe Royle and me.

Below: At Manchester United when I played for Manchester City.

Above: On the day of my release with my mates Peter McGuinness and Kevin 'The Egg' Hayes.

Below: A corporate lunch with other ex-players in late 2009.

Above: With my best mate Mick Tobyn.

Left: A shot of me from 2003.

Matt Jackson certainly had a very eventful first night out in Liverpool!

My nemesis had built himself a reputation for violence in our area over many years. He once allegedly settled a dispute with someone who owed him money by chopping off their fingers on a pub bar.

When we saw the knife, Waggy and I just looked at each other and ran like the wind in opposite directions. It was the start of a six-month ordeal – not just for me, but for Jane and Melissa.

I got out of my car at Bellefield on the Monday morning and was greeted by big Tommy Griff. Tommy knew the ins and outs of a duck's a*** and everything that went on in the streets of Liverpool. Remember, it was Tommy who told me at the PFA bash in London that I'd soon be signing for Everton while I was a Man City player. 'Do you know who you were fighting with the other night?' he asked.

'No,' I replied. Tommy told me the guy's name and said: 'He's not a happy man. In fact, he's very angry.'

Tommy gave me a brief history of The Blackmailer and what I could expect to be coming my way.

Over the next couple of days the word was about to be put out that The Blackmailer wanted £5,000 as compensation for the trouble he claimed I'd caused him at The Conty. He held me responsible for the loss of his gold watch, the ruin of his Armani suit and cuts to his face that required stitches.

What a load of b******s! There was no way I was going to pay a penny to him or anybody else. I'd stuck up for myself, just like always, and was never going to give in to demands, threats or intimidation. Footballers, especially full-backs, had tried to bully me on the pitch, but this was completely different. The heat was on.

I was training with the lads when Colin Harvey, Howard's assistant, stopped the practice session and told me there was an important phone call that I had to take. He took me from the pitch and into the office to speak to a solicitor who said he was representing the man I'd been fighting with. 'Mark, can we sort out this unfortunate fracas?' he asked in a polite, friendly manner.

He told me that if the money was paid to his client – 'reimburse' was the term he actually used – he would do all he could to ensure the incident was kept out of the papers. He added: 'You don't want this getting out, do you? . . . Drunk footballers fighting in a nightclub. You know it's the sensible thing to do.'

The phone calls from The Blackmailer's solicitor to the training ground went on for a while and although I never received any threatening calls at home, I felt I had to tell Jane what was going on. Liverpool is a big city but it holds few secrets and there are often times when it seems more like a village, where gossip travels fast.

My rift with this gangster became fairly common knowledge – even the Liverpool players knew about it because they also visited The Conty regularly on nights out. And nothing went on in the city without Howard Kendall knowing about it, so he pulled me in one day and asked what it was all about. His advice was to stay out of the city for my own good. He seemed annoyed with me for getting myself tangled up with such a known crime figure but when I told him the truth about what happened at The Conty that night, he was more sympathetic and told me to be careful and stay out of the city centre.

Dave Watson and I used to travel in to Bellefield together. Over the next six months I had numerous phone calls and a couple of visits from associates of The Blackmailer. One such meeting happened after training, when this big guy turned up unexpectedly in a large motor.

I got in the front while Waggy sat in the back with Dave Ash, the janitor at the training ground, who volunteered to come with us. Dave was a very hard man, a part-time bouncer and friend to all of us. Howard would sometimes take him on our trips abroad to look after the players. We drove the short distance to Croxteth Park and it was a scene straight out of a mafia movie. I didn't know where we were going when we left Bellefield but I felt a bit safer knowing Ash was with me and Waggy.

The Blackmailer's driver-cum-messenger never uttered a word until we reached Crocky Park, with its little nature reserve, and he'd switched the engine off. He turned to me and said: 'I'll ask you this once and once only. Are you going to pay the money, as he asks?'

I said: 'No.'

He didn't say any more before re-starting the engine and driving us back to the training ground in stony silence. I don't know who the man sent to collect me from the training ground was to this day, but he made me feel very uncomfortable.

The pressure on me became terribly intense and I was worried for my family. My good friend, Peter McGuinness, also became unwittingly caught up in the dispute. He'd been at The Conty on the night all this trouble began and saw what happened, although he didn't get involved.

About a week later, Peter had gone to the Hillcrest Hotel after watching an Everton home game and was suddenly confronted by a menacing figure. The Blackmailer had recognised Peter from The Conty and followed him into the toilets. The Blackmailer didn't inflict any physical harm on Peter but he left my mate feeling more than a little bit shaken.

'I want to buy you a drink and talk about this,' said The Blackmailer, before pouring Peter a glass of champagne. Once he had reassured The Blackmailer that he'd had played no part in the fracas at The Conty, Peter got out of there as fast as he could and then phoned me to tell me about his ordeal.

I felt awful for my family and Peter. The whole ugly saga came to a head after about six months – back at the same Hillcrest Hotel where Peter had come frighteningly face to face with The Blackmailer.

The hotel was just around the corner from my house in Cronton and one Sunday I was having lunch in there with Jane, brother Billy and his wife Julie. Just as I was tucking into roast beef and Yorkshire pudding, I noticed a man walking straight towards our table with a serious snarl on his face. I stood up but he told me to sit back down.

I realised it was The Blackmailer, who had obviously come looking for me. He went on to say that he couldn't sort anything out because my 'tart' was there, and so he promised to 'sort it tomorrow.'

He left the table and proceeded to the bar, where a giant of a man – his minder – was waiting. Jane and Julie were both petrified. We sat at our table for a good hour but, worryingly, The Blackmailer had still not left and remained alongside his henchman at the bar. To my amazement, Billy shrugged his shoulders and said to me: 'Mark, you have f****d him. I'll do the big fella if there is any trouble.'

HAMMERED

We left the two girls at the table and walked up to the bar to pay the bill. As I was about to produce my credit card, The Blackmailer stormed over to me, shouting threats that he needed things sorting out. Billy stopped him in his tracks by pushing his hand in his face and retaliating with his own verbal tirade. The minder was told to back off by The Blackmailer, who said he wanted to talk to us over a drink.

But he was told where to go in no uncertain terms.

To this day, I've never seen The Blackmailer since that meeting in the Hillcrest Hotel. I believe if I hadn't had the support and backing of certain men such as Tommy Griff, Gerrard Starkey, Dave Ash and Mark Quinn, the brother of Mickey Quinn, and my brother Billy, things could have been much, much worse for me.

After a harrowing six months it all petered out. The Blackmailer later claimed in a book he wrote that Everton eventually reached a settlement with him. That was total nonsense – no-one gave him a penny, and his memory of the incident at The Conty differs from mine.

Footballers and secrets go hand in hand. But it's fair to say that I wish that particular chain of events had never happened.

20. GOODBYE GOODISON

HOWARD Kendall's sense of humour was still much in evidence even after he'd resigned as Everton boss early in December 1993 in protest at the board's failure to grant him sufficient transfer funds. The team were lying 10th in the Premiership and despite a 1-0 home victory over Southampton, Howard had decided he'd had enough.

It wasn't until after the players had left Goodison that night that I heard the news. As soon as I found out I rang him straight away but he didn't sound too down in the dumps. In fact, he laughed as he told me that he was just clearing out his fridge at Bellefield!

Even though we'd been on a poor run, it was going to be very difficult for anyone to fill Howard's shoes. Reserve team manager Jimmy Gabriel was put in temporary charge of the first team, with Colin Harvey remaining as No.2, but results went from bad to worse over the Christmas period and it was obvious that a permanent successor to Howard was required. To most of us, Joe Royle, my former Oldham boss, was the obvious choice but the board turned instead to Norwich City's Mike Walker.

Walker had taken Norwich to third in the 1992-93 Premiership, behind Manchester United and Aston Villa, but it seems the Everton board were seduced by the Canaries' shock victory over Bayern Munich in the UEFA Cup, just a couple of months before his arrival at Goodison. That result thrust Walker into the managerial limelight and, as it turned out, took him way beyond his limits.

Just as my first impressions of Lou Macari at West Ham proved correct, so too was my quick assessment that Walker wasn't the manager we needed when he was appointed in January '94. He was a phoney from the start and, although he'd had an impressive 18 months at Norwich, I knew this job was just too big for him.

The tanned Walker was the complete opposite to Howard Kendall.

HAMMERED

He'd arrive halfway through training sessions, dressed in a suit, as if he'd just stepped out of Burton's window and stopped off at the sunbed shop en route to Bellefield.

Walker got rid of Colin Harvey and left his coach, Dave Williams, to do all the training and it wasn't long before the lads had major doubts about the new regime.

The defeat against Liverpool, in which I'd been left out, was the final straw for me. The squad trained at Goodison before the game at Anfield the next day. Walker got us all together in the middle of the pitch and named the team. Then he added that the subs would be from Barry Horne, Paul Rideout, John Ebbrell and myself.

I was absolutely fuming that he'd put 'Preki' – Pedrag Radosavljevic – in the side instead of me. The little Yugoslav midfielder would cry if you went anywhere near him in training and I knew he wouldn't get a kick in the white-hot atmosphere of a derby in which our Premiership future was on the line.

By also leaving out Barry and John, two strong, hard-working players who were needed in the cut-and-thrust of a big game, it showed the manager didn't have a clue. Maybe he'd been involved in derby matches as a player at Colchester United, or as manager when Norwich City met Ipswich Town, but he had no understanding of what a Merseyside clash was all about.

I'd already ruffled Walker's feathers at Bellefield a couple of days earlier. He was such a poseur that he'd instructed the groundstaff to paint his initials on his parking space in the car park. Everton had been led by club legends such as Harry Catterick, Howard Kendall, Colin Harvey and Billy Bingham through the years and yet none of them were vain enough to want their own name or initials marked out for all to see. I decided to show Walker just how pathetic I thought he was being.

I drove into the car park early on this particular morning and noticed the new 'M.W.' painted on the ground where the new manager clearly intended to park his car. So what did I do? I parked my BMW there! Well, I knew he wouldn't be in before me. I'd more than likely pass him on the way home afterwards.

After training, Walker summoned me to his office, where he abruptly demanded that I move my car out of the space reserved for him. He didn't see the funny side of my joke. He then indicated that I 'might be one of the subs at Anfield tomorrow' but I didn't want to be left hanging in the air like that, so I challenged him.

'Am I going to be a sub tomorrow?' I asked.

'I haven't decided yet,' he answered.

'Well *I* have,' I told him. 'I should be playing, never mind being a sub.'

'You have a bad attitude,' he told me.

'You're a bad manager,' I answered back.

'So you don't want to be sub?' he asked.

'No!'

I trudged away feeling absolutely gutted, knowing that Walker was going to ruin the club if he was left in charge for any period of time.

I never kicked a ball for Everton again.

My emotions were in turmoil – I felt so frustrated and angry at what was happening to the club I love.

I was banished to the reserves but I couldn't accept it. I'd never hidden away at any club before by playing reserve team football. Some shameless players couldn't give a toss and are content to see out their contract in this way, but it wasn't for me. I decided I needed to get away from Goodison, or Mike Walker to be precise, even on loan.

After training one day the whole squad was assembled by Dave Williams. The man from Burton's window walked onto the Bellefield turf dressed immaculately in his suit and his skin seemed to glow with a slightly more orange tint from a recent sun bed session. He was briefing the lads who were involved about travel plans to Tottenham the next day. 'Any questions?' he asked, ready to slope off quickly.

What was said next was the final nail in Walker's coffin at Everton as far as I was concerned. Big Neville Southall, clearly alluding to the fact that we hardly ever saw the manager, piped up: 'No questions, boss, but you must have the warmest bed in Liverpool!' Typical Nev – never afraid to tell the truth.

All the other lads started laughing and were all made up that the big fellow had told the manager what everybody was thinking.

Walker's reaction was pitifully weak: 'Well lads, I'll see you tomorrow,' was all he said before strolling off to his car. He'd failed to take on Nev in a battle of wills, never mind reprimand him for undermining the manager's supposed authority.

He was already finished at Everton in the eyes of most of the players but not before he nearly took the club down into the second tier for the first time since 1954. It took Graham Stuart's bizarre winner, a tame shot that bobbled past Dons' keeper Hans Segers nine minutes from time, to clinch a last-gasp 3-2 home victory against Wimbledon on the last day of the season that meant relegation had been avoided.

I should have been there, fighting for the cause alongside my team-mates, but in March I'd decided instead to go out on loan to Birmingham City until the end of the season.

Millwall manager Mick McCarthy wanted me on loan and I was going to the New Den until I got a call from David Sullivan, the joint-owner of Birmingham City. Birmingham was much nearer home for me and David told me that if City managed to stay up, there would be a £50,000 bonus in it for me.

Barry Fry was Birmingham's manager at the time and I also received a call from him. It went like this: 'Mark, I've followed your career since your Northwich days . . . come and show these c***s how to pass a ball!'

He went on: 'We're already relegated but come and enjoy yourself anyway.'

Barry is one of the game's great characters and I liked his honesty and enthusiasm for wanting me to help out. The Blues hadn't won in three months and were staring relegation from Division Two in the face. I knew I could make a difference. I was very fit and just wanted to play first team football for a side that had gone 14 games without victory.

My debut for Birmingham City, on March 26, 1994, ended in a long-awaited 1-0 win over Middlesbrough, who were flying at the time. I ran the show from central midfield and afterwards Barry was full of praise.

I was determined to do my utmost to try and keep Birmingham in the division. I got on great with Barry at first and he was different to any manager I'd worked under. He was my kind of man – straight to the point and very much in your face. In fact, to some of the players he was intimidating with his trademark ranting and swearing.

I really enjoyed the loan spell and gave it my all in the remaining nine games of that season. We won six, drew two and lost one. We produced a magnificent effort to win at Tranmere Rovers in the last game, only to see West Bromwich Albion – who also finished on 51 points – beat Portsmouth to stay just above us on goal difference. We dropped into the third tier along with Oxford United and Peterborough United.

I was sat in the big bath at Prenton Park after we'd been relegated by the narrowest possible margin, when Barry came and sat next to me. Although obviously gutted that we hadn't quite made it, he wished me all the best and thanked me for my efforts. Moving down a division came easily to me. I was able to dictate games from the centre of midfield and it wasn't as demanding as playing in the top flight.

I still had 12 months left on my contract at Everton but I wasn't looking forward to going back there in the summer of '94. Thanks to that last day miracle at Goodison – Everton had been 2-0 down to Wimbledon before goals by Graham Stuart (2) and Barry Horne saved the day – and with other results going their way, Walker had just managed to keep the club in the Premiership. He wasn't getting the sack just yet. Sadly, Joe Royle's Oldham, Swindon Town and Sheffield United went down instead.

It was only a short drive from Tranmere back to Liverpool, where Jane and I packed to go on holiday to the Cayman Islands. On the long flight to Grand Cayman the next day my wife and I discussed our future as well as my own. We weren't getting on that well and I hoped the holiday might help bring us closer together again. As we sipped our wine half way over the Atlantic, it suddenly dawned on me how close I'd been to collecting that £50,000 bonus David Sullivan had promised me. Money was never a motivating factor in my football career but missing out on such a massive bonus, on goal difference, was hard to swallow.

I hoped that the Everton board would sack Walker and I'd be able to pull on the blue jersey once again at the start of the 1994-95 season. But, sadly, I'd definitely played my last game for the club.

21. WHO'S THE JOKER?

THE day I arrived back from the Cayman Islands, I was invited to a charity dinner held at the Moat House hotel in Liverpool city centre. The event was in aid of the Alder Hey children's hospital and I was the guest of Caber Developments Ltd – a building company owned by my mates Paul Downes and Barry Jackson, who had been kind enough to give my brother Billy and cousin Kevin some work.

Feeling completely knackered having travelled for almost a full day, I only went to the dinner on the insistence of Billy who told me I'd be okay after the first few drinks.

My brother dropped me off in my black suit and dickie bow for what turned out to be a star-studded evening. Ian Rush was on the next table to me, snooker star Tony Knowles was there and so, too, were comedians Jimmy Tarbuck and Kenny Lynch.

Compering the event was the well known Liverpudlian comedian Stan Boardman, who wasn't everybody's cup of tea. A professional Scouser or, to some people, a pain in the a***.

I was to have a big altercation with Stan that evening but the trouble between us had actually started months earlier, when I met him in a bar in Liverpool. Bill Kenwright, an Everton director at the time and now chairman, had invited me and a couple of mates to the after-performance party of his play, *The Blood Brothers*.

I've got a lot of time for Bill. He has Everton blue blood running through his veins and I was happy to accept his offer, attending the party with Peter McGuinness.

The cast of the show were all there, enjoying their evening, and I first noticed Boardman when I heard him shouting above the crowd: 'Someone get a box for Wardy to stand on, so he can get the ale in!'

I've always had the mickey taken out of me because of my size, so Stan's verbal assault was nothing new. But he wouldn't leave it there.

HAMMERED

He was drunk, and even his mate was trying to stop him from winding me up.

I turned to Peter and said that I was going to shut him up the only way I knew. 'Don't Wardy,' he said, 'that's what he wants you to do.'

I left the party telling myself I'd catch up with Stan Boardman one day.

At the charity dinner in the summer of '94, Stan was doing his usual stand-up act on stage but I really wasn't listening to his tired, old jokes about Scousers. After a long plane journey and no sleep, and with the champagne flowing, I became drunk very quickly.

Stan had actually played in the same football team as my dad – the Farmer's Arms in Huyton. He was a very good centre-forward and Dad always said he was a character in the dressing room. But on this occasion he went a little too far with his humour.

I was nominated to sing a song on stage, after a table of 10 all put in £50 a man, so I climbed up on stage, where Stan handed me a microphone. I was drunk, but not too far gone to forget the words to my party piece, *Summertime*. I could sing the song backwards and started my performance confidently – well, it was for charity after all. As I belted out my version of the George Gershwin classic, though, Stan started to ridicule me.

'No wonder Everton are s**t and Birmingham got relegated!' he shouted at me.

That was it, the spark I needed to finally shut his fat mouth. I turned quickly, grabbed him round the throat and, with all my strength, pushed him backwards. Stan went crashing into the drummer and I jumped on top of him, locking my arms around his head and not letting him go.

There were no bouncers or security present because it was a charity night – the last place you'd expect any trouble. All my mates and Stan's entourage tried to drag me off the comedian, who was screaming: 'Get him off me.'

I eventually let go, and was marched off by my mates to the reception area to calm down. Moments later, Stan appeared, aiming a load of threats at me. 'My son is going to f*** you, Wardy!' he shouted, so I just called back at him: 'Go and get him then . . .'

Paul Downes and Barry Jackson then took me to The Conty, where the beer and champagne continued to flow. Most of the celebrities from the dinner began to turn up, and Kenny Lynch grabbed hold of me and said: 'Mark, do you know what, son? You've done something tonight that millions of people have wanted to do for years – put Stan Boardman on his back and shut him up!'

I didn't make it home that night. I stayed in Barry Jackson's flat at the docks and woke up with a terrible hangover. I rang The Egg to arrange for him to pick me up and he arrived just before midday. I was already thinking up my excuse to Jane.

As we were leaving the city, The Egg asked me if I'd had a good night. I told him it was 'all right'. Just at that moment, the Radio City news came on at 12 noon. And the newsreader's first bulletin was: 'Stan Boardman is playing down a fight he had with Everton midfielder Mark Ward at the Moat House hotel last night.'

'F*****g hell, Egg, pull over!' I said. It was only then that everything came flooding back to me. I quickly got on the phone to Jane and she said: 'What have you been up to? Don't come back here – there's press outside the house and the phone hasn't stopped ringing.'

Boardman told the press that I'd forgotten the words of my song and was very drunk, and that the whole thing had just got out of hand.

'Lying p***k,' I thought. I wanted to see him again over his remarks but I was in deep trouble with Jane. She wouldn't let me back home for two weeks. In her eyes I'd f****d up again.

22. FRY-UPS, FLARE-UPS AND P**S-UPS

THE 1994-95 season was just around the corner and I was heading back to Everton – or so I thought. Out of the blue, I got a phone call from David Sullivan. The Birmingham City chairman and co-owner said how well I'd done on loan at the end of the previous season and although it wasn't quite enough to save them from relegation, he said he wanted to offer me the chance to become a player-coach at St Andrew's.

I had a massive decision to make. Stay at Everton and play for the reserves while waiting patiently for Mike Walker's inevitable exit, or drop down two divisions and attempt to help Birmingham City win promotion while taking my first steps in a potential career in coaching?

In the end it was no contest. I had zero respect for Walker and I loved a challenge, so I agreed to meet multi-millionaire Sullivan at his mansion in Theydon Bois.

I knew this lovely part of Essex well, having lived just a couple of miles down the road in Loughton during my West Ham days, but I didn't want to travel there alone, so The Egg said he'd drive me. My good mate Mick Tobyn was also going to meet us for a drink in the Sixteen Jack String pub, which is opposite Sullivan's palatial home.

It was a lovely summer's day as we pulled into the empty car park of the pub. Mick was already there, having travelled just a few miles from his home in Romford, and my two mates wished me luck as I strolled across the road and up to the big electric gates in front of Sullivan's castle.

I was greeted by his house-keeper and couldn't believe the opulence and grandeur of the place. It was very impressive. I'd met David during my time at West Ham and always felt comfortable in his company. His racing manager, Eamonn Connelly, was a big friend of mine, and the Birmingham chairman made it very clear that he was keen for me to sign for the Blues on a permanent basis.

HAMMERED

David walked me around his 14-bedroom home and it took an age as he showed me almost every room. It had a cinema, bowling alley, a bar area and its own nightclub. It's a magnificent empire, the result of all the millions he's made from the sex industry, as publisher of the *Daily* and *Sunday Sport* titles. One of the country's leading property tycoons, he was ranked No.114 in the 2009 *Sunday Times* Rich List with a personal worth estimated at around £450m.

We finally sat down in his oak-panelled office to talk over a cup of tea and some sandwiches. He was very straightforward and told me that he wanted me as his player-coach at Birmingham and that I would be on the same contract I'd had at Everton – Premiership wages in the second division.

We shook hands and I told him he had a new player-coach. Before I left, though, I asked him what Barry Fry thought about my appointment. 'Don't worry about Barry,' David said, 'he's behind the deal too.'

I walked out of David's idyllic world to meet my two mates in the pub, ready to celebrate a new start at Birmingham City. I'd been talking with David for well over three hours and thought that The Egg and Mick would be well on their way to getting drunk.

I walked into the bar to be greeted by two glum, sober-looking friends. 'You'll never guess what's happened to us,' said Mick.

The pair of them had been basking in the sunshine, waiting for the pub to open, when three police cars suddenly screeched into the car park. Before they knew what was happening, Mick and Kevin were man-handled by several coppers and told to put their hands on their vehicle and spread their legs.

They were being arrested on suspicion of burglary!

The police had taken a call from a resident near the pub who gave the number plate of Kevin's car. Obviously, it showed up as being registered to a Liverpool address, which set alarm bells ringing in this sleepy, little Essex village on the edge of Epping Forest.

Scousers, in a pub car park, miles from home, at 11 o'clock in the morning? They were obviously up to no good.

Mick and Kevin explained that I was being interviewed by David

Sullivan in his house across the road and that they were waiting for me, but their excuses fell on deaf ears. It was only after a phone call to Sullivan's house and confirmation from his house-keeper that the pair were allowed to go on their way.

They were shaken up by their ordeal but I was p*****g myself laughing!

* * * *

I signed a two-year contract for Birmingham City, who paid Everton £200,000 for me, just before the start of pre-season training. I saw it as a stepping stone, a chance to make my mark as a coach and eventually progress into management. It was a good start at a relatively big club that belonged in the top flight of English football, not the third tier. These were exciting times for Birmingham, with major ground redevelopment just getting underway and the team installed as pre-season favourites to win promotion straight back to the first division.

On my first day in my new dual role at the club I met up with Barry and his staff – first team coach Edwin Stein, reserve team manager David Howell, chief scout Lil Fuccillo and physio Neil McDiarmid. Barry told me that he just wanted me to concentrate on playing but I was adamant that I wanted complete control of the first team coaching.

I could feel resistance towards me from day one. My appointment as player-coach had pushed Edwin Stein's nose out of joint but I was sticking to my guns and knew I could do a good job.

The playing side came very easily to me but the resistance towards my involvement with the coaching was an annoyance. David Sullivan would ring me every day, asking my opinion on all the goings-on behind the scenes. I didn't realise it at the time, but he was then reporting my comments back to his managing director Karren Brady.

Maybe I was a bit naive, but I only told the truth and I wasn't happy with the way things were going. Players and staff, including Barry, were turning up late sometimes two or three times a week because they had to commute from London. It was no good. In fact, it was amateurish.

HAMMERED

I'd go to the ground, collect the balls, cones and bibs, etc, and be at training very early to organise the massive squad that Barry had assembled. We eventually had 58 pros on the books that season. Barry's dealings were legendary. He managed to accumulate no fewer than 22 players from his two previous clubs, Barnet and Southend United. It was like Piccadilly Circus at times and, with so many players around, it was no surprise that one or two cliques developed. I wouldn't go as far as to say that there was a racial split in the camp, but the white lads and black lads tended to socialise apart.

* * * *

At this point in my marriage, Jane and I were quickly drifting apart and I was getting home to Liverpool only once or twice a week. On August 23, brother Billy, Peter McGuinness and Barry Jackson came to watch an evening match against Shrewsbury Town at St Andrew's. It was the second leg of a League Cup tie, we won 2-0 to reach the next round and afterwards we had a great night out in Birmingham. The lads crashed out afterwards in my room back at the hotel where I was staying on the Hagley Road.

The next morning, which was my day off, they were ready to head back to Liverpool but before they left, I said I'd take them for some breakfast in the city. I walked ahead of them and entered an Irish bar before ordering four pints of Guinness. When the lads walked in, I said to them: 'Here's your breakfast, drink up!'

The truth is, I very much enjoyed their company and I didn't want them to go back to Liverpool, so after a couple more pints they decided to spend another night with me. What a big mistake that was.

We ended up staying out all afternoon and got back to the hotel to shower and change before heading on to a nightclub called Liberty's, which was further along the Hagley Road. It was recommended to us by a barman who had served us that day – he said it was full of women and the best place in town.

There was certainly plenty of 'action' in Liberty's but this proved to be a night to remember for all the wrong reasons.

Admittedly, all four of us were very drunk but we were all behaving well until Peter and Billy had a falling out over something and threw water from the champagne bucket over each other. That was the only bad behaviour I recall.

On the way out, Billy was approached by a bouncer, who told him that he had to leave. We were leaving anyway but as Billy got to the top of a small staircase that led down to the exit, the bouncer kicked him in the back, sending him flying down the stairs. He hit his head on a pillar at the bottom and there was blood everywhere.

I couldn't believe it. I rushed down the stairs to my brother's aid and his head was split in two. By this time, the other bouncers had arrived and, before we knew it, Billy and I had been ejected from the club through a fire escape door. Once outside, I looked at his head and it was an absolute mess.

We ran round to the front of the club, which had a big glass reception area. Whatever came over us that night, I do not know, but as a clubber was leaving we darted in through the door to confront the bullying bouncers.

Big mistake. It wasn't so much bravery on our part as sheer stupidity, and our foolishness was rewarded with a terrible hiding. They punched and kicked us out of the door and down the steps. I literally had to drag Billy the short distance back to our hotel.

Peter and Barry arrived a few minutes later with not a hair out of place. I couldn't blame them for not getting involved. It was sheer madness to try and take on the bouncers but I still had to calm Billy, who wanted to go back for another go. I reminded him that I was the player-coach of Birmingham City and didn't need the hassle or bad publicity.

Eventually we fell asleep and I was awoken the next morning by the phone. I went to grab it with my right hand but the pain was unbearable. There was a big swelling on my hand where I'd damaged the bone in the act of punching one of the bouncers. I answered the phone with my left hand and it was Karren Brady.

I thought I was going to get a serious b********g from the Birmingham MD but, instead, she was sympathetic and helpful.

'Mark, I believe you had some trouble last night in Liberty's,' said

Karren. 'We have had the press and television on to the club and think they have CCTV evidence of the trouble outside the nightclub. Leave it all to me, I'll deal with it. Are you okay, though?'

I immediately looked at my damaged right hand and then glanced in the mirror to discover a terrible black eye, but I told Karren that I was okay to train that morning even though I felt awful.

She added that she'd had trouble in the same club when she first arrived at Birmingham, and that I wasn't to worry about a thing.

I'd only been at the club for a few weeks and I'd already been beaten up. Not a good start. It was my fault, though, because I'd persuaded the lads to stay down for another day and we'd had a few drinks too many.

I arrived at training that morning and was greeted by the captain Liam Daish. 'F*****g hell, Wardy, what happened to you?'

I did look bad. I explained what had happened and Liam told me that Liberty's was an Aston Villa club. It was owned by Villa fans and they didn't like Birmingham players going there.

Barry Fry was okay about it, too. He just told me that as long as I didn't miss any games because of my injuries, then there would be no problem.

It turned out that I'd broken a bone in my hand and cracked my cheekbone, but I didn't miss a game.

After the incident, I decided to find a flat, put that unfortunate episode behind me and give the job everything I had. I rented a two-bedroom flat in Edgbaston, just off the Hagley Road.

But the internal politics at Birmingham City were never far from the surface. David Sullivan was still quizzing me every day about the running of the club and it all came to a head one day when Karren Brady came to see me before training.

I was only six weeks into the job and the results were going fine on the pitch. She told me that there was going to be a meeting that afternoon with Barry and his staff.

'Mark, he is going to accuse you of wanting his job,' she said. 'But David and I are right behind the decision to bring you to the club, so don't worry.'

I had no intention of taking Barry's job, although I felt he was showing signs of insecurity. I'd built up a great relationship with the players and I was playing really well myself.

I was a bit nervous going into the meeting because I knew how volatile Barry could be. But I'd seen his kind before. He was a verbal bully to the people he knew he could intimidate. Maybe he could get away with that at lower division clubs, but he wouldn't get away with it with me.

I walked into Karen's office and Barry and his staff were already there waiting for me. I could instantly feel that the knives were out for me.

'Right,' said Karen, 'who wants to start this meeting?'

Barry stood up and pointed straight at me.

'That c*** wants my f*****g job!' he said. 'I'm not having him talking to the chairman behind my back.'

Typical Barry, I thought, full of anger, hot air and losing the plot. I told him to sit down but he carried on ranting and raving, claiming that I'd already lined up Alan Harper, my former Man City and Everton team-mate, to help me run the club. What a joke.

Karren told Barry to sit down and behave. I felt under pressure but was comfortable in the fact that I'd told the chairman only the truth and given my honest opinion on certain issues.

She then looked at Edwin Stein and asked him how many games he'd played in the Premiership. 'None,' replied Edwin. She asked the same question to David Howell, Lil Fuccillo and even the physio. They also all had to reply 'none'.

She was just about to ask Barry how many games he'd played in the Premiership when he erupted. Banging the table, he screamed: 'That's not the f*****g point!'

Karren eventually calmed him down and said: 'That's exactly the point, Barry. We brought Mark here because of where he has been, for his playing ability and the experience he has. None of you have come near to what he has achieved, so just get on with the fact that he is here to coach. He doesn't want your job.'

And that was the end of the meeting. They couldn't argue with the facts but it only fuelled Barry's hostility towards me.

HAMMERED

The team itself was playing well, although, to be honest, we were entitled to win the title as Barry had spent far more on players than any other manager in the second division.

Ian Bennett, in goal, was different class, big Liam Daish organised the defence, I was playing in the middle of the park and Steve Claridge was our centre-forward. It was a solid spine for the championship battle and we were strong in every department. Despite the behind the scenes rumblings, we were on course for a successful season.

* * * *

A week after the aggro at Liberty's, I was still bruised and battered when I arrived back in Liverpool for the day. I was in town having some Sunday lunch when I was introduced to an Aston Villa supporter, who was intrigued at how I'd sustained my injuries.

The guy's name was Sean O'Toole and we hit it off straight away. He was very knowledgeable about the game and even more knowledgeable about the Birmingham nightclub scene.

He told me to give him my address and said he would sort out the trouble I'd had at Liberty's, as he knew Al Stevens, the top man who ran all the doors, who happened to be a Blues fan.

I gave him my address and thought nothing more of it. Later that week, I was sitting in my flat when the doorbell rang. It was Sean. I asked him in and then we went out for a curry, to talk more about football and life in Birmingham.

He introduced me to a club called The Hot Spot, which opened my eyes – I believe it was one of the first lap-dancing bars in the country.

Sean and I got on really well and I never felt the need to ask him what he did for a living. He was a lively character and I enjoyed his company.

In early December '94 I was summoned to Liberty's nightclub by Sean, who was in there with Al Stevens. I was just about to leave for St Andrews, where we were playing against Scunthorpe United in the FA Cup second round that Friday evening, but Sean was adamant than I met with Al there and then.

It felt strange walking into a nightclub full of women and bouncers at 6pm. Sean led me to the back of the club where Al was waiting. He was a gentleman and told me that he'd sorted the problem. His only stipulation was that 'the little bald fella' – my brother Billy – wasn't allowed in Liberty's or any of their other nightclubs.

I explained to him what had happened when the trouble flared but he told me that I'd be looked after while at Birmingham and it was me who had to live in the city, so therefore it was in my interests to accept his offer.

I wasn't happy with the fact that Billy was getting all the blame but Sean told me to look at it positively, and to shake Al's hand, which I did before rushing off to St Andrew's to play in the goalless draw with Scunthorpe.

I spent a lot of time with Sean O'Toole – even leaving him the keys to my flat whenever I went back to Liverpool to see Jane and Melissa. We had a good friendship.

Then, one day, I was asked by one of the stewards at Birmingham City if I knew that Sean had been in prison and was a major drug dealer in Birmingham. I told him I had no idea.

I arranged to meet Sean after training for a bite to eat and I got straight to the point. I told him that somebody had marked my card about him.

He was brutally honest and told me his story, explaining that he hadn't told me about his background before as he was worried it would damage or alter our friendship. I told him it wouldn't. We remained firm friends and I was glad to have known the man for the last two to three years of his life.

We kept in touch even after I'd left Birmingham and then I heard the tragic news about him. I was visiting my brother Andrew when I noticed on Sky News that a man had died of gun shot wounds in Birmingham. I immediately said to Andrew: 'I hope that's not Sean.'

Later that day they named the dead man as my friend Sean O'Toole.

Sean, 34, was apparently shot at point-blank range while drinking with an associate in the busy PJ's Moon and Sixpence pub in Birmingham city centre on December 21, 1997. I couldn't believe it. I could easily have been sat in the pub with him that day, because we'd had drinks in there together numerous times in the past.

HAMMERED

I was really saddened by his death and it took me a while to get over it. I realised then how you can meet people in this world and not know them as well as you think.

But I still say I was glad to have known Sean. He never spoke to me about what he did for a living and never put me in any kind of awkward position or tried to involve me in his drug distribution activities.

23. OUT OF THE BLUE

ALTHOUGH I didn't really see eye to eye with Barry Fry, we had one thing in common – we were both winners and wanted success.

I started to warm to him over the course of the season. He was a complete one-off – there will never be another Barry Fry.

He has his own unique style of management, which sometimes involves speaking and acting before he thinks. At half-time in most matches he would normally blow his top – tell everyone in the dressing-room they were s***. If we managed to win the game, everyone was brilliant when we got back in after the final whistle.

He was the complete opposite of managers I'd played under. The discipline of John Lyall, the expertise of Howard Kendall and the enthusiasm of Joe Royle and Peter Reid all made Barry look second rate, but he had that loveable rogue way about him.

I gave my all for Birmingham and Barry, and he couldn't leave me out because I was his best midfield player.

The supporters really took to me during my spell at St Andrew's and they were a fantastic crowd to play for. As well as reaching the final of the Auto Windscreens Shield, we also faced top flight Blackburn Rovers, who knocked us out of the League Cup before going on to win the Premiership, and took Liverpool to a replay in the third round of the FA Cup.

After drawing 0-0 at St Andrew's no-one gave us a chance at Anfield 10 days later. I told Barry I was going to watch Liverpool before the replay to see if I could identify a way of beating them. I believed that if we could stop the supply of passes to Steve McManaman, then we'd have more than a chance of getting a decent result.

I went back to Birmingham and told Barry that we needed to mark Neil Ruddock but his response was typical: 'What, you want me to tell Steve Claridge to mark a f*****g centre-half?'

HAMMERED

I'd noticed that Ruddock was passing a straight ball into midfield for McManaman, who was running inside from his wide position. He was therefore impossible to pick up and most of Liverpool's attacks began this way. Beefy 'Razor' Ruddock was under estimated on the ball, he had a good range of passes and even though Barry was against the idea, I told Claridge to get close to Ruddock whenever possible. He had energy to burn and could stop the big defender playing his passes into midfield.

Claridge was another character at Birmingham City. We nicknamed him 'Stig of the Dump'. He still lived in Portsmouth and would sleep in his car some nights rather than drive all the way back to the south coast. He'd turn up at training looking bedraggled and I'd send him to train with the reserves.

But he could play, and at Anfield he gave a masterly display with the rest of the team to earn a 1-1 draw in 90 minutes. We went for the win in extra-time and deserved to go through, but it went to a penalty shoot-out.

Barry had sent on the young Portuguese winger, Jose Dominguez, in extra-time. He was a very tricky little player with bags of potential and I told him to attack the Liverpool defence whenever he had the opportunity.

Unfortunately he had a terrible start, giving the ball away on numerous times, and, unbelievably, Barry's patience snapped and he decided to replace him with Steve McGavin – just five minutes after he'd stepped onto the pitch in the first place.

I was disgusted by the manager's decision to sub the sub but, from the middle of the park, there was nothing I could say or do in my poor team-mate's defence. I felt for Jose, who walked past me in the direction of the tunnel with tears running down his face and his confidence shot to pieces. Yes, Dominguez had been guilty of conceding possession too often but he still had the skill to turn the game our way and we needed creative, attacking people like him on the pitch against a side as strong as Liverpool.

Birmingham got a then club record £1.5m for Dominguez when they sold him to Sporting Lisbon a year or so later, but they should have got more from this player of obvious talent with a little more encouragement. Jose would sometimes come to me for little bits of advice and although I always rated him as a player, it wasn't easy to give any individuals too much time with 57 other pros to attend to.

Our efforts in the penalty shoot-out that night were a shambles. I took the first one at the Anfield Road end and struck it well but it shaved the wrong side of the post and I trudged wearily back to the halfway line.

Ian Rush was walking past me in the opposite direction to take Liverpool's first penalty. He was laughing, so I told him to miss. And he did! We had a second chance but failed to convert a single one of our spot-kicks and were knocked out 2-0 on penalties.

It was a very brave attempt, and we were consoled by the fact that we still had a Wembley date to look forward to. True, it wasn't the glamour of the FA Cup final, but the Auto Windscreens Shield final meant so much to so many at Birmingham City at that time. A 4-2 aggregate victory over Leyton Orient in the Southern Area final meant Blues were going back to Wembley to face third division promotion-chasers Carlisle United on April 23, 1995.

It was fantastic for the Birmingham faithful whose club had been on the brink of bankruptcy until David Sullivan and the Gold brothers, David and Ralph, bailed them out in 1993. It was fever pitch at the club's ticket office as some 55,000 Brummies clamoured to book their seat for Wembley. With their rousing old anthem of 'Keep Right On', they would turn the national stadium into a sea of blue.

After my bitter disappointment with Northwich in 1983, when injury drastically reduced my contribution in the FA Trophy final and I petulantly refused to collect my losers' medal, I was determined to come away from Wembley a winner this time. The 1995 final was the first game staged under the Twin Towers to be decided by the League's experimental, new 'golden goal' rule. If the teams were still tied after 90 minutes, the first goal in extra-time would settle it.

As the teams lined up in the Wembley tunnel ready to walk out in front of a sell-out 76,663 crowd (bigger than the previous month's League Cup final involving Liverpool and Bolton Wanderers), I heard a familiar Scouse voice behind me shout: 'Do you want that second round now, Wardy?'

I turned and, to my disbelief, there stood Stan Boardman . . . in his football kit! Stan had been playing in a celebrity match before the main event. I said: 'Yeah, come on then,' and chased him down the tunnel. I was still wound up over his comments to the press following our altercation at the Moat House hotel the previous summer.

Despite Carlisle missing a great chance very early on, Birmingham should have won the game in normal time and Barry was telling us to go for it in extra-time with the sudden-death golden goal coming into play. With 13 minutes gone in the first period, I knocked the ball wide on the left to our £800,000 club record signing Ricky Otto, who floated in a perfect cross for mad Bluenose Paul Tait to glance a header into the top corner.

Paul, a second half sub, famously celebrated by ripping off his blue jersey to reveal a T-shirt with the words 'Birmingham City S*** on the Villa' printed on the front. As well as repeating the title of a popular chant heard regularly around St Andrew's, it also highlighted the hatred that exists between die-hard supporters of Birmingham City and Aston Villa. The authorities were not amused by Paul's prank. As well as receiving a club fine, his actions also brought him a FA disrepute charge.

Paul was a bit of a rough diamond who could certainly handle himself, but we got on great and I always had a lot of time for him. I guess I could easily relate to the problems he'd got himself into during his youth, which led to him dabbling in cocaine and having to attend a drug rehab clinic for tests to check that he'd kicked the habit. He's been an avid Blues fan all his life, the local lad made good, and if he wasn't playing in the game himself, he'd stand with his mates in the Blues Zulu crew on the terraces to watch it. Paul and I have kept in touch to this day and I'm pleased to see that he has settled down now with a family.

Whatever the people who ran the club and the FA thought of his T-shirt gesture in 1995, they couldn't deny him Wembley hero status and a place in Blues folklore. Paul's winning goal brought the Carlisle players to their knees, for they knew there was no way back. Blues became the first club to win the trophy twice, having beaten Tranmere in the final four years earlier.

Receiving the man-of-the-match award was the icing on the cake for me but, overall, it was a fantastic experience for everybody – from skipper Liam Daish, a strong leader of men, to all the other players, and especially the long-suffering Blues fans who finally had something to celebrate after years in the doldrums. I was delighted for Barry, who leapt on me like a little kid, and the directors of the club.

All my family were there to watch me and I met Jane after the game in the players' lounge. She took me to one side and told me that Stan Boardman was in the lounge, before warning me that I'd better not start any trouble with him.

I had no intention of doing so in front of my family but a few minutes later I felt a tap on the shoulder and there, stood behind me, was Stan himself. He stuck out his hand to congratulate me on winning the game and earning the MOTM award. I had no alternative but to shake his hand and we made up over a beer.

Two weeks after our Wembley triumph, on May 6, Blues were crowned second division champions – four points clear of Brentford – after winning 2-1 with goals from Claridge and Tait at Huddersfield Town.

The 1994-95 campaign could hardly have gone any better . . . my first coaching role, winning the title at Huddersfield on the final day of the season and victory in a Wembley final. I'd done my job, played 41 league games and was already looking forward to life back in the first division.

There were celebrations, too, among my family of Evertonians back on Merseyside, after underdogs Everton – managed by Joe Royle – had beaten Manchester United 1-0 in the FA Cup final, thanks to Paul Rideout's winner. Many believed Joe should have been the man to succeed Howard Kendall in 1993 but his appointment didn't come for almost another year, when the Goodison board finally came to their senses and sacked Mike Walker. The team had gone 12 games without a win at the start of the season, Walker had won only six of his 35 games in charge and, in November '94, even new chairman Peter Johnson could see Walker was the wrong man to lead a club of Everton's stature. Sadly, his dismissal came too late for me – my Goodison career had already ended.

And my days were also numbered at St Andrew's. Despite all my efforts throughout Birmingham City's successful 1994-95 campaign, I wasn't rewarded with a new contract at the end of the following season. Barry offered all of his other staff new deals but we weren't talking by then and he left me out.

I'd missed games through injury in 1995-96 but even when I was fit to play again, he didn't always pick me. We barely spoke and I knew, from his attitude towards me in that heated showdown meeting in Karren Brady's office, that I wouldn't have a future while he was manager at Birmingham City. It was clear that Barry saw me as too much of a threat to his job and my time in the West Midlands had come to a premature and disappointing end.

I thought David Sullivan might have been more supportive of me but I didn't go to him or Karren for reassurances about my future or to ask why I wasn't being retained. The club always seemed to be mired in internal politics during my time there and not a lot seems to have changed over the years in that respect. It's a shame, because the club has great support and enormous potential.

* * * *

Once again, both my professional and private life was thrown into turmoil. Jane and I were still drifting apart by this time. I wasn't going home as often as I should have and, instead, I found myself spending more time going to the races with Eamonn Connolly.

One day we went off to Doncaster, where Eamonn was selling some yearlings for David Sullivan. The sales took place two hours after the races had finished and I was well drunk by then.

Eamonn told me to sit with all the other bidders and wait for one of David's horses to come into the ring. I was to bid for the horse until it reached 35,000 guineas. Once it passed that number, I had to quit.

I felt like a millionaire as the auctioneer added thousands on to the price of the beautiful yearling. Once the 35,000 cut-off point had been reached, I stopped bidding – and the horse eventually went for 50,000 guineas.

I'd had a share in two racehorses over the years with the Everton lads. One was called Dome Patrol – but it ran more like a donkey than a horse. I can't recall the name of the other horse, so it can't have been much better than Dome Patrol. I also had a share in a horse called Robeena, with the father of jockey Martin Dwyer. I think it finished third on its debut at Haydock Park but was forced to retire due to a serious leg injury.

I've got so much respect for all those flat and steeplechase jockeys who are totally dedicated to their sport. It's a very tough profession, especially considering the sacrifices they have to make in terms of maintaining their weight.

It was always my ambition to own my own horse outright but I'm not so sure now. When I look back on the lack of success I had with three horses I had shares in, and my bad experience when I bought my own bookies, I think I would have been so much better off if I'd been a jockey!

I was still determined to succeed in football but after Birmingham, it was all downhill for me from then on. It was going to be a steady decline in every way possible – in my career, my marriage and my life in general.

24. THE BIG FELLA

IT was during one of my return trips home while I was with Birmingham that I first met and got to know Everton and Scotland star Duncan Ferguson.

I'd spent the day at Haydock Park races and ended up in Liverpool city centre at an Italian restaurant called the Del Secco. I was with a couple of mates and noticed that Ian Rush was sat with some friends on a table nearby.

'Rushy' and I had a mutual friend, Dave Sheron, who is now a successful football agent. Back then, though, he was just one of the lads – albeit with good connections – and would get us tickets for the race meetings from jockeys and trainers, or hotel rooms whenever we needed them.

Dave had got involved with my move to Birmingham City and represented me along with a solicitor called Richard Hallows. However, we had a falling out over the payment for their services. Let's put it this way, I ended up paying them a lot more than we'd initially agreed. It still angers me now but I learned quickly after that and had to let the matter rest. I didn't hold Dave responsible but it did leave a bad taste in my mouth.

This particular evening, we all ended up on one table, drinking, eating and generally having a laugh. Among Rushy's group of 'friends' were two birds, who were loud and clearly very drunk. They were a couple of slappers, hangers-on.

As the meal progressed, Dave Sheron stood up and said that he was popping down to The Retro Bar to see who was in there. Ten minutes later, he was back to declare: 'You'll never guess who's in The Retro, absolutely bladdered, but Big Dunc.'

Duncan Ferguson had not long signed for Everton from Glasgow Rangers in a £4.4m deal that November and was staying at the Moat

House hotel. I hadn't met him yet, as I was usually down in Birmingham, but just as Dave finished telling us that he'd seen Duncan, the big fella walked into the restaurant, accompanied by Bob, a very drunk night porter from the Moat House.

Everybody turned to look at the big fella, who was more or less holding up the night porter. I pulled a chair over for Duncan, who shook my hand and told me he'd heard a lot about me. Duncan was drunk, but very much in control, and I was laughing to myself as Bob was slumped with his head on the table, completely out of it after a night on the champagne.

I was enjoying the big fella's company but as the evening progressed, Rushy started to have a dig at Duncan. There they were at opposite ends of the table, the two opposing centre-forwards of the city. I'd met Ian Rush on a couple of occasions and played against him numerous times. He was a Liverpool legend and without doubt the best finisher I'd ever played against.

But he was having a little pop at Duncan, asking questions such as: 'So how many goals do you think you'll get this season?'

Duncan was a perfect gentleman and full of respect for Rushy. 'Not as many as you, Rushy,' he replied. Rush wouldn't leave it there, though. 'How many? You must have a target,' he went on.

Again, Duncan was full of modesty and paid Ian a huge compliment by telling him he'd be happy to score half of his tally of goals that season.

I chipped in by saying that Duncan would also make plenty of goals for the team and then Rushy's mate, an Evertonian, commented that as long as he did better than Maurice Johnston, he'd be happy.

The two female hangers-on were still loitering, getting louder and more drunk by the minute. Upon hearing mention of Mo's name, the blonde one said: 'Maurice Johnston? I used to see him – he's a Charlie-head.'

As the blonde kept babbling on about Maurice, the atmosphere immediately changed. I'd spent a lot of time socialising with Maurice, and not once had I witnessed him taking drugs of any kind. I thought to myself, 'I can't let this slut get away with rubbishing his name.' If he'd been present that night, she'd probably have been all over him.

'Hey, that's my mate you're talking about,' I said. 'He's not here, so don't go talking like that about him,' I told her.

She just looked at me and said: 'Who the f*** are you?'

I was in a dilemma now. Rushy's mates were laughing and I just wanted to knock her off her chair. She turned away, which was a good thing because I wasn't the best at holding an argument, and I got back to talking with Duncan.

About half an hour and a few more drinks later, the blonde started spouting her mouth off again, trashing Maurice and directing her comments towards me. I was fuming now but, before I could respond, big Dunc stood up and leant across the table until he was just inches away from the drunken slapper.

'Hey, you wee slag,' he said, 'shut the f*** up. The wee man is not here to defend himself.'

The whole of the restaurant was stunned into silence. Like myself, Duncan knew Maurice and had heard enough of her derogatory comments. He plonked himself next to me and asked: 'Wee man, take me to The Paradox.'

We jumped up and left the restaurant with Duncan's words still ringing in everyone's ears – especially the blonde's.

I'd never been to the Paradox nightclub but we made a call and the bouncers let us in. We had a great night together and got on famously.

The next day, I was in the Watchmaker pub in Whiston when the phone rang. It was Everton skipper Dave Watson, who told me that Duncan wanted to meet me for a pint. He arrived after training and we sat down for a session.

Before long, everybody on the estate got wind of Duncan being at the pub, and we had to close the doors as there were kids everywhere. But he was the perfect gentleman, signing autographs for all the Evertonians, and we became big mates from that day on.

25. GISSA JOB

AFTER my two years at Birmingham City, I badly wanted to stay in football. In fact, I became so desperate that I ended up in hospital for 10 days and nearly lost my right arm.

The 1995-96 season was an uneventful one for me and it took until March '96 before I could get away from St Andrew's and join Huddersfield Town, who were placed higher than the Blues in the first division table and challenging for a place in the end-of-season play-offs. It wasn't far for me to travel across the M62 into West Yorkshire and I enjoyed the sheer enthusiasm of Terriers' experienced manager Brian Horton. After a long career as a player, most notably with Luton Town, he'd learned his craft as a manager with Hull City, Oxford United and Manchester City (as Peter Reid's replacement) before taking over at the McAlpine Stadium at the start of the 1995-96 season.

Brian was very animated and gave management his all. He'd argue with everyone during the 90 minutes, especially those in the opposition dug-out. I liked him, though, and it was because he cared and wanted to win so badly that his emotions would often take over. He kicked every ball from the sidelines.

I looked at this wholehearted man from the West Midlands, who clearly felt a great passion for the game, and wondered what sort of manager I'd be given the chance. For after my experience at Birmingham, I was determined to be a manager and I had my own ideas of how best to manage players. That was in the future, though. Being very fit, I'd always been advised to carry on playing for as long as possible before thinking of hanging up my boots.

Unfortunately, our final position of eighth left us eight points and two places below the play-off places. I'd played eight matches for the Terriers but, alas, there was no contract offer on the table from Huddersfield for the upcoming 1996-97 campaign.

At 33, I still felt that I had much to offer but I was starting to think about life without football and it scared me. The game had been my life since leaving school at 16 but I feared that my career was already coming to a premature, quick ending.

I hadn't been clever with my money over the years. There was no plan for life after football. Now that the end was just around the corner, I became increasingly desperate to find a coaching or management position. When I left Everton for a fresh start at Birmingham, I thought it would be a step in the right direction, the start of a new chapter.

But even success in my first player-coach job counted for nothing. Footballers who had played at the top level were finding it more difficult to find a club to pay them a decent wage and give them a contract to see out their playing days. Having played at the highest level, ageing pros like myself were always going to be regarded by our managers as a threat wherever we ended up playing.

That's what happened with me and Barry Fry and there have been countless other examples where veteran pros have been allowed to drift out of the game simply because the managers at those clubs don't want them hanging around the place when their playing days are over. It's often all about insecurity and self-preservation on the part of those managers already in jobs, rather than building a strong management and coaching team.

What a waste of all that wealth of experience and knowledge accumulated over many years. It's not really an issue in modern professional football, because most of today's players – even those in the lower divisions – can live comfortably long after they've stopped playing and don't need to try and stay in the game in a coaching or management capacity. For those who have basked in the riches of the Premier League or the Championship during the past decade or so, they need never work again. They're made for life – and good luck to them. I don't begrudge players the money they earn today.

You certainly won't see any of them going anywhere near the only two business ventures I got involved in. While recovering from injury at Everton, I had another mad moment and bought a small, independent bookmakers next door to the Labour Club in Whiston. Stan Oakes had it for years but he'd sadly died, so I bought it for £10,000 and installed brother Billy as the manager, while Uncle Tommy and The Egg also helped out.

Why on earth I bought a bookies, I'll never know. Maybe I was bored when the opportunity presented itself? It didn't make a penny. It was okay for a one-man business but it didn't turn over enough to pay staff wages and I realised I had to close it as soon as possible. After six months, I met the area manager of Ladbrokes, who had a shop just across the road from mine, and I ended up selling it to them for a small profit.

My next ill-advised business venture was to buy the Watchmaker pub, my late father's favourite old haunt in Whiston and where he enjoyed his last drink the night before he died in 1988. It had a bad reputation for trouble but whenever it kicked off in there, it was always sorted out between the locals. The police were never called to the Watchmaker while I owned the place.

Jane and I were still struggling to keep our marriage going but my decision to buy the Watchmaker was the last straw for her and we were divorced six months after I took over the pub.

Too often I liked a bet and a drink – not exactly a good idea if you own a bookies and a pub – and I was steadily going off the rails. I'd drink in the pub until the early hours of the morning, especially on the evenings when we showed the major late-night fights on the big screen. There must have been more than 100 people crammed into the pub the night Frank Bruno fought Mike Tyson in Las Vegas in March 1995 and we held regular lock-ins until three or four o'clock in the morning.

Mind you, the best fights took place in the Watchmaker *before* the boxers had even entered the ring in the States! And most of the time it was women, who couldn't handle their drink, who caused or even started the violence!

As my drinking got worse, I sank deeper into a depression brought on by the demise of my football career and the effect it was having on my personal life. I'd lost the love of my wife and my other love – football – was quickly slipping through my fingers, too.

HAMMERED

But my League playing days weren't over just yet. In September 1996 I had a call from an agent and went to third division (fourth tier) Wigan Athletic, who had been bought the previous year by ambitious JJB Sports chain owner Dave Whelan. Former Manchester City and Norwich City coach John Deehan was the Latics' progressive, young manager. He'd been Mike Walker's assistant at Carrow Road but, despite his previous ties, I got on well with him.

He signed me for a month and I was determined to make an impression to earn myself a contract until the end of the season. Apart from playing matches, it was great to be back in training and just experiencing the everyday existence of being a footballer again.

Wigan won four of their five games while I was with them but I didn't play for them again after sustaining a nasty hand injury in the 3-2 home win against Torquay United. I went into a challenge with Jon Gittens and he unintentionally trod on my right hand as we fell.

The broken bone needed surgery and metal wires inserted into the hand to help it mend. With the ends of the wires protruding from the side of my hand, it meant I'd be out for at least two to three weeks.

The day after undergoing surgery I was called into John Deehan's office, where he told me that the chairman didn't want older ex-players and the club's aim was to build a young, up and coming team. John apologised and thanked me for my efforts. Wigan had picked up 12 out of 15 points in my short spell at Springfield Park – they would go on to win the third division championship that season and make it all the way to the Premier League in the next eight years – and I felt absolutely gutted. I thought I'd done enough to at least secure a contract until the end of the season but things can change very quickly in football.

What now? I had no other club to go to and, even if I could find one, who would take me on with a broken hand? I was really in a mess, physically and mentally. Jane and I were finished – I moved out of the house in Widnes and it was later repossessed – and I was terrified of what the future held for me. I knew then that the break-up of our marriage was down to my bad behaviour. As well as my wife, I knew I'd also hurt Melissa, who was 14 at the time Jane and I split up for good, although my daughter told me later that she also felt relieved because she was fed up with her parents' constant arguing.

If Jane and I hadn't divorced then, the fact that I was staring retirement as a player in the face and unable to earn money from the game on a regular basis, was only going to put even more strain on our relationship. I started to drink even more heavily and was shagging different birds left, right and centre. I was really off the rails by now.

My broken hand still had the wires in it when I received a call to play in a game for Dundee, who were top of the Scottish first division at the time. During this very unsettling period on my travels, I'd briefly trained with Motherwell and made one trial appearance for Ayr United without it leading anywhere.

But Dundee seemed the most hopeful option in Scotland. After all, they agreed to pay me a one-off fee of £1,000 to play in their home league game against St Mirren at Dens Park on Saturday, November 2, 1996.

I had a tricky decision to make. Do I cut off the wires with a pair of pliers, or tell them I'm not fit to play? I knew I could get away with saying I'd simply sprained my wrist if I cut the wires close to the skin, and then put a small bandage over the damaged hand. I was so desperate to play, that's what I decided to do. I cut off the wires and set off on the Thursday to Dundee, intending to train on the Friday and then make my debut for the Dark Blues the next day.

When I first agreed to travel north of the border I didn't know the first thing about Dundee – who their manager was or the names of any of the players. All I knew was that it was a bloody long way from Liverpool – just less than 300 miles. In fact, when I pulled up in my car outside what I thought was Dundee's ground, the stadium turned out to be Tannadice Park – the home of their city rivals Dundee United! Well, it's easily done if you're a stranger – the two grounds were a stone's throw apart in virtually the same road!

When I eventually arrived at Dens Park I was greeted by club captain Tommy McQueen – a familiar and friendly face, as he'd played a number of games for West Ham at left-back in the latter part of my second season as a Hammer, in 1986-87. Tommy stuck out his arm and grabbed my broken right hand, gripping it tightly in typically firm Scottish-style. I'd forgotten about the wires until the Dundee skipper screamed out loud and pulled his hand away from mine.

He was sucking the blood off his fingers, where the wires had made him bleed. I immediately apologised to Tommy, explaining I'd broken my hand and that there were wires inside that still needed to be taken out very soon. Although I had a small bandage covering the end of the wire, the end of the metal wire had obviously penetrated the skin on Tommy's hand. What a welcome to Dundee!

Tommy agreed to help me to conceal the full extent of my injury to the management and players because I didn't want it to jeopardise my chances of playing the next day.

I trained with the squad on the Friday and the first time I felt any discomfort was when I went into a tackle and knocked my hand. I felt a little soreness at the time but during the night in the hotel in Dundee I couldn't sleep. The hand became very warm and by breakfast time on the Saturday it was throbbing.

I removed the bandage and examined the hand carefully. The two tiny holes in my hand where each end of the wire had been inserted during surgery had swollen up and looked very red. The actual wires had disappeared into the hand itself!

I knew I was in trouble but I thought that if I could just get this first game out of the way and get back to Liverpool to sort it out, then everything would be fine.

During the game – played in blustery conditions and in front of a crowd of just 2,631 – the pain and heat from the hand became unbearable. I don't remember doing anything of note in our 1-0 defeat but I shouldn't have played – full stop. By not telling manager Jim Duffy just how bad my hand was, I'd been unfair to him, the club, my team-mates and the fans, who had every right to expect more from me.

Afterwards, I was summoned to the manager's office and he gave me my money for playing. As I admitted the full extent of my injury, I told Jim I shouldn't be getting paid anything. He wasn't happy that I'd pulled the wool over his eyes but he realised how desperate I'd been to play. He wished me all the best and advised me to get the hand treated as soon as possible.

I drove away from Dundee on that Saturday night in unbelievable pain. For the last half of the 300-mile return journey to Merseyside I drove with my hand dangling out of the driver's window, to try and cool it down.

Back in Liverpool, I went straight to hospital, where a male nurse examined the injury. By this time the redness had travelled up the arm, beyond my elbow and was spreading to my shoulder. He rushed me to a doctor and I was quickly admitted to a ward, where they treated me for blood poisoning.

I ended up staying in there for a week. The infection was so severe that I lost all the skin off my right hand and had surgery to remove the wires – but I was very lucky. I was told that if the infection had gone past my shoulder, the whole of my body could have been poisoned. And if that had happened, they would probably have had to amputate my arm. I've heard of giving your right arm to play professional football, but this was going too far!

I lay in hospital feeling deflated, angry and at war with myself. How had it come to this desperate state of affairs? I didn't know the answer but it was only going to get worse from now on.

26. FOREIGN FIELDS

WHEN your career is ebbing away and it's almost time to hang up your boots, there is a panic that sets in. Well, it did with me. I wanted to play for as long as I could and it didn't really matter where. After my painfully short-lived experience in Dundee I was desperately seeking another club when a Chinese agent somehow got in touch and told me that a club named Eastern, in Hong Kong, were willing to pay my flight and put me up in an apartment with a three-month playing contract.

I didn't know what to expect and had a meeting with the agent at Heathrow airport before signing the contract a couple of hours before our long flight. My mate Mick Tobyn had agreed to come with me for two weeks and I was looking forward to visiting Hong Kong. My father had spent two years stationed there in the army, based in Kowloon, and when I was a kid he'd tell me all about this fantastic place and urge me to go there some day.

Mick and I were both quite drunk when the flight landed in Hong Kong and I had to quickly try and sober myself up for the welcoming party. As we passed through customs there was a mass of photographers and a tiny Chinese man shouting out: 'Ma-War, Ma-War, Ma-War! Who is Ma-Wa?'

Mick stood there, all 18 stone of him, and said that he was Mark Ward. The little Chinese fella stood amazed and shouted back, 'You not Ma Wa – you too fat!' We both burst out laughing as I shook our small 'minder's' hand before being rushed into a taxi.

The scale of the reception had caught me by surprise but, despite the amount of drinks Mick and I had consumed on the flight over, we managed to stay in control and lucid. Hong Kong amazed me with its high-rise buildings, masses of people and exotic food smells.

The tiny Chinese 'minder' employed by the club took an instant and unjust dislike to Mick, saying, 'Why he here with you? He not play football!' Mick was becoming very angry and warned what he would do to the 'Tiddly' if he spoke to him so rudely again!

I didn't have much time to rest. Training was scheduled for the next day at the local racecourse – after the horses had completed their morning run. I was introduced to two other new players, a lad from Holland and a centre-half from South Africa. Our team coach wore a Liverpool kit and organised the squad into two teams for a small-sided practice game.

It was a great setting but the playing surface was terrible and the Chinese coach had only one point to repeatedly put across to his players. Speaking in broken English, every other minute he'd shout: 'We not Wimbledon, we pass ball like Liverpool.'

Mick watched the training session and I could see him laughing his head off. We both agreed that this trip was not about the football, but the chance to enjoy Hong Kong, the food, the booze and the sights.

There was a game the very next day and I wasn't looking forward to it at all. The rain was torrential and when I saw the size of our goalkeeper, that was it for me. He was 5ft 6in and looked like a little kid between the sticks.

After our warm-up, we were all gathered in the middle of the pitch, where the coach spoke to the team in Chinese before explaining in English that the owner of the club was going to address the players before kick-off.

At that moment a very old Chinese man was led onto the field with two enormous minders either side of him carrying umbrellas and keeping the rain off the frail-looking owner. He spoke only in Chinese and after his little speech the players all clapped him off the pitch. I found out that he'd told the team that if we won the game, there was a bonus of 2,000 Hong Kong dollars for each player.

'Good,' I thought, but then as I lined up to face the tough-looking opposition it dawned on me that we had one of Ken Dodd's Diddymen in goal. The match was a farce – we lost 1-0 after the Diddyman had been chipped from 30 yards – and I was soon asking myself what I was doing there.

That night Mick and I went to The Gene, the notorious bar where Paul Gascoigne made front-page news back in Britain by sitting in the 'dentist's chair' and having copious amounts of alcohol poured down his throat during England's build-up to Euro '96. When we were there the bar was full of girls – I've never seen so many in one bar – who were obviously attracted to the place due to the free drinks for women. At £6 for a pint of Guinness, who could blame Mick and I for getting the local talent to collect a few freebies for us, too!

Yes, of course I tried the infamous dentist's chair for size and after knocking back tequila and untold other spirits, we were certainly the worse for wear by the time we left there.

The next day Mick and I were told that we were to be moved to another hotel, in Kowloon. I asked about the apartment the football club had promised me but didn't get any response. Already they were moving the goalposts.

A Scots lad that played for Eastern's second team told me that the football clubs in Hong Kong were owned by triads and clubs would change hands regularly as part of the island's gambling culture.

I was glad I travelled to Hong Kong but the football was dire and it became just another p**s-up for Mick and me. I made an excuse that I had to travel back home for family business and was never to return to fulfil my three-month contract.

I hadn't been back in Liverpool long when I received a phone call out of the blue from another agent, Kenny Moyes, the brother of current Everton boss David Moyes. He asked me if I was interested in going to Iceland to play for a Reykjavik-based team called FC Valur, who needed an experienced midfield player to help get them out of trouble. They were bottom of the league at the time and had never been relegated before. It was only for the last few months of the season, so I agreed to go.

The club was professionally run and I loved the friendly people there. I had a perfect start on the field, too, when we beat the league leaders. The relief of the Valur players and directors was overwhelming. They prided themselves on having never been relegated and I felt that I could adapt to the team and help them achieve their goal.

Arnor Gudjohnsen, the father and agent of Eidur Gudjohnsen, was in the team and what a player he was even at the veteran stage. Capped 73 times for Iceland, he'd been a goalscoring hero for Belgian giants Anderlecht and also played for Bordeaux in France as well as a couple of top Swedish sides. This stocky, white-haired Icelandic legend was 18 months older than me and he knew the game inside out.

At that time Eidur was playing for KR Reykjavik and I remember watching him play – he was outstanding at that level and it wasn't long before he signed for Bolton Wanderers, before going on to enjoy great success with Chelsea and Barcelona.

I'll always have fond memories of my time in Iceland. Valur stayed up that season and I enjoyed being in a different place and experiencing the Icelandic culture. On my return to England, there was a new challenge for me much closer to home.

27. ANGER MANAGEMENT

FOR many of us who have played at the highest level, dropping down into the non-league scene is unthinkable. But I didn't see it that way at all. I'd swallowed my pride before, when I was given the push by Everton at the age of 18 and rebuilt my career with Northwich Victoria. After my professional playing days were over and I returned from those overseas jaunts to Hong Kong and Iceland, I jumped at the chance to extend my playing days at two more northern non-league clubs.

In October 1998, I'd turned almost full circle by joining Vics' long-time rivals Altrincham, playing 15 Unibond Premier League games, plus nine cup ties, for the Cheshire club. Alty lost only one league match in my first spell there and went on to win the championship that season but I wasn't there to collect my medal. I'd left in the February following a fall-out with manager Bernard Taylor that came to a head after our FA Trophy defeat at Boston United.

As well as managing the team on match days, Bernard also ran the social bar at Altrincham but he wasn't a football man as far as I was concerned. Despite going on to win the league, we were tactically inept and I thought he was out of his depth. In fact, on this particular afternoon at Boston, I told him to 'Get back behind the bar, where you belong,' and I left the club soon afterwards.

I moved to Lancashire-based Leigh RMI in October 1999 and my midfield contribution proved a key factor in their first-ever promotion to the Nationwide Conference at the end of that season. But, like Taylor at Alty, Leigh manager Steve Waywell was not my cup of tea as a manager. Another key member of the side that season was Steve Jones, a brilliant right-winger from Londonderry who was quick and went on to enjoy spells with Crewe Alexandra and Burnley as well as gaining 29 full international caps for Northern Ireland.

HAMMERED

I recall Steve once having a go at 'Jonesy' at half-time and what he said was utter nonsense. He told him: 'You're getting caught in two-man's land' when, of course, he meant to say 'no-man's land'. I use that as an example of some of the embarrassing things he'd say to the players.

There was talk of me being offered the role of coaching assistant at Hilton Park the following season but a much better alternative had already presented itself. Instead of staying with Leigh RMI and looking forward to playing for the Railwaymen one division below the Football League, in May 2000 I received a more attractive offer – to take over as Altrincham's player-manager.

Alty had just been relegated from the Conference under Bernard Taylor when chairman Gerry Berman approached me to get them immediately promoted back to the top tier of non-league football. I didn't apply for the position – Gerry just phoned me one day and asked if I fancied the job.

Taylor was to stay on as general manager but it was made clear that he'd have nothing to do with the playing side. As far as I was concerned, he could get back to looking after the nightclub at the ground, although the Taylors no doubt had influence behind the scenes at Moss Lane. Bernard's son, Anthony, was ominously on the Altrincham board of directors.

I treated this new millennium chance as a very important first step on the managerial ladder. If I could be successful with Alty, then it would obviously bode well for future jobs higher up the League pyramid. Dealing with players and men has always come easy to me and, from my own playing perspective, I adapted my game to suit the more physical demands of non-league football.

Despite having played in front of massive crowds at the best stadiums in England, in the big derby games in London, Manchester and Liverpool, and on the same pitch as some of the true greats of British football, I certainly never thought that turning out in front of a few hundred hardy souls in a ramshackle stadium in one of the non-league backwaters was beneath me.

But, as I soon learned, that was the easy part of being a player-coach at this level. Little did I know when I was appointed on May 20, 2000 that Altrincham, one of the most famous clubs outside the Football League, were already in financial freefall.

Gerry Berman had been bankrolling the Moss Lane club for years and the wage bill was the largest in the Unibond League – twice as big as that of any other club in our division. Relegation just before I arrived had come at a massive cost. Not only had I inherited a poor team but the players were on too much money for the level they were playing at.

We had three centre-forwards – Leroy Chambers, Phil Power and Keith Russell – on £450 per week each but none of them was much good. Power had been a fine player in his heyday but he was now past it. Chambers had a tattoo on his back saying 'Only God will judge me'. I judged him after five minutes – and sent him out on loan to Frickley Athletic. He wasn't up to it. And neither was Russell.

Gerry told me the wage bill for 17 contracted players was £7,500 a week and that I had to reduce it to £5,000.

The club's ailing finances then started to directly impact on the players and myself. We weren't getting paid and it was becoming a nightmare.

I did all I could to steady the ship. I brought in some good, young players. I put Ian Craney, who went on to play for Accrington Stanley, Swansea City, Tranmere Rovers and Huddersfield Town, alongside me in the centre of midfield at the age of 16. But it was a constant battle trying to balance my ambitions for Alty with the club's perilous financial plight.

Despite my pre-season hopes, it quickly became obvious that we had no chance of winning the division as I had to sell our best players. Left-back Danny Adams went to Macclesfield Town for £35,000, club captain Gary Talbot moved to Northwich and Kevin Ellison, our left-winger, to Premiership Leicester City.

Kevin was already at Altrincham when I arrived. Quick and athletic and our leading scorer with nine league goals in 17 matches, he was better than Unibond standard. Loads of clubs were interested in him but it was Leicester who wanted him most.

The board needed the sale of leading scorer Kevin to pay an

outstanding tax bill. I hadn't been involved in the transfer negotiations until I got the call from Colin Murphy, the assistant to Leicester City manager Peter Taylor.

Altrincham needed £50,000, and quickly, so I set off with Kevin and his agent Peter McIntosh to get the deal done. On arrival at Leicester I was called into Peter Taylor's office and he told me point-blank that if he had to deal with an agent over the transfer of a non-league player to his Premiership club, then the deal was off.

Leicester's offer was not particularly generous. Kevin was on £400 at Altrincham and they were offering him £200 a week more. However, if he made the Leicester City first team, then his wages would increase substantially.

I stood with Kevin and his father at Filbert Street and told them of the time I went from Northwich Victoria to Oldham Athletic and took a drop in wages because I was so desperate to play in the Football League. To be fair to Kevin, he had a great attitude and responded by saying that he'd have signed for Leicester City for a tenner.

Finally, the deal was done and Alty got their much-needed first instalment on the £50,000 fee to keep the club afloat. I still get reminded from time to time that I'm the only manager ever to sell a player from the Unibond Premier League – the fifth tier of English football – to one of the Premier League's elite.

Kevin was never good enough for the top grade but the kid found his level and I'm pleased to say he's had a successful career in the lower regions of the Football League with Stockport County, Tranmere Rovers, Hull City and Chester City.

With players having to be offloaded to cut costs, it meant our scouts had to be on the ball if we were to remain competitive, if not the title-chasing team I'd envisaged when I took the job. Tony Murphy, my good mate from my Northwich days and a veteran of the non-league game, came in to help out. He had an encyclopaedic knowledge of the non-league scene and was good at getting players in on the cheap, which was just as well because the money had clearly run out at Alty.

In January 2001, Gerry Berman issued an amazing public apology to me. He went on record as saying he was 'deeply sorry' he and his board had been unable to give me the sort of backing previous Robins bosses had enjoyed.

Berman told the *Manchester Evening News Pink*: 'Mark has done nothing wrong in his short time in charge here and what upsets me is certainly not him but rather that the club and the board haven't been able to back him to do his job to the best of his ability. He has known for some time, as we all have, that he has weaknesses in his squad but, unfortunately, due to financial circumstances, he has not been able to fill the gaps with players of the required standard.

'That's not the way of Altrincham Football Club, as people well know, and it's certainly not typical of me as a chairman.

'But, when we appointed Mark last summer, we didn't realise we'd have these problems, otherwise I'd have laid the law down to him and insisted he cut the wage-bill immediately.

'As it is, Mark has had to offload as the season has gone on. The board have not been able to support him properly – and I feel I've let him down.'

The chairman added: 'As far as I'm concerned, Mark is no different to the likes of Jan Molby and Mark Wright, who have both come into non-league management and are earning rave reviews. Mark should be in that category and it's desperately unfortunate for him that he has joined us at a time when we are experiencing serious difficulties.

'But we'll emerge from them and Mark will come out a stronger manager, just wait and see.

'Never for one moment has it crossed my mind that he isn't the right man for the job here. And neither is it now.

'Mark would already be up there with the Wrights and Molbys if we'd have been there to back him, as we have previous managers.'

I certainly felt let down. Words of public support are one thing but I wanted deeds. The players and I having to go unpaid for six weeks was a terrible state of affairs and I'd had enough. The beleaguered chairman kept promising me he'd turn up with our cheques but he let me down time and again.

The last straw came one Thursday night after training. I angrily rang Gerry's mobile after he again failed to turn up with the players' wages.

HAMMERED

It wasn't as if they could all afford to go without money either. Some lads couldn't even get to training because they didn't have enough cash to buy petrol.

The chairman's phone went straight to answer-phone, so I threw it down on my desk in disgust, while shouting abuse at what I'd like to do to him.

To my amazement, Gerry turned up for the next home game on the Saturday. He came into my office and passed me his phone. 'Listen to this, Mark,' he said.

On the voicemail recording I heard myself screaming all sorts of abuse at him. I was gobsmacked. When I'd thrown down my mobile after training, I obviously hadn't turned it off first, so Gerry's voicemail picked up my whole rant and every obscene and offensive word I'd directed at him. And, believe me, there were plenty of F's and C's among that barrage of expletives.

I handed him back his phone and he said: 'Now what have you got to say about that?' I just blurted out: 'It's true – I meant every word of it!'

He was shocked and dismayed by my defiance but there was a happy outcome to this unfortunate exchange between chairman and manager when Gerry pulled out all the cheques to cover what was owed in wages.

Managing at non-league level can be very difficult a lot of the time. It must be great to get a job with no worries about money and being able to buy and sell whatever players you want. Sure, the likes of Sir Alex Ferguson, Rafa Benitez and whoever is managing Chelsea next week are under pressure to deliver trophies – but I bet they don't have to hurl abuse at their chairmen to ensure their players get paid! Now that's what I call anger management.

Having said that, I did actually enjoy managing. I relished the challenge of working with a young group of players and pitting my wits against the opposition boss but, at Alty, whatever we did on the field was overshadowed by the club's relentless struggle to stay afloat.

Dwindling attendances – down to around the 600 mark despite the fact that we won eight and drew four of our 14 home league games before Christmas – and a decline in commercial activity left the board unable to continue bridging the gap between income and expenditure. They were apparently £450,000 in debt, including directors' loans, and it was claimed that one former director had threatened to bring a winding-up petition against the club.

In December, the directors used the local press to urge fans to come to Moss Lane and also pleaded for new investors, but none were forthcoming by mid-winter and the club was on the brink of going out of business. It was a far cry from the late '70s and early '80s when Alty captured the Conference title and FA Trophy twice and earned national recognition for FA Cup exploits that included a 2-1 humbling of then top flight Birmingham City at St Andrew's in 1986.

Following five years at the helm and less than two weeks after giving me his full public backing, Berman, the club's former saviour and majority share-holder, resigned to make way for a big boardroom shake-up that would reportedly see a business consortium bring new investment into the club.

Acting chairman Mark Harris, who brokered the takeover deal, warned at the end of January that 'things were likely to get worse before they get better.' Harris told *The Non-League Paper*: 'Mark Ward has done a superb job in very difficult circumstances but even at its current level the club cannot sustain the wage bill it is paying.

'Further cuts are going to have to be made. We are going to have to bring a new feeling of realism to the club and only spend what we can afford. But I would like to pay tribute to Mark Ward, who has done an exemplary job, and the players whose attitude has been first class during a difficult period.'

Even so, I sensed that my days were numbered and, sure enough, I didn't have to wait long for the extended new board to make its next decisive move.

On Sunday, March 18, 2001, the day after our emphatic 3-0 home victory over Droylsden, I was summoned to the ground to be given a letter by the Harris stating that I'd been sacked. Anthony Taylor, who was promoted to assist Harris, wanted his dad back in charge of the team.

HAMMERED

Even though I knew that Gerry Berman's departure left me vulnerable, I still couldn't believe I'd been sacked after just eight months into the job. Bernard Taylor – assisted by former Alty player Graham Heathcote – was reinstated as manager and it was all thanks to his son who fancied himself as a big shot and wanted everyone to call him 'Anton'.

When Harris informed me of the board's decision, it was a horrible, gut-wrenching moment. I felt immediate and overwhelming anger, a sense of betrayal and it was so very unjust. I had great difficulty keeping my emotions in check.

Enraged, I drove straight round to the home of Vic Green, Alty's kit man. Vic had been at the club for years and I don't mind admitting that I cried with rage as I showed him the letter. It was an awkward situation for Vic, as he was married to Bernard Taylor's daughter, but even he couldn't believe the appalling way I'd been treated.

The next day I rang the PFA's Mick McGuire, who was Gordon Taylor's right-hand man at the time and a former team-mate of mine at Oldham, who said I could use the PFA's solicitors, free of charge, to fight my case for unfair dismissal.

I went back to the ground at Moss Lane to collect my personal belongings and to say goodbye to the squad. Anthony Taylor pretended to be nice to me but I told him to 'f*** off' and then vowed to fight for all outstanding monies due on my original two-year contract. The idiot responded by saying I wasn't a member of the PFA because I was no longer a full-time pro. When I pointed out that ex-pros remain PFA members for life, he shut up.

It took me months to get over what happened to me at Altrincham – who finished that season in seventh place – 32 points behind champions Stalybridge Celtic – and it still angers me to think about it even now. I received a financial settlement from the club in the end but the money wasn't the main issue. I'd been well and truly shafted.

The damage the b******s who were behind my sacking achieved still haunts me when I think about it. It was my first job in management and for the sake of putting his father, who didn't have a clue, back in charge, Anthony Taylor's despicable actions damaged my reputation as a manager before I'd barely had the chance to get going.

At 38, it was a defining moment not only in my career, but my life as a whole. If I'd been left alone to run the team at Alty, I remain convinced to this day that I'd have gone on and enjoyed a decent career in football management. If I hadn't been unfairly sacked by Altrincham in March 2001, I'm sure I would have done good things there the following season, possibly got them promoted, and my fledgling management career would have gone from strength to strength.

I was mentally torched over what happened and unable to sleep properly for weeks. The overall feeling of frustration and anger really got to me and I felt bitter about it for a long time afterwards.

Two years later, I did get a little satisfaction from a phone call I received from a good friend of mine who was abroad at the time. 'Anton' Taylor had left Manchester and was abroad when he bumped into friends of mine. He was looking to do business with them but slipped up when he tried to do a bit of name-dropping and mentioned to my contact about 'having worked with Mark Ward at Altrincham'.

My mate rang me to ask about Anton's credentials. I told him in no uncertain terms not to do any business with the pretentious p***k. 'That will do for me,' he said. So, indirectly, I did gain a little bit of revenge.

But my time at Altrincham should have been the stepping stone to better things and the start of a promising new career in football management. Instead, I was sliding faster down the slippery slope.

28. ARMAGEDDON

TIME was running out for me and after my bad experience at Altrincham I was desperate to get another coaching or management role. But in football, as in many different walks of life, it's often not what you know, but who you know that matters most. Maybe my reputation was now counting against me on the job front but I believed then – as I still do now – that I can coach well and get the best out of players. But men, not groups of children, as I discovered on an eventful trip to the USA.

It was well into August 2001 and I'd been invited by Dave Jones, who had been involved with me at Leigh RMI, to coach kids in New York. He'd been coaching youngsters in NY for a year and was constantly badgering me to come over and give it a go.

To be honest, coaching children had been never my cup of tea – I didn't have the patience nor the communication skills to get the best out of them. But with nothing else lined up at the start of the 2001-02 season, I booked my ticket to America for a month – and what an experience this turned out to be.

'Jonesy' was a very likeable bloke and had been renting a room off Brian, a Bolton lad who had been living in the States for 12 years and had an interesting job coaching the under-18s women's university team. Dave, though, was working for a guy originally from Liverpool – I can't even recall his name – who had lived Stateside for 25 years.

This fella recruited 34 coaches from South America and Europe and he was delighted to have an ex-Premiership footballer join his coaching staff. But there was something I didn't like about him from the start. He was a phoney but, for the time being, I just let him babble on and gave him the benefit of the doubt.

My first day of work for him was a nightmare. I had to coach football – or soccer, as they call it – to 34 kids all under the age of eight. It wasn't really coaching, though – babysitting on a massive scale and I couldn't manage it successfully. And as I found out, none of the other coaches could either. The sheer number of children was overwhelming and, not surprisingly, I found it very difficult to teach proper skills and pass on my knowledge and experience to any of them.

After the first session the owner of Kiddies Soccer took Jonesy and me for a pint. Me being me, I told him straight that what he was doing, and what he expected his army of coaches to do on his behalf, was cheating the mums and dads, because the coaches he was employing weren't able to do their jobs properly. Needless to say, we had a big fall-out. I'd only been working for him for a day but I told him to stick his job. It just wasn't for me.

Back at Brian's house later in the day, Jonesy told me I'd blown my chances of working there after my forthright comments to the owner. On the other hand, Brian was made up that I'd spoken my mind, as he'd had a falling out with the same guy years earlier and gone his own way. 'I'll tell you what, Mark,' he said, 'I'll send an email to everyone I know here – I've got a soccer coaching database of over 300 email addresses.

'I'll say: "Ex-Premiership footballer, here for one month only, willing to do one-to-one coaching". How much do you want an hour?'

We agreed a fee of $70 an hour, bearing in mind Kiddies Soccer had been paying me $25, or would have done if I'd hung around with them for longer than a day. Brian said the Americans loved one-to-one coaching sessions and that $70 wouldn't be a problem.

The next morning Brian woke me up to say there had already been 25 responses from families wanting to hire my services.

'Get on the phone, Mark, and make yourself a few bucks,' he said enthusiastically.

I sat and phoned all the numbers from the email enquiries and most of the mums I spoke to had two children for me to coach. After an hour on the phone that morning I had a full coaching schedule lined-up.

It was great meeting all the parents, who always stayed to watch me take the kids and help them with the basics of coaching. I'd give them exercises to do that I'd done a million times and try and pick up on their weak spots. Just a simple instruction on how to run up to the ball makes all the difference to some kids.

One father was so impressed that he offered me his indoor astroturf gym in the winter to use for coaching. It was all going swimmingly … until the morning of September 11.

Jonesy was helping me coach four youngsters who were related. Just as we started the session, one of their dads came charging on to the field shouting: 'We're being invaded.'

He scooped up his kids and bolted off to his car. The other parents all quickly whisked their children away, too, leaving me and Jonesy to gather up a load of footballs. We'd heard sirens and also noticed helicopters above. We packed our gear away into the car and switched on the radio to hear those immortal words: 'The Pentagon has just been hit.'

'F****** hell, Jonesy,' I said 'You've brought me to Armageddon!'

We rushed back to the house and were amazed at what we were witnessing on TV. Everyone will remember where they were and what they were doing as that awful day of 9/11 unfolded.

I was just six miles from Ground Zero and the destruction of the Twin Towers, where official estimates reported that around 2,800 people died, devastating the people of America. We didn't move out of the house for two days. My family couldn't get in touch – all the phone lines around us were down – and all they knew was that I was working somewhere in New York.

It really was a life-changing experience seeing people, who couldn't get back into the city, crying in the street not knowing if their loved ones were alive.

Obviously, all my coaching plans collapsed there and then, but what did that really matter in the grand scheme of things? This catastrophic event that destroyed so many lives will never be forgotten.

It took me more than two weeks to get on a flight back to the UK. I thanked Jonesy and Brian for all their help but, in truth, my timing couldn't have been worse and it had been a disastrous trip for me financially. The reality was that I'd not had enough time to earn any decent money and I had to pay £800 for my return flight. I had a stroke of good fortune, though, when I was upgraded to business class on the way home. As I pondered my future, I was pampered by the cabin crew and got very drunk.

A month or so after returning from the States I returned to play non-league football, back at Leigh RMI. My second spell with them lasted 14 months but I found that I was no longer enjoying the playing side. I'd had surgery on a cartilage injury and as well as that, the legacy of the ankle I'd badly broken while playing for Everton at Blackburn eight years earlier was also now taking its toll.

On December 11, 2002 I played my last game of competitive football at the age of 40. The next 18 months were really just a blur as I tried desperately to fill the empty void left by the game I love. It had gone badly in the USA but surely, I kept telling myself, there were other places I could go to try and earn a living.

I knew for sure that I needed to get away from Liverpool.

29. UP TO MY NECK

AFTER my divorce from Jane in 1996, I got the opportunity to travel to Australia and spent four months in Brisbane. I'd hoped to spend a season playing there, or maybe even stay permanently if things went well. I travelled to Oz with a mate called Barry Jackson, who had previously lived there for 18 years and was on his way back hoping to re-settle in the Queensland capital.

I loved the laid-back Aussie way of life and used my time there to soak up the sun and try and get myself established in the game they call soccer. I met Frank Farina, manager of the successful Brisbane Strikers club, who was keen to sign me on but their season was nearly over and it would have taken too long for a work visa to come through for me to play any part in that National Soccer League campaign. My short visit did me good, though, and I was very impressed by the whole Australian experience.

In spring 2004 I got the opportunity to travel Down Under again but this time I was determined that I wouldn't be returning to England. I'd been offered the chance to go and stay in Coogee Bay, Sydney with an old school friend, Peter Jones. He had been home to Liverpool visiting family when I bumped into him in a pub. We reminisced about times we spent playing in the same football teams as kids, and he was adamant that a fresh start in Oz would be perfect for me.

He could see how difficult life had become for me in Liverpool. We had a good chat over a few drinks one night and he actually warned me that I could end up getting myself mixed up in a bit of bother if I didn't get away from the environment in which I'd grown up and lived for most of my life. He thought I'd do well as a soccer coach in New South Wales, especially in the development of kids.

I kept in touch with him after he returned to Sydney and things came to a head when I received a letter telling me that my time for claiming social security was up. I suppose I must have been drawing the dole for around a year but it was no good – I had to sort myself out and get back into full-time employment one way or another. It was an easy decision for me to go and stay with Peter on the other side of the world – once I'd worked out how I could afford to get there.

Billy and most of the family encouraged me to take the plunge. Once again, Billy was willing to give me enough money to tide me over until I got on my feet. Mum had also heard of my opportunity to start a new life and she, too, wanted to help.

I arranged to meet her and went by train to Wolverhampton, where she picked me up from the station. She took me for a coffee and we had a good heart-to-heart about my future. She said I had 'flown too close to the sun at times' and I think she had a mother's intuition that I could end up in trouble if I stayed in Liverpool much longer. She had always said that when I was a kid, if I got bored I'd always find time to get myself into bother. How right she would prove to be.

I'd become close to Mum again at that stage, having not spoken to her or seen her for 16 years after she had left Dad in very sad circumstances.

My reconciliation with her came about because my girlfriend at the time – she's asked not to be named here – kept on at me to arrange to see Mum, or else, she told me, I'd regret it for the rest of my life. My ex was friendly with my youngest sister, Ann, and they both chipped away at me until I relented.

I wanted to meet Mum again on my own terms – alone. My girlfriend and I travelled down to Wolverhampton to stay with my eldest sister Susan, and it was arranged that I'd meet Mum in a pub car park. As I drove into the car park, I saw her sat in her car. I opened her passenger door and noticed how well she looked for her age. It felt awkward for a few moments, so, to break the ice, I told her to 'start speaking English,' as her Scouse accent had been replaced by a Black Country dialect.

It was a strange feeling, seeing and being with Mum again after spending so many years apart. We talked and listened to each other's differences and I soon felt very comfortable with her. At the end of the day, she is *my* mother and I'm her eldest son, who she felt very proud of. She had missed out on so much, especially my success as a footballer, and I'd been the only one of her seven children stubborn enough to have maintained my distance. I think that stemmed from that horrible day I was with Dad when both our lives were turned upside down.

Mum was so keen for me to go to Australia and stay with Peter Jones that she very kindly offered to pay my air fare. After coffee we visited the travel agents, where she paid for a flight that would be leaving Manchester for Sydney in two days' time. She even bought me a big suitcase especially for my trip.

As she drove me back to Wolverhampton railway station, I started to feel very emotional. We both hugged each other not knowing when we'd see one another again. She had been out of my life for so many years simply due to my stubborn streak and I wanted to make up for so much lost time. As I walked away from Mum that day, I glanced back and saw her crying. I shed some tears, too.

The plane touched down in Sydney on May 2, 2004 and I was excited about my decision to start a new life in New South Wales. We'd arranged for Peter to pick me up at the airport and, being a Friday night, I knew there would be a pub full of expat Scousers in Sydney waiting to greet me.

I passed through passport control and waited for my cases to re-appear on the airport carousel. As I loaded my second case onto the trolley, a woman customs official approached and asked me to follow her. I was dying for a pint and couldn't understand why they had singled me out.

After being told to open my suitcases, I stood back and watched and then I was approached by another officer who wanted to check my leather soap bag, containing my mobile phone, which was my hand luggage. A few minutes later a more senior officer emerged and asked if I could explain why there were traces of cocaine found in my soap bag? I was gobsmacked.

My heart started pumping and I knew I was in a serious situation. They were demanding an explanation, plus full details of where I'd be staying and my personal background. I was s******g myself.

HAMMERED

They X-rayed everything I was carrying, including bottles of lotion, toiletries and even the shoes I was wearing. The most senior official came to speak with me, pointing out that the swab they had just taken could detect even the tiniest trace of drugs and that their test was coming up positive in my soap bag – even though there was no physical evidence of drugs.

I started to get my head around what must have happened. I told them of my last night in Liverpool, spent in my brother's pub. I know some of the lads in there took my mobile from me to insert their numbers into my phone's memory. I know so many people, some of them good friends, who use coke and smoke cannabis. I have never touched or sampled drugs but whether you approve or not, it's part of modern culture – not just in Liverpool but throughout Britain and society in general.

The logical explanation was that the residue of cocaine found on my phone could have been transferred there from the hands of someone who had used my handset on my last night in England. As my phone was transported in my soap bag, that explained why the airport check had come up positive. Thankfully, when the customs officer heard my explanation, he finally let me proceed.

It had taken me two hours to get through customs and I needed a drink. Peter, who was still waiting patiently for me in the arrival lounge with his girlfriend, Kirsten, said: 'I knew they'd stop you.' He told me that a lot of lads travelling alone from England are routinely stopped because customs officers believed there would be a fair chance of them carrying drugs.

I arrived in Sydney with £2,000 courtesy of my family's kindness and Peter and his family and friends made me feel very welcome. On the football front, I made many contacts with the aim of starting a soccer school. I also gave a live interview to the local radio station about the upcoming European Championship finals to be held in Portugal that summer and met a guy in the top sports television network who was in charge of *The Premiership* show that covered English Premier League matches. He told me that if I could obtain a visa, there was a chance of me being asked to make regular appearances on his show.

But I soon realised that without a work visa, a foreigner can't legitimately gain employment in Oz. I needed to be all above-board, especially as I'd hopefully be working with and coaching kids in the future.

As I said, it was my original intention to stay and live in Australia but I started to run out of money and after three months, I thought it was best to return home, get my visa sorted out properly and then return to Oz and fulfil my dream.

I don't have many regrets in life but I wish now that I hadn't returned to Liverpool in the summer of 2004. If only I'd stayed put in Sydney, I wouldn't have written this book from a prison cell.

I didn't stick it out in Sydney because I couldn't bum around and rely on others for hand-outs – it wasn't my style. Before I flew back to England, Peter managed to find me two weeks' working for a Scottish brickie known as Dessie, so at least I'd be able to travel home with some money in my pocket. Or so I thought.

I'd never worked so hard in my life. I ended up looking after and labouring for three bricklayers. Keeping one happy was hard enough, let alone slaving away for three of them. I was still very fit at the time but I discovered muscles in my arms that I never knew existed.

On my last day at work I was told to meet them in the pub where I'd be paid. I was travelling home the next day and had been looking forward to pay day. I showered and went off to the pub on that Friday night to enjoy a pint with my work colleagues – Peter, Tommy, Griff and Nib – but there was no sign of Dessie.

Unbelievably, he didn't turn up to pay the wages I'd grafted so hard for. My mates went berserk but nobody could get hold of Dessie. The b*****d knew I was about to go home to Liverpool. I felt gutted as I was driven to the airport with a mere 10 dollars in my pocket.

Ironically, two months after I returned to Liverpool, Dessie sent me a text message saying he was sorry for not having paid me. *Sorry!* What he did to me was despicable.

Much as I was looking forward to seeing my daughter Melissa and grandchildren Zach and Deri again, I returned to find that nothing had changed in Liverpool. I was welcomed home with smug comments like 'we knew you'd be back' and 'what a waste of time going there'. One thing my visit had proved to me was what a s***-hole England was compared to Australia – and I was determined to return to Oz as quickly as possible.

I would very soon have good cause to bitterly regret my return to Liverpool in more ways than one. Things were going well until I awoke one morning in November with a tremendous pain in the back of my head. It was excruciating – the worst I've ever experienced – and it got worse by the minute. I was sweating profusely and had pins and needles in my hands and feet. I was further alarmed to see my feet turn purple.

My girlfriend phoned for an ambulance and before I knew it I was in the local hospital at Whiston undergoing tests. The doctors tried to find out what was wrong with me but I had them baffled. The symptoms pointed to either viral meningitis or bleeding to the brain – an aneurysm. As I lay there, for the first time in my life I feared that I was a goner.

The doctors performed a lumbar puncture on me to try and detect whether there had been any bleeding to the brain. It was just my luck that a trainee doctor performed this delicate procedure – and luckier still that the consultant was overseeing him. I was tucked up in the foetal position, to open up my vertebrae so that he could locate the spinal cord before inserting the needle. I knew he was struggling when I heard the consultant say: 'No, not *there*, you're going into the bone!'

After spending five days in Whiston Hospital I was transferred to Walton Neurological Hospital. The doctors were adamant that I'd suffered bleeding to my brain and they wouldn't allow me to be moved. I wasn't permitted to get out of bed and they even wanted me to use a bed-pan, but I wasn't having that.

I would hang on until I was bursting, then sneak to the toilet. I was soon found out, though. A nurse called Debbie said to me: 'Mr Ward, I have had to pick dead men off that toilet floor just because they wouldn't listen. Do as you're told – and use the bed-pan until we know what's wrong with you.'

I was taken to the operating theatre, where they pumped a dye through the artery in my groin, which then passed along all the arteries in the brain. There was a risk that the operation could cause a stroke but I probably didn't realise quite how ill I was at the time – I just wanted to get out of there as fast as I could, so I went along with everything. It's a weird sensation, looking at your brain being pumped full of fluid while lying on a bed in the operating theatre.

After surgery that night, my tenth in hospital, I commented to Melissa that I felt as though I was in prison.

It was November 11, 2004 when I finally left hospital. I was told to take things easy and had to go and see a blood and heart specialist for a check-up. Christmas was just around the corner and I was dreading it. I like to buy presents for all my family but this year it was impossible. I felt as miserable as hell and was glad when Christmas had passed. I just wanted the chance to return to Australia and was determined to start the New Year in a positive mood.

* * * *

I'd be lying if I said I didn't have acquaintances who have been involved in criminality. Pro footballers and other high profile people seem to attract friends and hangers-on from every walk of life and it's so easy to become involved with them. I've had many friends who have taken different paths and indulged in various forms of criminal acts. Some have been sent to prison as a result of their actions.

Where I come from in Huyton, it's virtually impossible to walk through this part of Liverpool, take in the local pubs and not bump into somebody who has committed some crime or other – or is quite possibly about to!

Early in January 2005, I reluctantly agreed to rent a property on behalf of a friend – not a close mate but someone I'd socialised with. I'll refer to him from now on as Mr X because I won't reveal his true identity. He asked me to do this favour for him and his associates because, in his words: 'You're an ex-Premiership footballer and there won't be any questions asked.'

I realise now that he knew, as a lot of people did, that I was struggling financially, vulnerable and therefore an easy target. The reason why I agreed to his request was the thought of 'earning' easy money for six months. My heart and mind was set on returning to Sydney and I thought this private, short-term arrangement was going to be my passport back to the Aussie sunshine and a fresh start.

Mr X was well known to me. As I said, we weren't exactly bosom pals but we'd had the occasional drink together. He was doing well for himself, drove a nice car, wore smart clothes and although I knew he was 'connected', I'm a great believer in taking people as I find them, at face value. I'm man enough to tell somebody where to go if I don't want to be in his or her company.

Mr X and I spoke about my recent illness and my dream of returning to Australia as soon as I could afford to. It was then that he offered me the opportunity to earn £400 a week simply by renting a house on his behalf. Over a pint and a Chinese meal, followed by a few girls back at his place, he wore me down and I finally agreed to accept his tempting offer. As he put it: 'I'd have a few quid in my pocket for doing f***-all.'

Naturally, I did ask him what he wanted the property for, and his response was: 'For a stash.'

'Stash' is defined in the dictionary as 'a secret hideaway for valuables, usually drugs', so that's what I thought would be placed in the house. In truth, it didn't really concern me at the time what was being kept there – it could have been tobacco, cash or even guns.

It was a terrible lack of judgement on my part and I'll always regret it.

Acting on his behalf, I was to offer the local letting agency four months' rent in advance – £1,800 – for 11, McVinnie Road, a two-bedroom, semi-detached place in Prescot, not far from where I was living at the time. This normal-looking suburban house was on a nice estate and unlikely to attract undue suspicion from neighbours and passers-by.

On January 11, 2005, he handed me the money and drove me to Castle Estates in Allerton Road. The agency didn't bother to make any credit checks on me – there's no way I'd have passed had they done so – because I made the advance payment in cash. To the staff who dealt with the transaction I must have looked financially well off, when nothing could be further from the truth.

I passed Mr X the keys, so he could get a spare set cut, and in return he gave me my first payment of £400.

I felt great that night, pulling the wad of notes from my pocket to get the ale in at The Eagle and Child pub owned by my brother Billy. I wanted to buy everyone who had looked after me a bevvy, in return for their kindness. I remember one of the barmaids actually commenting on my generosity as I happily got the drinks in. She asked: 'Have you had a good win on the horses, Mark?' I snapped back: 'No! Aren't I actually *allowed* to have money?'

I felt my first pang of guilt at my new-found wealth but, I admit, it felt good to have a few quid in my pocket again.

The next day Mr X handed me back the original keys and asked me to arrange for window blinds to be put up throughout the house. He also wanted two timers to be fitted for the lights – one to go in the main bedroom and the other in the living room. He asked me to visit the house as often as I could, to 'make it look as though the house was being lived in.'

Already he was asking me to do things that I'd not agreed to. My suspicions aroused, I pressed him on this but he placated me by saying that there would be another few quid for me to follow next week.

Like a complete fool, I just did as he asked.

It's difficult for most current or ex-players of high profile clubs to do things secretly or to blend easily into the background, even after your career has long since finished. I was reminded of this when I rang a firm of window blind specialists. It turned out that the lad they sent round not only knew me, but also our Billy, Uncle Tommy and the whole Ward family! He never shut up, bombarding me with a million questions. After a while, I had to say to him: 'Are you a detective?' I made up a cock and bull story that I'd be moving in there because I'd fallen out with my girlfriend.

At first I went round to the house in McVinnie Road maybe twice a week but then the s*** hit the fan when I entered the place early in March 2005. Nothing had changed in my relationship with Mr X up to this point. On this particular day, though, the smell as I opened the door was one I'd never experienced before. It was an overwhelming mixture of chemicals and a musty pear-drop concoction.

I walked into the kitchen and it was as if somebody had been baking a cake on a huge scale. There was a food blender plugged in with white powder around its edges. There were plastic bowls, spoons, containers, plastic bags, tape and traces of white powder everywhere – as if it had been snowing in the kitchen. The work surfaces where covered in a film of dust.

It was obviously drugs and I started to panic, big-time. I rushed upstairs and nearly ran into a vacuum packer machine plugged in at the top of the stairway. I knew what it was, as our Billy had used one to seal meat when he had his butcher's shop.

I walked into the main bedroom and saw that heavy machinery had been brought in to the house. There was a large block of metal with a pump by the side – a hydraulic press, as I learned later. It was used to repress cocaine into one kilogramme blocks.

My heart began to race and I couldn't believe the state of the place. I ran downstairs and rang the guy who was paying the rent. 'What the f*** is going on here?' I demanded to know.

'Calm down, Mark,' he said. I went on to tell him what I'd just found. He told me to stay put and he'd ring back as soon as he could.

I sat, trance-like, on the sofa and the dire situation I'd got myself into was slowly sinking in. I'd had my usual Lucky 15 bet earlier in the day but this time the horseracing, on the screen a few feet away from me, was a complete irrelevance. I knew there and then that if what was going on at that house was ever detected by the police, I was totally f****d.

My mobile phone rang. 'Mark, I've just spoke to the big fella and he says he's sorry and it won't happen again . . . and he wants you to clean up everywhere and put it all out of sight.'

'F*** off!' I told him angrily. 'And you can tell the big fella, I want to see him to tell him to get everything out of the house.'

I was warned by Mr X that I'd be very foolish to ask to see the big fella. It was made clear to me that he takes no prisoners and I'd be better off just getting on with cleaning the house and letting the lease run its course, by which time all the incriminating stuff inside the place would be well gone.

Mr X knew my weakness, though, and he exploited it again when he hit me with: 'I'll see you tomorrow with your wages . . . and a bit extra.' Every time I mentioned something I wasn't happy about, he used money as the weapon to shut me up. I can't say it wasn't effective.

I opened all the windows and started to get stuck into cleaning up the mess that had been left. I then dragged the heavy machinery into cupboards and out of sight. It would normally have taken two strong men to have carried that hefty metal lump upstairs but my adrenalin was pumping and I just wanted to finish tidying up and get the hell out of the house.

To get my head round this frightening situation, I drove to Billy's pub to have a pint and consider what I should do. I just wished I had enough money to have got on the next flight out to Sydney. I knew I was in a very perilous position – my whole future was at stake. I wrestled with the problem over and over in mind before coming to the conclusion that I'd have to ride out the storm – and pray that my luck lasted.

But I was still angry and called Mr X to arrange a meet the very next day. I drank solidly for the rest of that day and was very drunk by the evening, desperately trying to erase the realisation of the dangerous situation I had foolishly got myself into. I'd never been an angel on or off the pitch, and I liked to play on the edge. I suppose that is how I lived my life off it, too. This, however, had gone beyond living on the edge.

I was up to my neck in it.

I remembered Mum's words on the day she had paid for my flight to Oz: 'Mark, you can fly too near the sun too many times.' How right she was.

My meeting with Mr X the next day led to another £500 sweetener being stuck in my hand. I protested that I still wanted out but he kept reassuring me and told me not to worry because the big fella had sorted out the problem. He said: 'The house won't be left like that again . . . just carry on and it will soon be July and the lease will be up, plus you'll have more money to help you get back to Australia.'

My life had become a roller-coaster ride yet again. I'd gone from being in Sydney and trying to make a new start in life, to coming home and being seriously ill and confined to hospital for 10 days. Now there was a very real risk of being arrested if events went horribly wrong for me again.

If things were looking already bad for me, they were about to get much, much worse.

30. MY WORST NIGHTMARE

THE 12th of May is a date that will live with me forever, in more ways than one. Firstly, it was the birthday of my late father, William Joseph Ward, who sadly died in 1988, aged just 52.

It was also on this day in 2005 that I was arrested for a serious drugs-related crime.

I believe that if Dad had still been alive on that Thursday to celebrate his 69th birthday, then I wouldn't have got myself into the nightmare situation that unravelled so dramatically. I had so much respect for my father and was always terrified of letting him down, but I certainly did this time.

Billy Ward had always been very anti-drugs and I can imagine him turning in his grave at the circumstances surrounding his eldest son's dramatic fall from grace. Our dad would have killed his kids if he'd caught any of us smoking either in or outside the family home, which is why none of us have ever smoked cigarettes.

Although I'd been through tough times, financially, in the previous few years, a big win at the bookies the previous day had put me in a more positive mood when I awoke on that warm and sunny May morning – even though it wasn't a happy occasion.

I was attending the funeral of Patricia, the wife of a nice fella I knew called Stevie Adare. The service was held at St Agnes Church in Huyton, the tough area of Liverpool where I was born and grew up. After the funeral my Dad's brother, Uncle Tommy, and two of his friends shared a lift in my Rover MGZT for the short drive to the crematorium at St Helens.

As I pulled into the car park at the crematorium, my mobile phone rang. It was a woman calling from the Castle Estates letting agency, who had leased me the property in nearby Prescot. She explained that the police were outside the house and that the burglar alarm was going off. She said that as I was the sole tenant of the property, the police wanted me to go there straight away to turn it off.

I told her that as I was nearby, I'd go to the house immediately. I apologised to my uncle, saying that I had to leave him there because something urgent had come up.

Uncle Tommy looked me in the eye and asked if I was okay, as if he sensed something wasn't right. I couldn't tell him the truth because, apart from those directly involved, nobody else knew of the house I'd rented on behalf of a third-party. I left him looking confused and told him I'd meet up with him later, back in Huyton for a drink at The Quiet Man pub.

I didn't know it then that but it was going to be a very long time before I would be enjoying his company again, chatting over a pint and a bet and being amused by his dry, cutting wit.

The drive from the crematorium to Prescot took no more than five minutes. I tried to remain calm and prayed that it was nothing more sinister than a faulty burglar alarm, or even a minor break-in, and that the police just wanted me to check if anything had gone missing from the house.

But, deep down, I was concerned that it could all go horribly wrong. And it did.

People have asked me since: 'Why did you drive to the house – why didn't you just disappear when you got the call from the letting agency?' There was no point – the police could easily have traced me anyway. After all, the house in question was rented in my name.

By now it was around 11.30am and I was driving on to the quiet estate where 11 McVinnie Road was located. I stopped at a T-junction and then looked to my right in the direction of the house, where my worst possible fears were confirmed. Parked outside the property, just 25 yards or so from where I was sat in my car, were two big, yellow police vans, a couple of patrol cars and up to a dozen officers congregated in front of the house, which was nearest to the corner.

There was no burglar alarm to be heard – the police had lured me there with the help of the unwitting letting agents. The only alarm bells I remember hearing when I drove up to the house were ringing very loudly inside my head.

I found out later that they'd had the house under surveillance for some time and, armed with a warrant, they had burst in to discover the drugs they had expected to find there. Inside, they also found the tenancy agreement document and a council tax bill with my name on it

My heart was poundng and I couldn't think straight. 'What do I do now? What have they found? Do I drive off or go to the house and find out what all the fuss is about?'

In a split-second, I decided to drive off as discreetly as possible without attracting attention, hoping that none of the police had recognised me at the wheel of the silver-grey Rover. I turned left onto McVinnie Road – in the opposite direction to the house that was swarming with coppers – and drove away from the scene.

Brother Billy owned The Eagle and Child pub close by, so I headed for there. I desperately needed to talk to someone I trusted who could give me honest advice.

As I turned right into the next road, I was horrified to see two police cars with their blue lights flashing coming towards me at high speed. It seemed that half of Merseyside police were chasing me.

I accelerated, overtook a van and took a sharp left into a quiet cul-de-sac. I thought that if I could dump the car there, I'd get to the pub on foot. I walked towards The Eagle, which was only about 300 metres away. I was frantically ringing the pub doorbell just as two police cars whizzed past but it was still only mid-morning on Merseyside and before opening time. I got no answer. I also tried to contact Billy by phone but there was no answer there either.

Alongside the entrance to The Eagle was a builders yard, where I took refuge as the wail of sirens continued to fill the sunlit noon air all around me. There was a massive pile of sand in the corner of the yard and the thought flashed through my mind: 'I wish I could bury myself in there and hide for a few hours.'

Unable to make contact with my brother, I had to accept that the chase was over. As I walked round to the other side of the pub, there were four coppers waiting for me. I found myself surrounded by plain-clothed and uniformed officers and I knew the game was up. There was no struggle.

I'll never forget the look on the face of the policeman who had the duty of handcuffing me. He was breathing heavily and bore the look of someone completely and utterly stunned. As he fastened the cuffs behind my back, he said: 'What have you got yourself involved with here, Mark? You're in big trouble.'

He cautioned me and said I was being arrested on suspicion of possession of a controlled drug with intent to supply. At least one media report subsequently claimed that police had found a quantity of drugs on me, but that wasn't the case. The 'possession' on my charge sheet was in reference to the property registered in my name.

I was led away in the direction of where I'd left my car. As we walked, the copper told me he used to be a season ticket holder at Everton and had watched me play. It's amazing the silly things that go through the mind in moments of crisis. I had a flashback and wondered if he'd been at Goodison and cheering for me on that day, in September 1993, when I scored against Liverpool in the Merseyside derby. No wonder he looked shell-shocked.

My head was spinning but I tried to remain as calm as possible. Back at my car, police were already conducting a search of the vehicle and found two additional mobile phones inside the glove compartment.

The Evertonian copper began to search me and took cash out of my rear trouser pocket. He counted the money in front of me and it added up to £750. He also retrieved my phone from my trouser pocket.

With three mobile phones and such a large amount of cash in my possession, it didn't look good for me. A quip of 'Footballer to Drug Dealer' from one smarmy officer immediately hit home.

A crowd started to gather as I was put into the back of the police van. The journey to St Helens nick was one of complete calmness and no words were spoken. Although I knew I was in trouble, I kept telling myself: 'Just tell the truth and it will be okay . . . stay calm, you haven't done anything bad . . . you haven't killed or physically harmed anyone.'

If I'd committed any crime at all, it was the fact that I'd rented a property and given access to others to use it in my absence. I was confident of satisfactorily explaining my minimal part in the whole episode. If the police had found drugs on the premises, they were most certainly not mine. And I had no part in putting them there.

At the same time, I also knew I couldn't reveal the identity of the person I'd rented the property for. No way would I ever grass on him or his associates.

There was a welcome party awaiting me at the police station. The phones and money were produced on the desk in front of the sergeant. 'That's a lot of money to carry around,' he said. I replied by saying that I was going to buy everyone a drink after the funeral.

The fact is, only one of the phones belonged to me. The other two had been left in the glove compartment of my car by the mourners I'd given a lift to church. I explained that I was carrying such a large amount of cash on me because I knew I'd be out and about for the whole day and, besides, I'd won the money legitimately on a Lucky 15 accumulator bet I'd placed on the horses the previous day.

I may have got lucky to have backed four winners and gained such a good return on my £30 stake, but my luck had now well and truly run out.

I didn't know at that stage what police had found at the house, although I remember one of the officers sarcastically remarking: 'What's he been trying to do, raise money for Everton's Champions League campaign!'

I was taken to a cell, told to strip off and put on a white paper suit. There was a box in front of me where I was instructed to place my funeral clothes, including the new black cotton Armani T-shirt I'd bought the previous day especially to wear for the funeral. As I undressed, I heard a copper say: 'F*****g hell, with the time he's going to be looking at, he may as well keep that stuff for his own funeral.'

The cell door was slammed shut behind me and I lay down trying to come to terms with my nightmare ordeal. The awful, long wait to find out what exactly had been found at the house was frustrating and I feared that I could be in serious trouble.

I found it impossible to sleep on what seemed like the longest night of my life. Knowing it was Dad's birthday, I wondered how he'd have reacted to my arrest had he still been alive. He would have been furious with me, to say the least.

I had to be strong for my 22-year-old daughter Melissa and the rest of our family. Even then, I felt ashamed that I'd not only let myself down but being arrested was going to alter my whole life – whatever the outcome.

Friday the 13th is considered by some to be unlucky – and that morning in May 2005 certainly proved that way for me. Without managing any sleep the previous night, I felt dirty and tired. A duty solicitor called Paul Durkin came to see me. He knew I'd been a professional footballer and he was friendly enough, but his words were straight to the point and chilling: 'Well, Mark, they have found four block kilos of cocaine and adulterants for the cutting and re-packing of cocaine and other paraphernalia.'

Mr Durkin's direct manner and revelations hit me hard. 'You're in s*** street, mate,' he continued. 'They've analysed the blocks of cocaine and have taken 60 items from the address.'

He told me the three options I'd face in the police interview to follow:
'Say nothing at all.

'Answer some of the questions but refuse to answer others.

'Or make a written statement and answer 'no comment' to the questions.'

Looking back, I would prefer to have said nothing at all but when you're in a desperate, highly pressurised situation like the one I suddenly found myself in that day, you don't always do the sensible thing. Foolishly, I chose to make a written statement.

I was brutally honest – far too honest for my own good, as it turned out – and wrote: 'I had rented a property for a third party – for a stash.'

Mr Durkin was simply a duty solicitor and, in hindsight, I wish Lenny Font, the solicitor who later represented me, had been present from the beginning. When Lenny read my statement, he came straight to the point. He said that what I'd written for the police had given my defence team nothing to work on.

The statement I wrote at St Helens police station ultimately condemned me to prison for the next four years – even though I had nothing at all to do with what was found in the property and stated that I deeply regretted my very limited involvement in what was clearly a much bigger crime.

My police interview lasted about four hours, with breaks at half-hourly intervals. Most of the questions the detective sergeant put to me were pathetic and pointless.

'Are you Mark Ward who played for Everton Football Club?'

'No comment,' I said.

'How old are you?'

'No comment.'

'Do you have any brothers or sisters?'

'No comment.'

He also asked me if I'd been forced to take any action against my will, or if I'd been the victim of extortion, kidnap, blackmail, assault . . . anything like that, to which I also replied 'no comment.'

The 'no comment' response to every question put to me over the course of four hours became very boring, although I tried to inject a little humour into proceedings in between one of the breaks. I turned to DS Green, who was asking the questions, and remarked that he looked like Teddy Sheringham. 'I never thought I'd find myself being questioned by another footballer in a police station,' I said.

He wasn't amused, though, and countered with the comment: 'I never thought I'd be questioning Mark Ward about being a drug dealer.'

His comment was cutting and, as it was off the record, in between a coffee I pointed out to him that I was not a drug dealer. He was clearly annoyed that I'd chosen to answer 'no comment' to every question but I'd made my written statement and was entitled to keep my silence.

Not that my stonewalling tactics did me any favours. I had already given them all the ammunition they needed to charge and eventually convict me with my ill conceived written statement.

Honesty has often got me into trouble in the past. Our Billy and other members of my family used to say that if I was thinking something, I couldn't help but say it out loud. I suppose I inherited this trait from Dad, who always called a spade a spade and suffered the consequences later. Mum once told me that in one of my school reports, the headmaster said I was 'very impetuous', and I have to agree that he was right there.

When the interview finished I shook hands with Paul Durkin who had organised Huyton-based solicitor Pat McLoughlin to represent me in the magistrate's court the next day. He was very positive and confident that I would be granted bail, as I'd never been in trouble with the law before. I was banged up again but not for long. My cell door reopened about an hour later when I was formally charged with three offences:

Charge 1: Possessing a controlled drug of class A with intent.
Charge 2: Possessing a controlled drug of class A with intent.
Charge 3: Being concerned in the production of a controlled drug of class A.

Charge 1 was for the possession of cocaine; Charge 2 related to crack cocaine; and Charge 3 was for allegedly being concerned in the production of crack cocaine.

I was shattered by the charges. If there was crack cocaine present at 11 McVinnie Road, and the stuff was being manufactured there, I knew I was f****d – big-time. I felt totally defeated and was left reeling after the hours of interrogation. Nothing I had experienced in the past had prepared me for the turmoil that engulfed me in the custody suite at St Helens police station.

Yes, of course my problems were all self-inflicted and I had made an appalling mistake by getting involved and effectively sub-letting the property out to criminals for ill-gotten gain.

But I was not a drug dealer. The drugs were not mine and I was determined to fight my corner. While I knew I was looking at time in prison, I hoped my sentence wouldn't out-weigh my crime. I have always been realistic when faced with bad situations and although I knew it looked dire for me, I just kept hoping that I would get bail and be able to extricate myself from this nightmare, once I was on the outside again.

I was put back in my cell but that night of Friday, May 13 seemed longer than the previous one. The trauma surrounding my arrest prevented me from getting any sleep, a factor not helped by the noise from the other arrests as the night progressed. The drunks babbling on and protesting their innocence – even arguing with themselves! – remained constant throughout the night.

My thoughts were for my family and friends, especially my daughter Melissa, who I knew would be distraught. I'd only been able to make one call from the police station and that was to Billy. My brother was great, just like always. Although gutted, he reassured me that he and the family were trying to get me the best possible legal representation. Billy assured me that he was going to put up his pub as surety for my bail the next day. He didn't question what I'd got involved in. He just said that he and all the family were right behind me and that they would be in court to see me the next day.

When Saturday eventually arrived, I felt even more dirty and unkempt – those two days in a police cell were a horrible life-changing experience. I was put in a prison van to go less than 100 yards across the road to the magistrate's court. I could hear the other arrested lads in the van talking to each other about whether they would be granted bail. The consensus was that the magistrates don't give bail out 'because they're all knob heads.'

My solicitor came to my cell below the courts and told me he was putting in an application for bail. He was hopeful based on my clean background and believed that this should be regarded as a positive in my favour.

However, he also pointed out that the charges against me were very serious and I may have to make a bail application at the Crown Court, because – as the lads in the prison van were saying – the magistrates hardly ever grant bail.

I felt very nervous as I was led into the court. As I climbed into the box I was asked to state my name and address. I scanned the courtroom and to my left I saw Melissa, her partner Kevin, Billy with his wife Julie, Uncle Tommy and Auntie Helen. I remember the haunted look on their faces, especially Melissa's. I knew she was hurting very badly just seeing me in the dock and knowing I was at the mercy of the magistrates.

I sat down to be amazed by what I heard. The prosecution explained what, at that time, they believed to have been found at the property – including four kilograms of cocaine plus half a kilo of 'crack' that was being prepared and found in the freezer. The prosecution originally claimed that the estimated street value of the drugs found at 11 McVinnie Road was somewhere between £1.5 million and £2.5 million. It was only later that the true extent of their find was revealed.

Police also discovered a vacuum press, a cutting agent and drug paraphernalia when they entered the premises.

The female prosecutor went on to describe the house as a 'drugs factory.'

I just wanted to stand up and yell out 'that's a load of b******s' when the woman then said that the prosecution was opposing bail on the grounds that I may interfere with witnesses and abscond.

My solicitor told the court of my unblemished background and made the point that, as an ex-professional footballer who had played in the four major cities of London, Liverpool, Birmingham and Manchester, it would be very difficult, if not impossible, for me to abscond anywhere.

When he'd finished defending me, I started to feel more confident that it would all blow over and I'd be free to leave the court and fight my case from the outside.

I was led away to the cell for 10 minutes but then brought back to hear more bad news. The magistrates were refusing bail and remanding me in custody until May 19. I looked across at my daughter and the rest of the family and the sight of Melissa's tears rolling down her face will haunt me forever.

I had handled pressure, on and off the field, all my adult life as a fairly high profile professional footballer for Oldham Athletic, West Ham United, Manchester City, Everton and Birmingham City. I'd played in more than 400 league games at the biggest and best grounds in England over a league career spanning some 13 years. Now, more than ever, I needed to show the same strength that had characterised my playing days to get me through whatever was to follow.

Before I knew it, I was being loaded onto the meat wagon, along with other criminals, for the journey to the notorious Walton jail.

As the van turned into the prison entrance, I wondered what kind of reception awaited me – not only from the inmates but also the screws. I knew the shock news about the ex-Premier League footballer nicked on a serious drugs charge would lead to big headlines. The press had been present in court that morning to report on my shameful appearance, so news of my imprisonment was bound to spread rapidly.

I kept telling myself to remain focused, be strong and not show any weakness – just as I did throughout my playing career. I knew lots of lads who had been sent to Walton, so I was aware that I had to keep my wits about me. I thought I might become an easy target. But I'd never let anybody bully me on or off the field and it wasn't going to happen now.

Walton is one of the largest prisons in Europe with a capacity of 1,600 prisoners. It is over-populated and, consequently, has a strict regime.

As the gates closed behind the prison van to accept its latest guests of Her Majesty, I was moments away from being known as Prisoner WARD NM6982.

31. PRISONER NM6982

I COULDN'T believe it when they told me on arrival at HMP Liverpool – or Walton Prison, as everyone calls it – that I'd be put on A-wing, where the most dangerous prisoners serving life sentences were all kept.

Why lifers' wing? Surely that's for the evil b******s – the murderers and rapists – not me? I wondered if being sent there meant I really was looking at a long-term sentence.

A surge of anger came over me – and, yes, there were feelings of grave injustice too. Sure, I'd been a f*****g idiot in agreeing to rent a house for criminals who, as it turned out, were using the place to manufacture hard drugs.

But I wasn't a druggie. And I didn't sell drugs to anybody either. I was no more than an accomplice but it still felt as if the whole world had turned against me.

It's amazing the things that go through your mind in times of emotional crisis. I even started to question whether they had put me in with the lifers because the prison screws were all Liverpool football fans out to punish me in the worst way possible!

After the ordeal of my first strip-search and giving away much of my 'welcome' bag of treats to the smack-heads on arrival, the screw told me to move on as he shouted the next prisoner's name. I stood by the door waiting to enter the heart of the prison. Another screw told me to follow him, and not to stop to talk to anybody.

The walk to lifers' wing had to take in B-wing, the remand wing. To my amazement some of the prisoners were out of their cells, 'on association'. Association is what they call the hour in which you're let out of your cell to play pool, table tennis and to use the prison telephone. This was done on a rota basis.

By now the whole of Walton knew I'd be arriving and the prisoners were waiting to get a glimpse of the shamed former footballer. I walked close behind the screw, concentrating on not dropping the bundle of clothes and bedding I was holding. My first impression was how small and condensed it all was. B-wing was narrow but very high, with five landings. Everything seemed so claustrophobic.

And then I heard the first shouts coming from the prisoners. They were shouts of encouragement and recognition.

'Keep your head up, Wardy, lad.'

'You're one of us now, Bluenose.'

'Great goal in the derby, lad.'

I just kept walking and was aware of everybody's eyes focused upon me. As I approached a group of prisoners sat together, one stood up and shouted to me: 'Mark, it's Paul McGrath. I'll try and get you over here with me.' Stood next to Paul was Ian Hughes, who gestured to keep my head up.

Paul McGrath, who was also in on a drugs-related charge, played in the same Whiston under-12s team as me. Ian Hughes had grown up with me and my brothers. I knew both lads very well and it was encouraging for me to see them there. But, already, I felt how intimidating and claustrophobic the prison was.

As I left B-wing, a screw was stood in front of a big red door with the words 'A-Wing Lifers' painted on it. A gut-wrenching feeling shot through my body. What was behind this door? I was dreading my entry into prison life.

The prison officer on lifers' wing took me into his office. 'I bet you never ever thought you'd end up in here, son?' he said. He went on to tell me that they had taken the decision to put me on lifers' wing because it was more disciplined and the atmosphere subdued compared to B-wing. Here the prisoners are all doing long sentences and so they tend to get on better with each other. There is an air of acceptance and relative stability to the place. But then Baghdad during a bombing raid is more peaceful than B-wing. It was everyone's worst nightmare.

The screw told me that I was to be put in a cell with a young lad from Newcastle. He advised me: 'I don't know if you will be moved on to B-wing next week but keep your head down and you'll be okay.'

I left his office and went off to find my cell. I was approached by a big, black prisoner, who introduced himself as Martin Jackson, and said he knew a mate of mine called John Brougham. He also told me he was the wing listener – somebody I could go to if I had any problems.

I found my cell on the ground floor of the wing, where I was greeted by a lanky Geordie called Chris. He was polishing the floor of the cell. It was immaculate and the floor gleaming. He was very friendly and instantly made me feel at ease.

Chris told me that two Scousers wanted to see me upstairs. I walked up the metal staircase and was met by Paul Hannon and Mark McKenna, who were in for a drugs conspiracy. Paul was a big Evertonian and he sat me down to explain how things worked on the lifers' wing. Their insight into prison life was important to me and Paul stressed I needn't fear trouble from anybody. I never felt intimidated by others, although I avoided eye-contact with other prisoners.

Paul warned me, though, that I'd be looking at a sentence of eight-to-10 years. His estimation shocked me but, as I was to discover, he was spot on.

Mark went to fetch me two brand new prison T-shirts. I almost laughed to myself as they were in the colour of West Ham's famous claret. They both told me to try and stay on lifers' wing, because B-wing was very violent and volatile.

Paul pointed out that prisoners were coming and going on B-wing every day and, consequently, there was no discipline among the prisoners, who were in a state of constant turmoil. There were little gangs from different parts of Liverpool always taking each other on. And it was full of smackheads.

* * * *

It was Saturday, May 14, 2005. I'd been in custody for three days but it seemed more like three months. That night, when the prison door was banged shut, I felt really down and it dawned on me that I was looking at a long sentence. News of my arrest was announced on the radio and television and I realised it was big news that an ex-Premier League footballer had been nicked.

HAMMERED

I talked to my cell-mate Chris from the bottom bunk and he gave me good advice about how to arrange for money to be sent in from the family and how to book a visit. I couldn't wait to see my family and organise a decent solicitor to sort out a case for my defence.

But there was one burning question repeating itself over and over in my mind: How long will I have to spend in prison? One night in Walton was enough for me to realise I'd made a very terrible mistake.

Paul Hannon and Mark McKenna worked behind the wing servery. Paul was a typical Scouser – loud and funny. I was in the queue waiting for dinner when Paul spotted me. 'Here he is, lads . . . scored against the s***e in the derby. Right Wardy, what do you want?'

As I passed over my metal tray with its tiny compartments, Paul just loaded my tray with everything that was on the menu. I tried to tell him that I wasn't that hungry and I struggled to carry the mountain of food to the table. The food, if you could call it that, was awful but I knew that everything from now on in my life was going to be different.

I sat around on the Sunday listening to Paul explain who was in for various murders and telling me about those who had committed other evil crimes. He pointed out an old fella who was stood nearby. 'See him, Mark, that horrible little b*****d dressed up in his mother's clothes and murdered his family. He is never getting out.'

It was unreal thinking about the men around me and learning of their appalling crimes that had brought them to Walton. The lifers were from all over the country but mainly from the north-west. A few came up to me and shook my hand, telling me of the matches they had seen me play in. They were fans of Man City, Birmingham and loads of Evertonians came to have a close-up look at the ex-footballer in their midst.

Just before I was allowed to settle down with the lifers, I was told on the Monday that I would be moved to B-wing, because that was the remand wing and I was a remanded prisoner.

Paul Hannon tried to have a word with the P.O., in an effort to keep me on lifers' wing, but to no avail. Just before I left for B-wing I received a visit from Robbie Fowler's father-in-law. He was in on fraud charges but had been moved to the lifers' wing for his own protection – because of his relationship with the famous Liverpool striker. His parting words to me were: 'Do what you can to stay on here, because B-wing is f*****g barbaric.'

I packed my belongings and was helped the short distance to B-wing by Paul, who told me that he'd got word to a few of his mates on B-wing to look out for me.

I was taken to the office and immediately noticed the difference in the two wings. The noise level was louder and there was much more going on in B-wing, which held 250 inmates. I was allocated Cell 21 on landing four. I walked up to my cell carrying my bedding and noticed how dirty the landings were compared to those on the lifers' section.

When I arrived at my cell I got the shock of my life. It was disgustingly dirty. The furniture was broken, there was no glass in the toilet window and the toilet itself was literally full of s***. The floor looked as though it had never been cleaned and, even worse, was the sight of the biggest cockroach I've ever seen. It scuttled across the floor and escaped into a hole in the wall. It made my flesh itch and I just wanted to be at home with my family.

Before I could dwell on my misfortune, my new cell-mate appeared at the door larger than life. He was a young Scouser called Tommy. He threw his belongings on the top bunk and asked me if I had a roach. I didn't know what a roach was. Was he asking me for a cockroach? When I told him that I didn't know what he meant, he laughed and explained that a roach is a makeshift cigarette filter made out of cardboard, to put in a rolly.

F*****g hell! A smoker! First s*** and now smoke in my cell. I wasn't having it.

I went off to find my old mate Paul McGrath. What a stroke of luck. His cell-mate, an old man called Alfie, had just been sentenced to life for murder and was being moved to lifers' wing. Alfie was a big Evertonian and told me he'd have a word with the PO for me to move in with Paul. Thankfully, the PO was OK about me moving in with Paul and I felt so much better.

I quickly moved my stuff into Cell 4-06 and what a difference this place was. It was clean and there was no s****y smell. There was even a window in the toilet, but it wasn't glass. It was an old snakes-'n'-ladders board that had been cut perfectly to fit in the window.

Paul and I had so much to talk about.

32. DEATH IN THE WALLS

I WASN'T sleeping. My mind was in turmoil. The noise throughout the night was unbearable. Deafening music, and prisoners shouting to each other from their cell windows. 'Hey kidder' or 'You're a grass' or 'I'll see you in the yard tomorrow.' Idle threats, but they had the desired effect in the early hours of the morning.

I was used to having complete silence at night in the freedom of my own bedroom. Now I was in a zoo with noise emanating from every corner.

However, it wasn't only the shouting, the music, or even the snoring of my cell-mate Paul McGrath that prevented me from sleeping. The grave reality of my situation and the thought of spending a long, long time behind bars raced constantly around my mind.

I'd already been warned by numerous inmates that I could be looking at 20 years. I laughed it off at the time but, on reflection, I knew deep down that I was in a lot of trouble. If what the press had claimed was true – that a 'drugs factory' manufacturing huge quantities of crack cocaine had been found – then I was facing a hefty sentence.

It wasn't long before I witnessed my first sight of physical violence inside. I got up for breakfast and was queuing with the other prisoners for our cereal or porridge, when someone was suddenly punched flush on the chin by a lad two places in front of me. He fell like a sack of spuds and the bowl full of cereal and milk flew up in the air and all over everyone stood nearby.

That sparked a mad rush from the screws. The prisoners were told to get back behind closed doors as the whistles for more back-up rang through the wing. It was an hour before we were allowed to go back and finish our breakfast, and the poor lad was still out cold. Paul told me that this kind of thing happened most days, and I began to wonder if it might happen to me at some point soon.

HAMMERED

I could hear some of the prisoners pointing me out. 'That's him, the footballer. He's f****d, they're going to throw away the key.' It was tough to hear but I told myself that I had to remain strong and ignore any taunts.

At that point, the only thing I was looking forward to was my first visit, on the afternoon of Wednesday, May 18. Melissa, Billy and Tommy were coming in to see me, and I couldn't wait to see their familiar, friendly faces.

All the lads who had visitors that day were let out of their cells in the morning for a shower and then, just before 2pm, led over to the visiting area, which was situated in the new part of the prison. Even though I'd only been in prison for a week, feeling the fresh air as we walked between the two buildings brought a tremendous sense of relief. It was a gorgeous May day and just to feel rays of sunshine on my face again and to breathe in the air was an unbelievable delight.

I felt like a right scruff in a pair of black leather shoes, black Nike tracksuit bottoms and a sky blue cotton crew-neck jumper. These were my only personal belongings, which police retrieved from the house in McVinnie Road. I'd have to ask Melissa if she could send in some new clothing for me.

It was pretty intense to be stood in a small room with the other prisoners, waiting to be called in to greet our loved ones. I looked around and could tell how much they were all looking forward to the next hour of their lives.

My name was called and I was given a designated table to sit at, marked clearly by a number. Once all the prisoners were seated at their tables, the door was opened and a swarm of bodies just rushed through, their eyes darting around the room as they searched for a familiar face.

I was beginning to feel very nervous about seeing them again face to face when I instantly spotted Melissa. She was heavily pregnant, and my heart just sank as I saw the hurt and upset on her face. I just wanted to burst out crying there and then but, instead, I stood up to hug my little girl and assure her that I was okay. Melissa is an emotional person and I wasn't surprised to see how upset she was. She said how tired I looked and asked if I'd been eating properly.

Billy and Tommy shook my hand and also asked how I was coping. They all felt gutted for me and just wanted to do all they could to help. I was to appear in Huyton magistrates court the next day, hopeful that I'd be granted bail. Billy was putting up surety for bail and, as a well-known footballer who had never been in trouble before, I felt I stood a good chance.

Typically, Tommy tried to make light of the situation. There was a prisoner, much older than myself, aged about 70, sat at the next table and my uncle looked over at him and said to me: 'F*****g hell, lad, you'll be as old as him before you get out of here!' Our Billy went mad at him for cracking a joke at my expense, but I didn't mind. I've always appreciated Tommy's sense of humour. Melissa told me months later that as they left the prison after their first visit, Tommy put his arm round her and said: 'He'll be all right.'

When visiting time ended at 3pm, it was the hardest thing in the world to have to say goodbye to my daughter. I was so choked up. That first visit was going to be one of many but I'll never forget it because it went so quickly. The hour vanished in what seemed like 10 minutes.

The reality of my situation, and what it was doing to my family, really began to hit home. I was ashamed and disgusted with myself for having put them all through this ordeal. I couldn't look behind me as I left the visit room and was led back to the crazy world of B-wing, praying that I'd get bail the next day.

When I reached my cell, Paul – who had been in two months before me – sat me down and gave me his advice on getting the best legal representation. He told me that to get on in prison you have to conform, keep your head down, take any opportunities that come your way, and work hard to move on after being sentenced.

Sentencing was a long way off. I started to keep a diary after that first visit, writing down my memories, thoughts and feelings on paper.

The ever-present question in my mind was: 'How long will I be in prison for?'

Billy arranged for a solicitor named Lenny Font, from the Liverpool firm Hogan Brown, to visit me in prison. My trip to the magistrate's court was a waste of time because I was remanded in custody until June 16. I didn't apply for bail at that point because Lenny – whose company specialise in criminal defence – advised me that it would be better to put my application before a judge in the crown court instead.

I began to feel angry with myself. I'd somehow got myself into an unbelievably pathetic position and I was trying to come to terms with the idea of spending a long time behind bars.

I was just praying that my sentence didn't out-weigh my crime. The courts were in the habit of dishing out heavy sentences for drug-related crimes. And the charges against me were serious.

One day, while coming back from the shower room, I was approached by a prisoner who handed me a big parcel and said: 'There you go Mark, keep your chin up.'

It turned out he was an Everton supporter, and had given me a big box of goodies containing cereals, tins of tuna, mackerel, coffee, biscuits and shaving cream. I was so glad to receive that box of necessities.

One thing I noticed straight away was the togetherness and camaraderie between some of the prisoners on B-wing. The prisoners known as 'The Filth' or 'The Scum' – the paedophiles, rapists and really evil b******s – were on K-wing, also known as VP-wing (Vulnerable Prisoners). Most of the inmates on B-wing were in for robbery, fraud, violence and – like myself – drug-related crimes.

Not surprisingly, many of them were smack-heads. And they were a bloody nuisance. They were forever getting filled in for robbing stuff from cells, and would constantly pester you for everything and anything.

'Have you got a skinny, fella?' 'What the f*** was that?' I thought. Turned out it was a skinny, home-made cigarette.

They would do anything for a sachet of sugar and, feeling sorry for them, I'd end up giving my stuff away.

There was also a rule on the wing known as 'Double Bubble'. The way it worked is that if you gave someone an item, say a tin of tuna, they would have to give you two tins back the following week. The smokers would borrow tobacco and trade in this way. I soon discovered that tobacco was the most valuable currency in prison.

Paul was already coming to terms with life on B-wing, and he told me it would take two months before I could sleep more normally and feel a little better about my situation.

I was just so glad to be sharing a cell with someone I knew and could get on with. Paul had also been involved in drug-related crime but his story was incredibly sad. He lost his young son, Paul jnr, who died of a heart defect at the age of 12. The tragedy hit him hard and he found it very difficult to carry on with his job and normal life.

He made a bad decision similar to mine, getting involved on the fringe of a drugs-related crime, and was eventually made to serve the same eight-year sentence. Looking at Paul's personal plight, I soon realised there were so many people worse off than myself.

I decided to start writing a book to pass the time away. And more significantly, I used the half an hour out of my cell each day to keep myself fit. I was already doing press-ups and sit-ups in my cell, and now I started to walk around the exercise yard as fast as I could. I wanted to run but the amount of bodies made it impossible.

One of the worst sights in Walton were the huge cockroaches that climbed the walls. The way they were swarming all over B-wing made me feel sick. Some prisoners referred to them as 'Jaspers', although I didn't bother to ask why. I couldn't even manage to eat my food if one crawled past.

I had days when I felt desperate but somehow I managed to stay positive. I started to write to people to say how sorry I was for what I'd done. I wrote to all my family and started to receive letters back giving me support.

The weekends were the most difficult, being banged up for 23 hours a day.

Early on in my days on B-wing, there was a definite undercurrent between two rival gangs, who were on different landings. One gang was from Speke and the other from over the water in Birkenhead.

Every day there were attacks launched from both sides, usually just quick, physical assaults whenever they got the opportunity to have a go at one another – at breakfast, in the shower room or in the exercise yard.

This simmering feud came to a head later in the summer and

virtually everyone on the wing knew it was going to all go off in the exercise yard on this particular day.

I was sat down against the fence with Paul and some other prisoners. The yard began to fill up and six of the Speke lads were congregated together. Just as the Birkenhead boys came through the door and out into the yard, they were attacked.

It was a bloodbath. Somehow the Speke lads had got hold of chair legs and metal bars. It was no contest. One officer got caught up in it all and it took what seemed like an age before he and the Birkenhead lads were rescued by an army of screws running into the yard.

The violence left one screw with a broken arm and led to a full lock-down for all prisoners that lasted two days. There was no 'association' and we were only allowed out at meal times.

At this point I was receiving a couple of visits during the week and one at the weekend from members of my family. They felt like a lifeline to me but it was difficult to find a way of passing the rest of the time.

I still hadn't been to the prison gym. I'd applied and put my name down but, as with everything in prison, you have to wait your turn. I'd use the prison phone as often as I could, to speak to Melissa and the family, but the credit was so expensive and it was a battle just to use it due to the lengthy queue of prisoners waiting to make the most of their only contact with the outside world.

The hardest phone call I had to make was to Mum. I'd been putting it off, but I knew I would have to speak to her sooner or later. It was May 27 and when I rang her she was so upset at hearing my voice. I knew I'd let her down.

I was just glad that Dad wasn't around to endure what she and the rest of the family were going through. I already knew that the biggest victims of my crime were my family and the people closest to me.

I told Mum my prison number – NM6982 – so that she could write to me, and I'll never forget her parting words on the phone that day: 'Mark, why are you still naughty?'

I laughed out loud, thinking that only my mum could say that. She wanted to visit me but I told her to wait, as I remained hopeful of getting out on bail before long.

I was now known as 'NM6982 Ward'. Well, they got the NM right – Naughty Mark!

I met solicitor Lenny Font for the first time on June 3. A lot of solicitors were interested in representing me but Lenny's name cropped up because he'd been involved in a lot of high-profile, drug-related cases.

I took to him straight away. I told him I wanted a solicitor to be straight with me and honest about my predicament. Lenny was adamant that I should never have given the police a written statement. But he was all for my honesty and he thought that would bode well for my bail application.

The bail application was a story in itself but, after going to the crown court later in July, I was turned down even though there had been significant developments in relation to the charges levelled against me.

By now I was being charged with one single offence – possession with intent to supply cocaine, based on evidence police found at the house. The other two charges – relating to the supply and production of crack cocaine – were both dropped because no crack-cocaine was found at the address.

The original police estimation that the drugs haul at McVinnie Road had a street value of between £1.5m and £2.5m was also well wide of the mark. In fact, it had been drastically reduced to £645,000.

On one hand, I obviously felt relieved that two of the charges against me were dropped. But on the other, I felt outraged that they had been made in the first place and that the original estimation of the drugs found was as high as £2.5m. Given all the bad publicity surrounding the case, with talk of a 'drugs factory', if I'd pleaded not guilty and take my chances in front of a jury in court, I wouldn't have stood a chance of escaping an even bigger sentence than the eight years I was given.

Despite the change in circumstances, with the second two counts now dropped, and my renewed optimism, they still refused me bail. In hindsight, though, I'm now glad they did. I would still have had to do the time I'd have spent outside prison on bail and, once I began to settle down to prison life, I grew to accept it. It would have been murder to have spent months back in the free world, only to find that I'd have to return to prison once I'd been sentenced.

I now understand how my background and previous career as a former professional footballer stood me in good stead for anything that prison threw at me. Coming from a big family and being around a group of men throughout my life, dressing rooms full of banter, meant that prison probably came a bit easier to me than many others, who simply can't cope with being banged up. The football dressing room can be a cruel place. You have to stand up for yourself on and off the field. I was still very competitive and hadn't lost that fire in my belly. My temperament was going to help me survive in this horrible place.

One of the most demoralising aspects of being held behind prison bars was coming to terms with all that you miss out on – everyday things that people on the outside take for granted. Melissa gave birth to Isabella on June 6 and my daughter cried her eyes out when I spoke to her on the phone. She was sad and upset that I was unable to see my new-born grandchild but I was just glad that both her and the baby were fit and healthy.

However, as one life began, another very close to me was about to end in horrific fashion. Three days after speaking to Melissa, 31-year-old inmate Daniel Rowland was found dead in his cell. I heard the screams from his cell-mate, who had returned from the shower to find Rowland hanging from the bars over the window.

Just two days later, on Saturday, June 11, 42-year-old Patrick Bailey reached the end of the line and he, too, decided to take his own life.

Prison becomes just too much for some people to bear. They are brought in from the courts and when that big iron door gets slammed behind them, it becomes a huge test of character. It's never easy to stay focused and positive and some just aren't strong enough to handle it.

There were often cell searches from the security screws. You were stripped, searched, and then ordered to stand outside your cell as they looked for anything that shouldn't be in your possession – mainly drugs, mobile phones and dangerous objects. It's unbelievable the weapons that can be made from objects as harmless as a pen or a CD.

Razor blades were used for shaving, and they were another lethal weapon favoured by certain prisoners.

One day, a suspected paedophile had to run a gauntlet of hate past the cells from the exercise yard, with all the prisoners punching, kicking and taking their fury out on him as he raced along the corridor. How he survived I don't know. He must have somehow slipped through the net, because the paedophiles were usually well protected and kept well out of reach of the other prisoners. I was all for the paedophiles getting a kicking, but if they weren't protected then there would be so many more deaths in the prison system.

June 14 was a roasting hot day. Royal Ascot was on the television and I was thinking of all the memorable days out I'd had at the famous Berkshire racecourse with ex-wife Jane, my good mate Mick Tobyn and his wife Kathy.

Me and Paul both liked a bet and I told him I was thinking of getting a mobile phone so that I could keep in touch with the family and place a few bets with the bookies on the outside.

If you were caught with a mobile phone in prison, you found yourself in big trouble. You could be forced to serve more time, so it was a big decision for me to take on. I'd not even been sentenced yet but, in all honesty, the positives outweighed the negatives.

I got on well with a big prisoner called Metan, who told me he had played professional football in his native Turkey. He told me there was a mobile phone available on A-wing and that the lad selling it wanted £350.

Without hesitation, I told him to get it for me. 'What the hell,' I thought. I could keep in touch with my loved ones, place the odd bet and ring people I needed to talk to. I knew I was breaking the rules but I was willing to take my chances.

Paul and I watched a horse owned by the well-known football agent Willie McKay win the big sprint at Royal Ascot – hosted that June at York racecourse due to redevelopment at Ascot – and land him around £300,000. I turned to Paul and explained how, years earlier, Willie had offered me the chance to go into partnership with him in his new football agency, but I'd turned him down. What a decision that turned out to be! The Monaco-based McKay has gained a reputation as one of the game's most controversial characters, but he's made a fortune from transfer dealings and looking after the interests of numerous top-level players.

I thought I was on my way to a small fortune myself one afternoon. Paul and I would study form in the papers delivered into prison on a Saturday morning, I'd make my selections and then phone Uncle Tommy from my cell and ask him to put on my usual bet – a £1 Lucky 15 involving four horses. Relatives of prisoners would pay the local newsagent in advance to ensure papers were delivered and I'd always look forward to reading the *Daily Mirror* on a Saturday.

On this particular day it was looking good for me when my first two horses both won – at very long odds of 20-1 and 16-1. The 15 bets that form a Lucky 15 are one fourfold accumulator, plus six doubles, four trebles and four singles. I worked it out later that after my first two horses had won, I had £791 running on to the third and fourth races. With the starting prices for my chosen horses in those latter two races at 8-1 and 6-1, I stood to win £31,679 if they all came in.

And so, full of excitement after watching my first two gee-gees romp home, I thought I'd give Tommy a quick call to tell him the good news that I was halfway to my biggest ever windfall.

Only when I dialled Tommy's number, there was no answer. 'That's strange,' I thought, knowing he'd usually be at home watching the racing on TV. I phoned Billy instead – and he gave me bad news. Apparently, Tommy was so unimpressed with my choice of long-shots that he didn't even bother to place the bet!

And then when the first horse had won at 20-1, he panicked and shot round to the bookies to back my other three selections! That's why I couldn't get any answer when I phoned his house. As it happened, my remaining two runners didn't win anyway – much to Tommy's relief! I had to laugh about it afterwards. At least I didn't end that Saturday worrying about what to do with 30-odd grand in winnings!

I was starting to take a few liberties, though. On a Saturday, I'd collect half an ounce of tobacco from any of the prisoners who wanted to have a bet on the live horse racing that day.

Around 20 prisoners entered the competition, where they were awarded 10 points for a winner, plus the SP of the winner. The prisoner with the most points after the last race won the tobacco.

As both Paul McGrath and myself are non-smokers, we didn't care about the tobacco – it was just a bit of fun to us. We stuck a big chart on the wall of the cell with everyone's name and their horses written down.

The screws would turn a blind eye to the gambling but one Saturday there were five prisoners in with a chance of winning the competition. Our cell was absolutely rammed full of lads, all shouting at the big telly. The half-ounce of tobacco represented a big prize for the winner, especially if they happened to be a smoker. They could sell it for 'Double Bubble' and get twice as much back in return, although I never did take advantage of that unwritten rule.

After the race was over and I weighed in the winner with his snout, I was summoned to the mess. The PO told me to shut the door behind me and then asked if I knew that gambling of any kind was against prison rules.

I pleaded ignorance. But he was giving me a chance and told me to just keep it quiet – not have my cell looking like Ladbrokes on a Saturday afternoon.

We carried on with the competition.

* * * *

Not long before I'd been arrested, I met a girl called Nicola Kelly, who worked for Billy in the pub. I liked her a lot. We never got the chance to get close but I had strong feelings for her and was gutted that my arrest prevented me from getting to know her better.

However, even though we had only known each other for a short while, Billy brought her in to see me. It was great to see her again but I was thinking to myself: 'I bet she's glad she never got that serious with me'. I told her to forget about us but she was adamant that she still wanted to be involved.

I couldn't believe what I was hearing but I enjoyed her company so much that I agreed she could still come and visit me.

HAMMERED

Soon after, I took possession of the mobile phone that Metan had told me about. I was shocked. It looked like one of the first Nokia phones ever made. It was massive. 'How the f*** am I going to hide that?' I thought.

I'd been done over. I'd got someone to take £350 to an address in Liverpool and in return I'd been given an antique house brick.

However, using the phone after 'bang-up' of an evening was a welcome relief from the boredom. I was on the phone every night to Melissa and Nicola. They kept my spirits up and I can truly say that the big, ugly mobile phone kept me sane at times.

Television was another way of killing time. Paul had a habit of watching our portable TV until late at night and then falling asleep without turning it off. I'd regularly wake up and have to switch it off while he was snoring loudly.

But in the early hours of Sunday, June 26, I was awakened by a different noise – the sound of a woman crying and sobbing uncontrollably. 'F*****g hell', I thought, 'Paul has left the telly on again.'

I turned to face the TV but it was off – and I could still hear the woman's cries. I realised it was coming from beneath our cell, on the ground floor of B-wing.

It turned out that it was one of the woman screws I'd heard crying. I could hear lots of talking and movement down below, prisoners had started to wake and, before long, the news spread from cell to cell, landing to landing. The female PO had found the Number One prisoner, a guy known only to us as 'Dava', hanging in his cell.

The Number One prisoner and occupant of Number One cell had the privilege of having extra time out of his cell. He was given various duties, including compiling the prisoners' diet sheets, arranging newspapers and helping the officers to allocate cells for new prisoners on arrival from the courts.

One of the perks of being in Number One cell was that it had a big TV with Teletext and was considered the best cell on the wing. More importantly to me, its occupants were given access to the prison gym.

Dava – real name Timothy Davenport, 40, from Cheshire – was a quiet, polite man and helpful to other prisoners. I discovered later that he'd been given a six-year sentence for manslaughter in 2002 but he was due for release just five weeks after taking his own life. Apparently, he was too scared to leave the prison, frightened of reprisals on the outside.

The mood among the prisoners on the day Dava killed himself was very sombre. Even the screws, who had seen it all before, including three suicides at Walton in the space of just 17 days that month, were devastated.

With his cell-mate given compassionate home leave that day, Dava had the opportunity to hang himself alone that night. How sad. This place had death in its walls. It was the worst experience of my life, and I wouldn't wish a term of imprisonment in Walton on my worst enemy.

Even big Metan, the Turk, reckoned Walton was worse than the hellish Turkish prison depicted in the hit movie, *Midnight Express*.

Late one evening, I was speaking to Nicola on the mobile when I heard a key go in the cell door. I instantly shoved the phone under my pillow and was greeted by the PO. He stood in the doorway and asked Paul and I if we would be interested in moving to the number one cell the following day.

'It's a lot of responsibility,' he said, 'but you'll get more privileges.'

I looked at Paul and we both nodded in agreement. The PO shut the door and I breathed a huge sigh of relief that I hadn't been caught with the phone.

Nicola said she had heard the whole conversation and I realised then that I'd have to be more careful to keep the phone hidden throughout the day. However, I was beginning to use my head a lot more, and knew that I'd have more chance of hiding it from the screws after landing the Number One job, albeit at the cost of another prisoner's life.

Our first few hours in Number One cell were spent thinking about Dava. It was only 24 hours earlier that his dead body had been discovered there. As we settled down for the night, the door suddenly swung open and a screw walked in.

'Right lads,' he said with a smirk on his face. 'That's where we found the poor sod, over there under the sink, the belt tight around his neck, his eyes popping out of his head and his face all blue. Goodnight lads.'

With that, the p***k disappeared and locked the door.

I was disgusted by the way some prisoners were treated, especially those who I thought shouldn't even have been there after committing menial crimes.

As part of our special new privileges in Number One cell, Paul and I would be in charge of the server, where the food was handed out at meal times. It had a large bain-marie – a large kind of hostess trolley – that kept the food hot, but it was disgusting. There were 250 men on B-wing and if it wasn't for buying your own stuff from the canteen, then you would starve. A prisoner's typical diet consisted of canned tuna, noodles, tinned mackerel and porridge.

Violence seemed to lurk around every corner. One day I witnessed a terrible assault by two brothers from St Helens on an older prisoner. Nobody got involved to split them up, so I started to get up but Paul stopped me. He told me to leave it because it had nothing to do with me. He was right but it was sickening to watch.

However, I had to intervene when a fight kicked off in the yard one day in July.

Richie Harrison was a young lad from Huyton who had been put in a cell with me when I'd been separated from Paul for a few weeks. He was an Evertonian and a good lad. He'd been caught with cocaine in his van and when the police went back to his house they found 50 kilos of the stuff in a car on his drive. He was looking at a long time behind bars.

I was walking round the yard one afternoon when I noticed a scrap going on between two lads. As I looked more closely, I could see that Richie was involved – and the other lad was biting him on the back.

I rushed in and grabbed the lad around the neck before pulling him to the floor. It was all over before it had started, but Richie had made a mess of the kid's face. Apparently the fight was all over Richie accusing the lad of being a grass – the most common reason for a tear-up on B-wing.

A more pleasing memory from time spent in the yard came when I heard someone yelling: 'Wardy – over here'. At first I couldn't see where the voice was coming from but it turned out to be John Ryan, who was also doing time for a drugs-related crime. John's cell faced the exercise yard and after we'd exchanged pleasantries, I thought to myself: 'So I'm not the only ex-professional footballer in here, then'. John was at Oldham in the summer I signed for the Latics, just before he moved on to Newcastle United. He was capped by England under-21s and his brother, Dave Ryan, was in the same Northwich Victoria side as me.

* * * *

Mick Tobyn, my great friend since my West Ham days, paid a very welcome visit – even though he lived more than 230 miles away in Dagenham, Essex. I could tell by the look on his face that he was gutted for us to be meeting in these circumstances. It was only a month or so earlier that we'd been laughing and joking in Goa, where we'd stayed at the lovely house Mick owned.

That welcome break ended on a bit of a sour note, though, on April 16, when I was stopped by customs officers at Gatwick airport and they confiscated 25 cartons of cigarettes I was carrying – 5,800 fags in all. It summed up my financial state of affairs at the time that I'd intended to sell them for just a tenner a carton back on Merseyside.

I kept in regular touch with Lenny Font, who informed me that my committal papers – the evidence put forward by the prosecution – didn't look good. By this time, he'd also introduced me to Nick Johnston, the QC who would represent me at the committal hearing.

Our first meeting was one of total honesty . . . and came as a real kick in the b******s. Nick told me the candid written statement I'd given at the police station after my arrest would ultimately guarantee a custodial sentence, and that I would be looking at anything between six and 10 years – depending on the judge. His estimate was that I'd be going down for eight years.

The judge, he explained, is guided by the amount of drugs found at the address. And the 3.2 kilos of cocaine seized at McVinnie Road would warrant a sentence of eight years.

HAMMERED

There were four one kilo blocks of cocaine found at the house that had to be sent to a laboratory for analysis to determine the purity level contained in the drugs. The purity level came out at 3.2 kilos. It's the purity level – not the actual quantity – of the drugs found on a person or at their property that determines the length of the prison sentence.

When it comes to sentencing, the judge has guidelines to follow. Apparently, anyone found in possession of one kilo of pure cocaine can expect a prison sentence of between one and five years. They tend to add on up to five years for every kilo of an illegal class A drug involved.

Having weighed up all the police evidence and the purity of the coke, my barrister advised me to plead guilty to the one remaining charge against me.

We were convinced this was the right course of action to take because, just weeks earlier, there had been a significant change in the law. New legislation, introduced in April 2005, meant that provided you pleaded guilty as charged at the earliest opportunity and didn't pursue a trial by jury, anyone given a sentence of less than 10 years was likely to receive up to a third off. On release, the remaining half of the sentence would be 'on licence'.

I didn't want to accept any prison sentence but, as it was explained to me, my name on the rental agreement and subsequent written statement to the police gave me no hope of avoiding a jail term.

I was honest with the family, telling them exactly what the barrister had indicated. They were all worried that the judge might pass an even bigger sentence, to make an example of me, when it came to sentencing in October.

My attitude changed after hearing the brutal truth from Nick Johnson. I decided I was going to do my time as well as I could, and attempt to move on in the system as quickly as possible. Not to get into any trouble, and to write my story . . .

* * * *

Paul McGrath and I were constantly being tested for drugs because of our move to Number One cell but that didn't concern me. I've never taken drugs, so there was no way I was going to fail a p**s-test.

My first day in the gym made me even more determined to come through the prison process. I joined in with the circuit training squad – and what a mistake that was. My competitive nature took over and I tried to keep up with the fittest lads.

Even though I'd been walking each day and doing press-ups in my cell, I was completely out of condition. As I trailed in nearly last, one of the screws shouted: 'F*****g hell, Wardy, you're not fit mate. Thought you'd be fitter than that.'

I'd more or less spent the last three months lying horizontal on my back. Now I could put all my efforts into training. I was determined to show that screw who was the fit one here.

* * * *

After my hospital scare at the Neuro Centre in Walton Fazakerly in November 2004, I was due to see a specialist in the Royal Liverpool Hospital. Being in custody didn't affect the appointment in any way.

I didn't know about my hospital appointment until early one July morning, when I was awoken early by a screw who simply said: 'Right, Ward, hospital today.'

I was led to reception, where two big screws were waiting to take me to the Royal. They were very friendly and even joked with me as they put the biggest pair of cuffs on me you've ever seen – attached to chains, which, in turn, were attached to them.

A governor came to see me before I left and personally tightened the cuffs himself, telling me he'd heard that I could run. You'd have thought I was a mass murderer.

A taxi was waiting, and it felt strange to be sat between two screws in a cab driving the short distance to the hospital. As we pulled up outside the Royal, it suddenly dawned on me that we'd be walking in among the general public, who would all be looking at me as I walked in chained and cuffed to two big prison guards. I was totally and utterly embarrassed.

The hospital was chocker-block full. I was led up to the main desk as the screws asked for directions. I could see that everyone in the room was looking at me, and I knew what they'd be thinking. 'What has he done wrong? Is he a murderer, a rapist? He must be dangerous to have those great big cuffs and chains restraining him.' I hated every second of being in the hospital and, I never thought I'd say this, but I just wanted to get back to prison.

We walked over to the specialist clinic and I stood at the entrance to witness a very busy waiting area. Once again, everyone looked up and stared at the prisoner standing between the two massive screws.

I put my head down, but not before noticing a local lad sitting down wearing an Everton shirt. He recognised me straight away, and I don't think he could believe what he was seeing. I felt completely ashamed.

Luckily for me, I was rushed through to see the doctor. I lay on the bed to be examined but it was a struggle because the screws wouldn't take the cuffs or chains off me.

After the examination I was led through the hospital again, sensing all eyes burning into me. I felt like a monster. It was a humiliating experience and, to be honest, I couldn't wait to get back to the relative sanctuary of the prison.

I was using the phone every night, just to speak to Nicola and Melissa. However, the person I'd rented the house for – Mr X – had somehow got hold of my number, and one night he called me.

He must have been s******g himself in case I opened my mouth, but that isn't my style. He spoke a lot of s***e about what he would, and could, do for me. One day I'll see him again face to face, man to man, and my conscience is crystal clear. I kept my mouth shut and did the right thing.

33. PHONES 4 U

FOR all the privileges associated with being in Number One cell, the responsibilities that came with it could also drive you mad at times. The phone that I'd bought for £350 had obviously been in the prison for a very long time, so every Tom, Dick and Harry knew the number. I'd be lying in my cell late at night and the next minute the phone would vibrate to alert me to an incoming call.

A typical message would go something like: 'Hello Mark, it's Jimmy from Risley. You don't know me but my mate will be coming in on Monday – can you sort him out with some food and tobacco?'

I'd also receive calls from other wings within the prison. 'Wardy, it's Pancake here. I'm sending a parcel over in the morning for my mate who's due in tomorrow.'

You're either one of the lads or you're not. I've always been a team player and I'd like to think I'd do anything for anybody, especially in prison. There are times when you need the help and co-operation of the prisoners around you and a favour here or there is always welcome.

Paul and I were responsible for delegating which prisoners served the food from the big bain-marie that had to be wheeled onto B-wing from the kitchen some distance away. I helped out by serving at first but the screws complained that the portions of chips I'd been dishing out were too large, so they stopped me. If any of the food ran out, it meant them having to unlock all the adjoining doors between B-wing and the kitchen, escort me all the way, and then repeat the whole laborious process again when they fetched more food back! They hated it.

What the screws didn't know was that I started to stash away any phones that came our way in that bain-marie. Fortunately, my tiny hands would fit in a small gap so I could place the phones inside during the day and get them out again when needed. But if I'd been caught hiding them, my feet wouldn't have touched the ground.

HAMMERED

One morning Paul McGrath stood outside the serving area, keeping watch as I went to place my phone away in the bain-marie. I'd been given a present of a metal Swatch from a young Asian lad called Imran. He'd since been released and it was his way of thanking me. He'd been bullied terribly, had his £2,000 Rado watch stolen from him by fellow inmates and afterwards I took him under my wing.

I got Imran involved on the servery at meal times but one day he got a load of unnecessary abuse from a Scouse prisoner who wasn't happy that he'd been served a veggie burger instead of a leg of chicken. I confronted the Scouser and asked him what the problem was. He started moaning about Imran not giving him what he wanted to eat, so I explained to him that if, as happened in this case, a prisoner didn't fill in his diet sheet when he chose what meal he was going to eat the next day, then the rule was that the prisoner concerned would simply be given the standard veggie meal. It was a simple system to follow but sometimes one or two inmates couldn't be bothered to comply.

The Scouse lad wasn't happy about me sticking up for Imran and I found out later that, after our exchange of words, he'd pinned a picture of me up on his cell wall and wrote beneath it the words 'I Hate Mark Ward'. I've always stood up for myself and what I believe in, though. The main point is, he never picked on Imran again.

I'd never experienced any problems before when slipping my hand into the gap inside the bain-marie but as I placed the mobile phone and tried to release my hand, there was a mighty bang and a flash of electricity. My watch must have touched a live wire and it threw me right back landing on my backside.

My hair stood on end and the skin on my hand was burning – it felt on fire. The trouble was, my accident had also short-circuited the electricity throughout B-wing. Deafening alarm bells were going off everywhere and the screws were running around looking to find the source of the problem. Everyone was locked behind closed doors and Paul was laughing his head off at the commotion I'd caused. He commented how lucky I'd been and said he could just imagine the newspaper headlines 'Ex-Premiership footballer electrocuted to death – hand stuck in bain-marie!'

Every now and then the prison security staff would clamp down and early morning inspections were common. It was a constant battle to hide the phones and the Nokia brick had to be put away somewhere safe before I went to sleep in case of an early visit from security. I'd hide it in the back of a computer chair which I'd acquired from the officer's mess. I told the SO that because I was sat for hours doing his work – going through the prisoners' diet sheets and so on – I needed a decent chair. He let me have the computer chair and much more than providing a bit more comfort, it was also an ideal hiding place for the brick.

But things didn't always run smoothly. One morning the door was banged open and both Paul and I were strip-searched, told to put our clothes back on and then sent outside the cell while it was searched. Although I've never had a problem taking my clothes off, the strip-searches were a bit degrading, but you get used to them. To be honest, some of the screws seemed more embarrassed than the prisoners. Outside the cell Paul started flapping: 'They will definitely find the phone, Mark,' he said. I told him not to panic and said that even if they did find it, I'd take the rap.

After a good 20 minutes the search ended and we were locked up again. 'Good news', I thought to myself . . . but just as I was about to check that the phone was still tucked away where I'd left it in the back of the chair, the door reopened and in came a warder: 'I'll take the chair, thanks very much,' he said.

Now I was minus both my chair and phone. Paul started to panic even more and at that stage I, too, thought it inevitable that they would uncover the brick. It was hours later, after the searches throughout B-wing had finished, that we were let out of the cells again. Tony Kirk and a fella called Keith, a West Ham fan in the cell next door, greeted us and everyone was asking each other whether the screws had found anything. I was looking around for my computer chair when 'Kirky' told me that the officers had simply used it to stand on, to search a shelf high up in his cell. The chair had obviously then been taken back into the officer's mess instead of being returned to me.

Paul and I had the job of cleaning the officers' mess on a daily basis, so I walked straight in there . . . only to see 12 IDENTICAL computer chairs scattered around the room! Paul asked: 'How are you going to solve this one, Wardy?'

'Easy,' I replied, 'I've marked the back of my chair with a W!'

I soon located my chair that held the secrets of Number One cell and was just praying that my mobile was still in the back of it. I turned to the nearest warder and said: 'Hey Guv, that's my chair.'

'How is that *your* chair?' he responded.

I explained that it had been borrowed from my cell that morning so that his colleagues could use it to stand on during the security searches. I was testing him big-time now. 'But why have you got a computer chair in your cell anyway, Ward?' he went on.

'Because I sit there all day doing *your* job, that's why.'

'You cheeky b*****d. Take it and shut the door behind you,' he added.

I got the chair back to Number One cell and there, tucked up safely in the back of it, was the brick. I couldn't have been without it.

I sometimes managed to get to the gym twice a day. I was feeling more positive and by becoming fitter it gave me so much more confidence. I knew it wouldn't be long before anybody would be able to touch me on the circuit training. I was pushing myself hard on the running machine and just wanted my day of reckoning – October 4 – to come around. Lenny still visited me once a week and I was coming around to the idea that I was going to be sentenced to eight years.

I was taking too many risks, though. The favours I was being asked to do by other prisoners was putting me under increasing pressure. Everyone knew that I was always in the gym, so I was constantly asked to take things, such as phones or information, back to B-wing. I did this a few times but not after one such favour nearly landed me in big trouble.

I'd agreed to take a phone back for somebody and put it inside my sock. I had tracksuit bottoms on and usually we were taken outside to walk back around the prison. You weren't allowed to stop and chat with other prisoners as you walked through the different prison wings.

I came to realise how vast Walton prison is. As I was about to re-enter B-wing, the wing governor was walking towards me with another governor. I'd spoken with him a few times previously – he was a mad Liverpool supporter. On this occasion he stopped me dead in my tracks: 'Mark, can I have a word with you? I've got a disclosure letter in the office for you to sign from a West Ham supporter who wants to write to you,' he explained.

I stood frozen and, unbelievably, the phone in my sock started to ring and vibrate – the p**** who had given it to me hadn't turned it off!

My leg shot out sideways with the shock of the vibrating phone, although fortunately the ring was drowned out by the noise inside the prison. Even though he couldn't have heard the phone, I thought the governor must have noticed my strange behaviour. Thankfully, he didn't – but I made up my mind that I wouldn't take any more stupid risks for other people, especially those I didn't even know!

A number of lads I knew previously to being in prison ended up on B-wing following their court appearance. One of which was a friend of mine called John Smith. He'd been arrested on a serious drug charge and upon his arrival I went to meet him in his cell. He was fuming that he'd been remanded but he needed to talk to his family, so he asked to use a phone.

I handed the big Nokia to him, he dialled the number . . . and carried on walking out of his cell, as if he was casually strolling down the high street. I charged after him and pushed him back into the cell. 'F*****g hell, John, you can't do that!' He was so engrossed in wanting to talk to his family that he just forgot where he was. He was only in for a week before he got bail, although he eventually received an 11-year sentence.

I'd first met John many years earlier. He was a massive Evertonian and I played a few games for his Allerton team on Sundays after my playing days were over. He ran the team – a pub side from south Liverpool – like a professional set-up and he had some excellent players. The ex-Wigan Athletic and Bolton Wanderers midfielder Tony Kelly played for the team, as did Stuart Quinn, who was with Liverpool as a youngster.

HAMMERED

My first appearance for The Allerton was against near rivals The Pineapple and the game was watched by Robbie Fowler, who has an allegiance to that part of the city.

Receiving the ball straight from the kick-off, I let it run past my body before laying it off to our full-back. As I released the pass, I was hit hard and late by a midfielder who put his studs through my left bicep. My mouth was also bleeding from the impact.

Feeling stunned and dazed by the ferocity of the challenge, my midfield partner Tony Kelly came over and picked me up and said: 'Welcome to Sunday morning football!' After that reckless tackle on me in the opening few seconds of my debut, I soon enjoyed playing Sunday morning football.

This rude awakening forced me to treat the game as seriously as everyone else and I got stuck in just like the rest of the lads. Later in the game, I even scored with a left-foot volley from the edge of the box – the jammiest goal I've ever scored! 'Smithy' was jumping up and down on the line, delighted that his new signing had netted on his debut.

I was also pleased to score again, this time with a powerful header in the last minute of a cup semi-final to send the tie into extra-time. Stuart Quinn scored from a brilliant free-kick to win us the game.

For the final, Smithy produced a brand new kit and gave all his players blue towels with our names embroidered on them – I still have mine to this day. It turned out to be a great day as we beat The Sandon, who had Billy Kenny – my former Everton team-mate, who was playing up against me in centre midfield – sent-off.

That cup final victory, watched by a crowd of hundreds, was my farewell appearance for The Allerton. There was talk in Liverpool that Smithy was paying Tony Kelly and myself hundreds of pounds to turn out for his team, but that wasn't true. We didn't receive a penny but that didn't bother me.

A lot of nonsense has been said and written about my relationship with John Smith. Apart from those false claims that he was paying me to play for his team, others have put in print that he sorted out that trouble I had with The Blackmailer *(see chapter 19)* – another pile of bull***t. I didn't even know John at that time, although I wish I had! There were even rumours that I was working for him in his drugs network.

The truth is, John and I met through football and we enjoyed each other's company, but that still didn't stop me being linked with the Smith family for other, more sinister reasons.

John's brother, Colin Smith, was the victim of a gangland shooting in Liverpool on November 13, 2007. His death at the hands of a hitman was plastered all over the tabloids and the *Sunday Mirror* ran with the splash headline 'Gangland Drug War Over The Assassination of King Cocaine'. Alongside the article, they had pictures of Colin and his 'ex-boss' Curtis Warren.

But because Colin was an Evertonian, the paper reported how he knew Everton players and had used corporate VIP facilities at Goodison. They also thought it a good idea to include a photo of me in action for Everton. Within their two-page spread, the paper conveniently linked me to Colin's family again by saying how I'd been 'paid to play' football for his brother's pub team and, of course, how I was later imprisoned on drugs charges.

It was typical sensationalism and just another graphic example of how the media love nothing more than to link footballers – and ex-players – to criminal activity in any way they can.

34. GOING DO\

ON the night of Monday, October 3, I had a ____ of trouble sleeping, I can tell you. I'd been in Walton for nearly five months and now D-Day – my time to be sentenced – was looming large.

I spoke to Nicola and my family that night, and they told me they would all be at Liverpool Crown Court the next day to support me.

In the meat wagon on the way to court, it came on the radio that I was due to be sentenced that day. I didn't feel nervous during the drive there, or as I waited in the cells below the court dressed in the suit that Billy had brought in on a recent visit. But when I was told that they were ready for me, I began to feel very anxious.

Despite assurances from my barrister Nick Johnston to the contrary, it was always in the back of my mind that the judge might decide to make an example of me, throw the book at me.

Based on what Nick had indicated to me at our previous meetings, I went to court that day fully expecting to have to serve eight years. On a good day, I could have been given a more lenient six-year jail term. But on the other hand, if things went badly for me, I could've been given a 12-year stretch. It all depends on the judge and what mood he is in on any given day. It's ridiculous to think that a person can be condemned to an extra four years in prison depending on what side of the bed the judge got out of that morning, but that's the way it is.

There was one judge, in particular, that drug offenders were very keen to avoid. Apparently, his daughter died through drugs and he is notorious for coming down hard on anyone involved in a drug-related crime who comes before him in court. I was relieved to be told that I'd managed to avoid him and would be sentenced by Judge John Phipps instead.

After being led into a packed courtroom, I was amazed by how many press and police were present. I sat down, with Billy and Tommy

rectly behind me. I turned to look at them. Melissa was
ide the court, too upset to face the agony of waiting for the judge
o pass sentence.

Nicola was at work, although I didn't want her to be present anyway
– it would have been unfair.

Barrister Henry Riding, for the prosecution, tried to maintain that I
was the main man, that the drugs were mine and it was me who was
distributing them around Merseyside.

However, there was a much more important side issue to my case
that I can only talk about now.

The police and prosecution could not disclose in court on the day of
my sentencing that there was an ongoing police investigation called
Operation Vatican, which had started in June 2004.

They knew who was manufacturing the drugs. There had already
been three seizures at different addresses – one in Huyton, another in
Prescot and the third intercepted in a car travelling to Birmingham –
and they had considerable surveillance on nine members of a drugs
gang even before they got to McVinnie Road.

I'd been used in the process of storing the drugs by renting the
property, but the prosecution were willing to let me receive a big
sentence, knowing full well that police would be arresting others for
their much more significant roles in this crime in the near future.
Which is exactly what happened.

They knew all along that I was only on the periphery of the overall
crime – 'a foot soldier'. as the judge described me that day. Let's face
it, if I was as heavily involved and influential in this crime as the police
and prosecution claimed, then would I honestly have gone along to a
letting agency, registered the lease of a house in my name, paid £1,800
rent up front . . . and then thrown four kilos of cocaine in there?

In the real world that just doesn't happen. That's why these career
criminals, the people at the heart of these drug-distribution crimes, use
knob-heads like me to act for them.

In my eyes, the way the prosecution targeted me in court was a crime
in itself.

Of course, I'm not saying that I was completely innocent. I've

278

explained here what I very stupidly agreed to do and my part in this whole sorry saga. And I accept I had to be punished, too. But my gripe is that punishments should always fit the crime, and I don't believe they did in this case.

I stood in the dock and faced Judge Phipps, who went on to say how incredibly sad it was to see an ex-footballer fall from grace, and that for my crime I was to receive an eight-year custodial sentence.

He started with 12 years but because of my early guilty plea, it was reduced to eight – a third off.

Eight years, spot on – just as my legal representatives predicted.

But eight years . . . for what *I* did? Do convicted paedophiles, brutal rapists and those who commit other serious, violent crimes – callous b******s who inflict serious physical and mental damage on others and then, as often happens, put their victims through hell again in court – get eight-year sentences? No way. Sometimes they're not even expected to serve half the time I've spent in prison.

Turning to face Billy and Tommy, I could tell they were gutted.

It was a hollow feeling being driven back to Walton, realising that I wouldn't be free again until May 2009 – at the earliest.

To be honest, I was quite philosophical. For almost five, long months I'd had many sleepless nights wondering and fearing what sentence I'd eventually receive. The wait had been unbearable. To hear that I'd been given eight years, knowing I would be released after four if I kept my nose clean inside, left me with a sense of relief.

In the prison van on the way back to Walton, I ran it over in my mind: 'I've already served nearly six months . . . so that's three-and-a-half years to go' . . . and you start to feel more positive. Once again, though, Radio City kept its listeners fully updated with the news that I'd been sent down for eight years.

News must have reached Walton, because as I walked back through main reception a couple of the screws made a few comments, though mainly they were words of encouragement. 'You'll do that standing on your head, Wardy,' said one. 'It could've been worse, lad,' piped up another.

I arrived back at my cell to be greeted by Paul, who had been given an eight-year sentence just two months before me. A lot of know-it-all prisoners were telling me how lucky I was, and that I could have been handed a double-figure sentence.

'What a load of b******s,' I told them.

They were suggesting that, because I was an ex-Premier League footballer and a relatively high profile public figure, I should have been given a longer sentence than eight years. Why?

* * * *

My intentions now were to win the Christmas fitness competition at the prison gym and move on to a Category C prison in 2006. I wanted to move through the prison process as quickly as possible.

Believe it or not, I did actually feel much better once sentence had been passed. I was thinking of putting in an appeal but was advised not to by my barrister. Some clever p**** in prison told me that four years amounted to 35,000 hours. I nearly smacked him in the mouth.

The day after sentencing, you are given a sheet of paper detailing your dates for sentencing and release. All the dates are shown in total days, and it really hits home when you see that four years is, in fact, 1,460 days locked up behind bars. It scared me at first and I wondered how I'd cope. Somehow, I just had to.

Solicitor Lenny Font informed me that numerous tabloid newspapers had been on to him about doing an interview with me. He advised that Nick Harris, from *The Independent*, would be my best bet.

I spoke to Nick on the phone and he sounded very enthusiastic about doing a piece. I told him that if he wanted to write a story on what had happened to me he'd have to come in and visit me. I wanted to look him in the eyes when we spoke, so I sent him a VO (Visiting Order) and in November he came in to see me.

I'd never really trusted tabloid hacks ever since Steven Howard from *The Sun* stitched me up in my first season at West Ham some 20 years earlier. Nick was just a friend as far as the prison was concerned. He had no notebook or tape recorder with him and we just talked for the full hour.

I spoke honestly and told him he could go ahead with his story. I also agreed to do some of it by phone. He promised me it would be a balanced piece of journalism and he was true to his word.

The Independent ran their exclusive interview on November 16, 2005. It was a big article – three pages and 3,000 words long – and Nick said it was unusual to get that much coverage for a story of this nature.

I was happy with the article but the most significant part of it was that Nick – or his editor – had run the headline 'WARD NM6982' which was my prison number.

It very quickly had a positive knock-on effect. Just a week after the article appeared in the *Indie* I started to receive mail from all over the world: New York, Croatia, Sydney, Portugal, Ireland, Germany and various other places in Europe. They were all from fans who had followed the clubs I'd played for, mainly West Ham and Everton but some from Man City and Birmingham, too.

I thought I'd get a few dodgy ones but I can honestly say that I only ever received positive, kind letters, all telling me to be strong and keep my chin up.

By this time I'd also received letters from my old West Ham team-mates Tony Gale, Alvin Martin, Alan Dickens, Tony Cottee and Billy Bonds. It was great to hear from the lads and receive their support and best wishes. Paul Tait, my old Birmingham team-mate, also sent a note.

I received a letter from the book publisher John Blake. He told me that I had an extraordinary story to tell and that he'd be willing to publish my book. I also had other publishers send letters of interest.

I'd already made my mind up to write a book. I'd read a lot of footballers' autobiographies over the years and I knew that my story had 'added spice'. I sent John Blake a chapter I'd written, and he loved it. John was very keen to publish my story but I decided to enlist the help of somebody I'd known since my West Ham days and he was keen to go ahead.

Tony McDonald was my choice of publisher and I felt comfortable that, having known me throughout my career, he would be the best to help me to get my story across in the right way. Tony had already written and published a number of books and had done a great job with the autobiography of my old mate, Tony Cottee. We exchanged a few letters and Tony 'Mac' advised me to keep a diary of prison life and to write down my thoughts as the days, weeks and months slowly ticked by. He also encouraged me to maintain my fitness levels because he could tell, from our exchange of letters and occasional phone conversations, that it was doing a lot to lift my morale.

In the gym, I was starting to find myself at the front of the circuit class, and was pushing myself more and more for the fitness competition. There was a prize for the winner – £10 added to your canteen credit to spend as you wished.

It wasn't the tenner I was after, though. It was the prize and the honour of being the fittest man in Walton prison.

On December 14, 40 prisoners of all ages entered the competition and I was confident of winning a couple of the events.

One was the bleep test, in which you run between two markers spaced around 20 yards apart, making sure you reach each marker before the bleep sounds. As the test goes on the 'bleep' gets progressively quicker and I had done loads of these during my playing career.

Everyone except me and a young lad in his 20s had fallen away by level 14. I just pushed on, and he dropped out. I was still going when the gym screw told me to save my energy for the next exercises.

The rest of the competition consisted of press-ups, sit-ups, bench-jumps and squat-thrusts. At the end, all the scores were added up to find a winner. I pushed myself to the limit and won. It felt so satisfying, especially as the screw who only months earlier had laughed at my fitness levels was there to watch me collect my prize.

I didn't say anything to him. I just gave him a look that said 'Told you so!'

A sad footnote to this story was that the winner of the strong man competition in the gym, a lad called Andy Creighton, died in 2008 after being released from prison.

Andy was a big lad and, like most prisoners who wanted to bulk up even more in the gym, he was taking the dreaded steroids. They are very dangerous drugs, a recipe for disaster in prison, because they cause aggression and make the person taking them feel he is invincible.

It always made me laugh looking at the sted-heads, with their big arms and chest, and legs like straws. 'Weak as p**s!' I'd say to them.

* * * *

Christmas in Walton was dreadful. It really hit home how much I missed my family and loved ones. In the New Year, though, I was told that I'd be getting moved to a Category C prison.

I'd spoken to my probation officer Angela Corcoran, who had been good enough to visit me after I'd been sentenced. She told me to keep my head down and my nose clean. I had a release date of May 11, 2009 and wasn't on a parole sentence, so it was just a case of behaving myself.

Paul and I were both accepted to Buckley Hall prison in Rochdale and moved to our new home on January 25, 2006.

Before I left Walton, the faithful Nokia was passed on to someone else. I didn't seek any money for the big brick. It had never let me down and had served its purpose. It kept me in touch with loved ones when I needed them most to help me through my darkest hours.

That made it worth every penny I'd paid for the vintage antique.

35. TAKING THE P**S

THE journey to Buckley Hall was an uncomfortable one. Sitting handcuffed in the stinking prison van gave me the opportunity to reflect on my time at Walton.

I knew I'd never, ever be able to forget my first spell in prison. The long days and sleepless nights, the unbearable stench, the unbelievable sights and the deafening sounds. Not to mention the spate of suicides. And yes, those horrible cockroaches too. I can honestly say that I never want to endure such an experience again.

Paul McGrath travelled with me and we spoke on the 90-minute journey to Rochdale, wondering what was in store for us both at our new 'hotel'.

We had the option to apply for Buckley Hall or Risley in Warrington. I didn't fancy Risley because of its reputation for being rife with drugs. Buckley Hall had recently been converted from a women's prison to a Category C men's prison and, because it had been open for just over a month, only 100 prisoners were held there when I arrived.

Nothing could be worse than Walton and this was definitely a step in the right direction.

Arriving at the reception area of Buckley Hall was so different from my 'welcome' to Walton a year previously. It was just me and Paul being brought in this time, and everything seemed much more laid-back and friendly.

Straight away I noticed there were no high walls and the buildings were all pre-fabricated.

I was worried that I wouldn't receive as many visits from friends and family because of the extended travelling distance from Liverpool, but I knew that I had to move on in the prison system as quickly as possible. On first impressions it looked like I'd made a good choice.

After a strip-search and security check, we were allocated our cells.

HAMMERED

The prison comprised a division of eight billets situated on a hill. Paul and I were put on the induction wing, where we were pleased to be greeted by Paul Dunn.

Paul, from Huyton, was a lad we both knew well. He had arrived from a Category B prison in Nottingham called Lowdham Grange. He introduced Paul and me to the other Scousers who had arrived with him – Peter Wilson, Tony Molloy, Peter Riley and Andy Rogan.

The prisoners allocated spaces at Buckley Hall were all coming from Category B prisons – lads who were doing big sentences and still had a long time to serve. It soon became clear that there were some hard lads at Buckley Hall.

The good news for me was being allocated a single cell. To have my own personal space was a massive bonus. No disrespect to Paul, but I was relieved that I wouldn't have to listen to his snoring any longer!

However, the cells were flimsy compared to the old Victorian walls of Walton. You could hear everything that was going on in the cells next door because of the paper-thin walls. At least they had recently been painted and were clean. And there wasn't a cockroach in sight.

There were showers at the end of the landing and a room with a bath in it – a legacy of its days as a women's prison. The trouble was, everyone arriving from Category B prisons wanted to use the bath.

On my first night, Dunny sorted out the key to the bathroom for me so that I could have a nice long soak. I lay in the hot water, letting my body relax and enjoying the luxury that I'd missed so much. It was the best bath I'd ever had and I then realised that it's the simple things in life that you miss the most when they are taken away from you.

I was also pleasantly surprised by the food. A new kitchen had been added and the cuisine was Michelin star quality compared to the slop we had to suffer at Walton.

I rang Nicola that night and she wanted to visit me the following weekend. We were becoming very close now and I was looking forward to seeing her.

The three most important things in prison are your visits, followed by the gym and then your food. Well, those were my priorities anyway.

The prisoners at Buckley all seemed much more settled compared to those on B-wing at Walton. All had come to terms with their sentence and the majority just wanted to progress through the system and move up to the next level – a Category D prison.

* * * *

It was amazing how quickly Buckley Hall filled up. Within a couple of months it was bursting at the seams.

Paul and I had been moved on to the VTU (Voluntary Drug Testing Unit) billet. This was a billet to help prisoners come off their drug habits. We thought it would be a safe bet there because there would be no drugs available but, on the contrary, the complete opposite was true.

Because of the lack of security and low fences, the prison was full of drugs within a couple of months of opening, and the prisoners who were supposed to be trying to get off drugs were actually using them in the bathrooms at the end of the landings.

Smack-heads are dangerous men in prison and it made me sick to see them use the security of the bathroom to shoot up with heroin and abuse their bodies with other hard drugs. Before long, this practice was rife and I never lay in that bath again.

* * * *

On February 1, 2006, Mr X and eight others were arrested on conspiracy to supply class A drugs. I'd found out through Lenny Font that there had been an ongoing surveillance operation on the arrested nine, which had been code-named Operation Vatican – something that was not known to me at the time of my trial.

On March 21, I was taken to the reception of Buckley Hall to be greeted by two officers of the Serious Crime squad. I nearly s*** myself.

It was the good cop-bad cop routine straight from the off.

'Mark, we want to question you at Rochdale police station on conspiracy to supply class A drugs.'

My heart was pumping. I'd already been given an eight-year sentence. Why were the police questioning me again?

HAMMERED

On the way to the police station, the good cop in the passenger seat was giving me the full works. 'You'll be all right, Mark, we just want to question you on your association with certain individuals we arrested last month.'

On arrival at the police station, I got in touch with Lenny. He was in court and couldn't make it over to Rochdale, so he sent his colleague Alex Campbell to advise me on the situation.

While waiting for the solicitor I was drug-tested, which I found bizarre as I was already in custody. Apparently it was a procedure they did with everyone who arrived at the police station, with a DNA sample also taken.

The test was negative. Having to go through all this s***e was really p*****g me off. I was already serving an eight-year prison sentence. Hadn't they had enough?

Alex Campbell sat me down and told me that the police were going to ask me a load of questions concerning my association with certain individuals they had in custody. I was adamant – and Alex agreed – that I had been handed my sentence and was entitled to give a 'no comment' interview, so that's what I did.

For two hours I was asked a multitude of questions, as they attempted to connect me to certain persons and events. Just as it had been at my original police interview, my answer to every question was a simple: 'No comment.'

They were hoping I'd grass on the main conspirators who were known to me, but I refused to name anyone.

Later on that week, I discovered that police had simultaneously taken four others out of prison for questioning – all five of us having been sentenced for having drugs found at addresses or in our possession.

The nine other individuals were to be charged with conspiracy to supply class A drugs. The three main conspirators – Mr X, Y and Z – received nine, 10 and 11 years respectively, involving five seizures of drugs over a 24-month period.

I took my sentence of eight years bang on the chin but I'll always question why I was treated in court as if I was the 'main man' acting alone in the crime. How on earth could I receive an eight-year sentence when Mr X was only given nine years? Where was the justification of sentence?

I would have been better off facing the conspiracy charge along with the others. There was no way I would have been given a sentence of eight years when Mr X, who rented the property and put the drugs there, got nine years.

Even the police inspector commented after I'd been sentenced: 'Ward was a foot soldier in this operation, but we will get his Commander-in-Chief.'

After the co-conspirators were sentenced, I later received a letter from Mr Z, who received 11 years. He said to me that the police had had their cake and eaten it. They had dealt with me as the main man and then dealt with him as the main man, too. 'They can't have it both ways,' he argued.

But they did. The police and prosecution knew the tiny role I'd played in renting the property in my name. But on the day of my sentencing they couldn't disclose in court the fact that Operation Vatican was ongoing. That would have wrecked their surveillance operation and blown the whole thing wide apart.

I accept that I deserved to be punished for my part in the crime. But I'm bitter about the fact that the police and prosecution actually pushed for me to receive more than the eight years.

How criminal of them – they knew my limited role and who the drugs really belonged to. It turned out that McVinnie Road was the fourth seizure of drugs linked to the accused conspirators.

People tell me that I got eight years for being a former high-profile footballer. Maybe. But I think I got eight years for keeping my mouth shut. I didn't keep quiet because I was scared of repercussions – it was the way I was brought up. And I don't regret continuing to live by those principles.

Six months before I was arrested, there was a seizure of drugs in Prescot. The individual charged received four years for possession of three kilos of cocaine, with scales, paraphernalia and money found at the address. This person is now known as a grass and has to live with that stigma for the rest of his life. I got twice his sentence for the same crime. How can that be fair?

Leaving the police station in Rochdale to return to Buckley Hall, the two cops were still giving it all their s***e, and asking me questions 'off the record'.

I told the cop in the passenger seat: 'I watch *The Bill*, you know.' He just laughed.

Later, reflecting on the day's events in my cell, I realised it was a routine line of enquiry they had to follow, to tie up the loose ends of the case. But, as I say, they were getting zero information from me.

* * * *

I settled down at Buckley Hall and had progressed to working in the gym as an orderly. There was a little bit more freedom there compared to Walton but, when you weren't working, you were still banged up in your cell.

I was really pushing myself to the limit to improve my fitness even more, training sometimes for up to four hours a day. I'd start by completing a circuit and then do a long run on the running machine before moving on to weights in the afternoon.

I passed a sports science course, which I really enjoyed, thanks to the help of Adrian Fields, who organised it. In fact, my reason for doing it was to help me achieve the aim of becoming a personal trainer upon my release from prison.

The gym screws were easy to get on with. One was named Glen Fox and the other, Mark Hilditch, was an ex-pro footballer who had played centre-forward for Rochdale, Tranmere Rovers and Wigan Athletic. Mark had been employed as a screw for 13 years and also worked in Oldham Athletic's youth academy. He was still fit and was unbeatable at the game of soft tennis – tennis played on a small court with a soft ball. It was a great game, and I began to play it religiously whenever I could.

I became very good and won the prisoners' Christmas tennis competition. But I couldn't manage to beat Mark Hilditch. And it was getting to me. He had been playing for 13 years and had the edge with experience.

Andy Rogan became my sparring partner at Buckley Hall. He too was a gym orderly who was very fit and we would compete at everything. We both ran a half-marathon on the treadmill on behalf of Glen's charity, The Bethany Project.

I'd written to everyone I knew for sponsorship, and we managed to raise over £2,000 to help a children's home for orphaned, abandoned and abused kids in Tanzania, east Africa. Andy ran first, and I followed straight afterwards. Even this became a race – Andy finished in 100 minutes and I managed to do it in six minutes less. It was tough on the treadmill, in a small gym with very little air.

I have to thank everyone who made a donation, including Tony Cottee, who really helped and collected money from some of the ex-pros. Former West Ham United chairman Martin Cearns also sent in a cheque.

* * * *

The day I got a message saying that Howard Kendall wanted to see me, I became very nervous.

I sent out a VO (Visiting Order) and I knew he was coming in to see me with his good mate Tommy Griff and former Everton star Duncan Ferguson. The whole of the prison knew that two of the most famous figures in Everton's recent history were coming. Some of the screws even brought in football shirts for them to sign.

Walking down to the visit hall I remember feeling very anxious. What was Howard going to say about his ex-player's dramatic fall from grace?

I sat at the table waiting for the three men to appear. Duncan walked in first, shook my hand and said: 'Good to see you, wee man.' Howard greeted me with: 'You're looking fit son,' and Tommy said the same.

Their visit flew by and the one thing I'll always remember from it was Howard's words. He said to me: 'Mark, nothing has changed between me and you, son. I don't want to know how you got involved or any of the details. We'll be there for you when you get out.'

Those words from my former manager, a man I've always had the greatest respect for, meant so much to me.

The rest of the visit was built around stories from Duncan's six weeks spent in Barlinnie prison back in 1996. We had a good laugh and it really boosted me to see all three of them.

John Blake was still very interested in publishing my book. He even sent his *senior editor* up to visit me. But I'd already decided to go with Tony McDonald – somebody I could trust – who runs his own Football World publishing company from Romford, Essex.

I had to complete a Victim's Awareness Course as part of my rehabilitation. It was interesting, because I had to write down on a piece of paper who I perceived to be the victims of my crime.

I had no direct victims of my crime. I didn't force anybody to do anything against their will.

I listed the main victim of my crime as Melissa and other family members. Of course, down the line, there are thousands of victims of drugs, but I will always maintain that my family have been the biggest victims of my crime.

* * * *

Buckley Hall's drug problem meant I was constantly targeted for MDTs (Mandatory Drug Tests). When I raised this with an officer, he admitted that 70 per cent of the MDTs were coming back positive.

And get this . . . the screw told me I was being targeted because the prison was fined for every positive MDT and so they picked me out all the time because I was guaranteed to prove a negative!

The test procedure wasn't a nice experience. A strip search and then you stood over a toilet to p*** into a plastic cup.

By the time they demanded I took a third MDT in the space of one month, I'd had enough. I started to complain. Why weren't they testing the smack-heads? It wasn't hard to tell who was on drugs.

I was put in a room to calm down. I'd been plucked from the gym and was soaking wet with sweat. They left me there for a good hour and by the time I was back in the test room, I needed to use the toilet . . . and not just for a p***.

I told the officer that I needed to do a 'number two' but he said I couldn't!

With that, I just dropped my shorts and sat on the toilet. It wasn't long before the room stank.

There was no bog roll and so I just sat there until they brought me some. I told them I wasn't moving. The PO in charge of the p***-testing station arrived and he wasn't very happy.

I wiped my a***, provided another negative sample of p**s and then basically told them that if they continued to literally 'take the p**s' by asking me for an MDT every week, then they were getting my s*** too. They never asked me again!

* * * *

Big Warren Cox had followed Paul McGrath and I from Walton. He and Andy Creighton ended up on the same billet as the pair of us, and Paul became a big help to me.

Warren had got himself a mobile phone and allowed me to use it so that I could keep in touch with loved ones. I had my own SIM card – inmates would arrange for them to be passed over the low prison walls or smuggled in on visits and then sell them for a tenner each. Phones would cost a couple of hundred quid each and if you wanted one, you had to make your own arrangements to pay friends or relatives of those who supplied the goods on the outside. Or, rather than physically hand over cash, what tended to happen was that prisoners would get someone on the outside to buy them phone credit and then text the relevant details to their fellow inmates, who had an instant £10's worth of top-up credit on their mobile. Well, they don't have a shop in prison where you can buy phone credit!

But it was more difficult to use the phones in Buckley Hall than it had been at Walton. The screws were cracking down on the use of them, and it was difficult to conceal them in your cell or anywhere else in the prison.

I even resorted to hiding my SIM card within my foreskin. It may sound crude but it was the safest place, as the screws were searching the cells every day and had scanners that could detect mobile phone signals.

Warren had the phone overnight but I'd use it in my cell before bang-up and sometimes during the day. One afternoon I was on the phone to Nicola, who was actually in Australia visiting her brother. The battery was very low, and suddenly the phone just switched off. I gave it to Warren just before dinner so that he could re-charge it.

The previous night, Warren had been using the phone and had a major row with his ex-wife. While sitting in his cell, he received an incoming call. When he answered the phone, the caller said: 'Is that you Warren?'

'Who is this?' asked Warren, and at that very moment a screw opened the door and said: 'It's me, and I'll have the phone please.'

Caught, banged to rights. It turned out his ex-wife had phoned the prison following their row and grassed him up about the mobile phone. Warren received another month on top of his sentence for that misdemeanour.

People have often asked me how it's possible to charge a mobile phone in prison without a charger. The most common way is to use ordinary batteries, and simply run a length of copper wire from positive to positive and negative to negative, using sticky tape to keep it in place.

Certain electronic gadgets, like razors and hair clippers, have chargers that also fit some mobile phones. Prisoners can be very cunning and you'd be amazed at some of the improvisations they create in order to get by.

One of the most unbelievable acts I heard about in prison was the art of hiding a mobile phone . . . by inserting it up the a***. It's something I can honestly say I never tried, but there was a skinny lad from Manchester called Mather who apparently could fit two phones up his a***!

Many a prisoner would use this distasteful method to hide their phone, but I would rather run the risk of getting caught than attempt that disgusting test of pain.

It goes to show, though, the lengths that some prisoners would go to in order to retain contact with the outside world and keep in touch with their loved ones.

However, it came to my attention recently that an X-ray machine had been developed that could provide a scan of your rectum when you sat on it. So maybe the old phone-up-the-bum trick is no longer such a clever idea!

* * * *

I often listened to BBC Radio 5 Live in my cell during the day but on the morning of Wednesday, April 19, 2006, I was very shocked to hear of the sudden death of John Lyall, who had been like a father to me at West Ham. John had died of a heart attack at his farmhouse in Suffolk the previous night and I was upset that I couldn't attend his funeral in Ipswich to pay my last respects to the great man. The best I could do was send flowers to his bereaved family, which Melissa arranged on my behalf, and I was genuinely touched to receive a letter from John's wife, Yvonne, thanking me. It was the least I could do in memory of a man who meant so much to me as a football manager and as a person.

It would have been fitting if West Ham had won the FA Cup in his honour when the Hammers met Liverpool in the final at Cardiff just a few weeks after John died. With plenty of fellow Scousers in Buckley Hall, there was a lot of banter in the build-up to the game, with me and the other Evertonians obviously cheering for the team in white.

I watched the BBC's live coverage and couldn't believe it when my old team took a 2-0 first half lead, only for Steven Gerrard to deny them the trophy with his wonder goal that made it 3-3 in the dying seconds. Liverpool won it on penalties, which was a sad end to an emotional period for West Ham fans who had mourned the loss of another great manager, Ron Greenwood, just a couple of months before John passed away.

* * * *

I was beginning to look ahead to when I might be able to step up to category D status and move on to the last stage of my four-year prison term. I'd discovered that my ROTL (Release On Temporary Licence) date was May 11, 2007 – a quarter of the way through my original sentence. I was allowed to apply for open conditions 24 months before my release date.

But that was in the future. In the meantime, I had further reminders of the happy family occasions I missed out on.

Melissa married Kevin Coyle on August 17, 2006, and I was gutted to miss the wedding. I got to speak to her on the mobile after the reception, and she was so upset to hear my voice. I felt I'd let her down badly by not being there on her big day to give her away.

I'd already missed so much while banged up in prison. Two Christmases, the birth of two grandchildren – Frankie followed Isabella on January 15, 2007 – and now my daughter's big day. Instead of me being by Melissa's side, it was Jane who gave her away instead.

I sensed it was becoming hard work for Nicola and the family to visit me regularly at Buckley Hall. Instead of receiving visits every week, it now stretched to every fortnight. I was beginning to think that maybe she wouldn't be waiting for me when I eventually did get released.

At 28, she was a lot younger than me, and it must have been difficult for her. I'd seen, at first hand, many relationships destroyed because of prison. Not many women wait for their men but I was hoping that Nicola would because she was special to me.

* * * *

During my playing days, a favourite training game among the lads was head tennis – which is better described as volleyball with your head instead of your hands. I'd got all the lads at the prison gym into it, and the screws even held a head tennis competition at Christmas.

Being the ex-pro footballer, I was under pressure to win it. I was partnered by Peter Wilson, a big Everton fan, and we managed to triumph in the final to become the Buckley Hall Head Tennis champions.

In prison you set yourself little targets to aim for. It's very good for focusing the mind. I was desperate to beat the gym screw Mark Hilditch at soft tennis before I left Buckley Hall. I was edging closer and was a lot fitter than Mark but he had exceptional racket control. In March 2007, I eventually achieved my target, beating him three sets to two.

After the game he shook my hand and told me that it was his first defeat in 13, long years.

* * * *

On Thursday, March 8, a screw opened my door early in the morning and said: 'Pack your bag, Ward, you're out of here.'

It was great news. I was going to HMP Kirkham, an open prison situated between Preston and Blackpool, and two months earlier than expected. I assume they let me move on to category D status a little earlier due to my good behaviour. Kirkham was nearer to Liverpool, which was good in terms of visits from friends and family, but, more significantly, it meant I'd be going to open conditions and it would be my last prison before release.

I couldn't wait to get there.

36. FINAL COUNTDOWN

I ARRIVED at Kirkham on a bright, sunny day and it was a welcome sight just to see prisoners walking around the grounds. The reception area was very busy and after a security check I was allocated my billet.

Each billet was made up of 20 cells, with a shower room and toilet at the end of each building. The cells were small and basic but that didn't matter to me. I just wanted to dump my belongings and get out in the fresh air.

As I put my bag on the bed, a prisoner popped his head in and, after placing a loaf of bread, milk and coffee on the table, he said to me: 'My name is John. Anything you need, Mark, I am down at the end.'

I later got to know the guy as John Willis, a Scouser and mad Evertonian, who was soon to help me again in more ways than one.

Breathing in the fresh air and feeling the spring sunshine on my face, I began to realise what all the fuss was about when prisoners spoke about open prison and how cushty it is in comparison to institutions such as Walton and the barbaric behaviour that goes on in those places.

The prisoners who had been there for a while looked so much healthier while, by contrast, I noticed that all the lads who arrived with me had that classic 'prison grey' complexion.

It was unusually warm for the time of year, and I just sat in the sun, feeling the warmth on my face. Right outside my window was the running area, and I couldn't wait to put my running shoes on out in the fresh air, instead of the claustrophobic, compact gym I'd left behind at Buckley Hall.

There were ducks everywhere, waddling about in groups, and I also noticed a bowling green. What a contrast to the misery and draconian regime I'd left behind at Walton. It was a big shock to the system.

In the first couple of days, I was introduced to all the facilities at the prison. The gym area was excellent, with its well-equipped weights area, running machines and squash courts.

While I was walking around taking it all in, I noticed a lad following me. Before I'd left Buckley Hall, a prisoner from Bolton named Benny had told me that he had a fat mate at Kirkham who would smack my a*** at soft tennis, and that he would be waiting for me when I got there.

I turned to face this big lad following me and he said: 'All right, Wardy, I hear you play tennis.'

Without thinking, I replied: 'Oh, you must be the fat b*****d.'

'You cheeky t***,' he said, 'I'll show you who's a fat b*****d. When do you want to play?'

The lad's name was Lee Bonney. I said I'd play him the next day if we could organise it.

Just before bang up on my first day, I went outside for a run round the track and felt like a little kid again. It was an unbelievable sensation to have the freedom to run around in the open surroundings.

I'd arrived at Kirkham with still over two years of my sentence remaining. A long time to serve, even in open conditions, but as far as I was concerned I was going to use my time at Kirkham positively and do my utmost to be 100 per cent prepared for my release date of Monday, May 11, 2009.

I was given my release details once again and as I read down the sheet of paper this time, I noticed that I'd be able to apply for what they call a Town Visit on May 12, and a Home Visit a week later.

A home visit! Nobody had told me anything about going home. I showed the dates to a prisoner in the next cell and he pointed out that, because I wasn't on a parole sentence and had my release date, I was entitled to home leaves.

In two months' time, I was going home for four days, and again every month until my release. F*****g hell! I couldn't wait to tell the family. This place Kirkham was getting better by the hour.

* * * *

I'd been at Kirkham for precisely six days. I'd battered the running track and had never felt fitter. However, I had a rude awakening on the soft tennis court, where I well and truly met my match.

Lee Bonney, the fat prisoner who had challenged me to a game, smacked my a*** big time. Benny from Bolton was right – he was a freak. He was big and heavy, and I was sure that he wouldn't beat me – I'd be too quick and fit.

I never got a set off him. I shook his hand and told him what a good player he was. But that soft tennis defeat was really the least of my worries.

* * * *

On March 14, I awoke early but, as soon as I stepped out of bed, I was on the floor. I'd collapsed suddenly and fallen unconscious.

The sound of me hitting the floor in my cell had been heard by John Willis, who happened to be walking along the corridor. I remember waking up on the floor feeling very disorientated, with unbelievable pain in my neck and pins and needles in my arms.

John sat me up on the bed, told me I looked terrible, and rushed to sound the alarm. A screw arrived on the billet and John told him to ring an ambulance. 'I can't', said the screw, 'I'm on my own.'

'Ring a f*****g ambulance now, you p****!' said John, and with that the screw ran off to do as instructed by my fellow prisoner.

There were no chains this time as I was taken to the Royal Preston Hospital, where an Irish doctor examined me and said I'd be staying with them for a while. I had a cut on the back of my head from the fall but the doctors were more concerned about what had caused me to black out. I really didn't feel well at all.

Melissa, Billy and Uncle Tommy came to see me that night and were obviously concerned, especially remembering what I'd been through in hospital four years earlier. I was wired up to a heart monitor that took a telemetric 24 hour reading of my heart. I told the doctors and nurse about the suspected aneurysm I'd suffered in November 2004 but they didn't seem too concerned about that.

On my second night in hospital, I was woken up by a doctor who asked me how I was feeling. I told him I felt okay but he said that my heart-rate had gone down to 32 beats-per-minute. The next day, a consultant saw me and, after completing a load of tests, the diagnosis was that my heart was very healthy. They put the low heart-rate down to my high level of fitness.

It was quite surreal being in hospital knowing that I should be in prison. All the nurses knew that I was a prisoner and I remember overhearing a nurse on the phone saying: 'Yes, he's still here.' She told me later that someone from the prison had just called her to check that I hadn't escaped!

After I'd been in for four days, a couple of screws came to see me, asking me to sign a form declaring that I hadn't been attacked or assaulted while in prison.

There were ridiculously false stories doing the rounds at Kirkham about why I'd ended up in hospital. The rumours ranged from me being done in by another prisoner to injuring myself in a bad fall while attempting to escape through a window. Kirkham was like a Scouse village – I'd say three quarters of the prisoners were from Liverpool – and the rumour mill worked overtime. It was pathetic.

I thought I was going back to the prison when a young doctor came to examine me, but instead he asked me if they could perform a lumbar puncture, as it would determine if I had suffered a bleed or an aneurysm.

I'd knew from the lumbar puncture I'd had at the end of 2004 that it was unpleasant but I really wanted to get to the bottom of what had happened to me, so I agreed to it. I was told that if the results were negative I'd be able to leave the hospital.

I was fast asleep when I was woken again by an Indian doctor with nurses pulling the curtains around my bed. They told me they'd had the results of the lumbar puncture and *it was positive for a bleed.*

I was told I couldn't move from my bed and was put on medication every four hours. It was a nightmare. A nurse would wake me to give me tablets that would lower my blood pressure, just in case I suffered another bleed.

My hospital stay lasted for 14 days and I was only allowed to go back to the prison after having an angiogram X-ray of my brain, which proved inconclusive anyway. I wasn't really told what had happened to me – they just advised me to take it easy for a while.

From that day to this, I've never felt the same as I did before collapsing.

Walking around the prison for the first few days, I felt as if I was on another planet. Everything was all over the place. I was constantly losing my balance and I knew something was wrong. However, prison isn't exactly the best place in the world to fall ill – sympathy and care are not words you are likely to hear, even in open conditions.

My condition worried me. I'd been so fit before my hospitalisation, but now I didn't know if I'd ever feel well enough to exercise properly ever again.

Despite my mystery illness, I was looking forward to my first visit home. Nicola had not been to see me, either in Kirkham or during my hospital stay. I was gutted but at least she was willing to stay with me in a hotel during my initial four-day leave. I was supposed to stay at my designated Release On Temporary Licence (ROTL) address – Uncle Tommy's house in Huyton – but I needed time with the woman who had been so patient and caring towards me over the previous two years.

I couldn't sleep the night before I was released for my four days in paradise. It was Friday, May 18, 2007, I'd been locked up in prison for two years and was now going home for four days.

On my licence it stated that I couldn't drink alcohol, enter licensed premises, gamble or take drugs. Every single one of these conditions are normally abused within the first few hours of a prisoner's release on their first home leave.

Yes, I had a drink. I entered licensed premises and I had a bet – I also did the lottery. But no, I didn't take drugs.

Obviously when prisoners have been banged up for a considerable amount of time, they are eager to enjoy the most pleasurable things they have been denied behind bars. So they want to shag their birds, have a few bevvies and have bets on the gee-gees. And there will also be some who want to smoke cannabis or take hard drugs. It's human nature.

I had no curfew imposed on me and it was overwhelming to begin with as I tried to adapt to life on the outside. The family had organised a Chinese meal that Friday evening at Ho's restaurant in Prescot. I didn't make it to the main course because I was so drunk. I'd started drinking early with Billy and Tommy, and my tolerance level for alcohol was zero.

Despite that, I had a special time with the family. Melissa was made up to be with her dad again and I realised then that I would be able to handle the rest of my sentence easily, knowing I could go home once a month.

Those dark days and nights in Walton were behind me. I'll never forget things there but I was now being much more positive and just wanted to do the rest of my time.

It was hard leaving on the Monday to go back to Kirkham, though. Nicola and Melissa were upset but I told them I'd be seeing them again in three weeks. And it got better, because I was told that if you behaved yourself on the four-day leave, it would be increased to seven days. A whole week out of prison!

However, one special occasion I couldn't obtain release for was a dinner to honour the late John Lyall and Ron Greenwood at West Ham's ground. John's son, Murray Lyall, wrote to me and the prison governor asking if it was possible for me to attend. They let you out for family funerals but the prison wouldn't allow me to travel down to east London for the gala dinner on May 9. That was a shame, because I'd also missed out on a similar tribute dinner that the Boys of 86 had organised to honour our old Hammers boss at the end of 2007, although Tony Gale got a few laughs from the guests when he announced that I'd sent an apology for absence!

* * * *

Kirkham had its own prison football team that played matches against normal sides in a proper league, although, for obvious reasons, all games were played at 'home'. They had done very well that season and, with two games left, were in with a good chance of winning the division.

A Scouse lad named Nicky Ayres, the team captain, was constantly mithering me to play in the penultimate game. I would love to have played but I just wasn't feeling well enough. I managed to hide out of his way on the day of the match and I felt a bit bad when I heard they had got beaten 1-0.

A week later, they had the final match of the season against the team placed second in the league – a winner-takes-all clash for the title. The Kirkham side was full of Scousers – everyone bar goalkeeper Lee Bonney, from Bolton, and a defender Billy Moonie, a Glaswegian, came from Liverpool. The Mancs weren't allowed to play – it didn't matter *how* good they were!

On May 12, 2007, I was sat on my bed in the cell watching *Football Focus* on BBC1. The following day was a massive one for my old team West Ham United, who badly needed a result against Manchester United at Old Trafford to be certain of retaining their Premier League status.

I was looking back at the last two years of my life. It was two years to the day since my arrest. I was also remembering Dad, who would have been 71 that day.

The TV programme ran a big feature on West Ham's chances of survival, including interviews from Upton Park with the likes of Alvin Martin, Frank McAvennie and Tony Cottee. It was good to see my old team-mates again. They all looked a little bit older than how I'd remembered them but I couldn't help feeling envious.

They were filmed while taking part in the annual Boys of '86 corporate football tournament – one I'd played in with them numerous times prior to my arrest. I always enjoyed going back to Upton Park and kicking a ball around on the pitch that held so many happy memories.

The irony that day was that I'd agreed to play for the prison football team in the last game of the season. Whoever won this match would be crowned league champions. Never mind the enormity of the final game of the season at Old Trafford, with a reported £30m on the line for the Hammers, this was *the* big one!

I knew after playing that game that something was very wrong with me. I couldn't anticipate anything and my balance was terrible, but somehow I got through the 90 minutes and we won the match –

thanks to a goal by a lad named Russell – to seal the title. The other lads celebrated as if they'd won the World Cup final – it meant so much to them.

For the record, this was our line-up on the big day:

HMP Kirkham FC

Bonney

Bignall   Moonie   Boscoe   Bailey

Morgan   Woods   Ayres   McNicol

Ward

Russell

The refereeing by the screw was very strong. There were a lot of hard lads in the team. Nicky Ayres (aka Jan Molby) was a ferocious tackler. He couldn't pass water but he got stuck in and didn't need an invitation to intimidate the opposition. I didn't enjoy the game one bit. The symptoms I was getting after my spell in hospital were now worrying me.

At least West Ham fans had nothing to concern themselves about that summer. Having suffered relegation with the Hammers in 1989, I was made up for the supporters after Carlos Tevez scored the only goal of the game to keep them in the top flight, at the expense of Sheffield United. I knew what it must have meant to them and I was delighted to see how my old team did it when I watched Match of the Day later than night.

I'd been working in the prison as a billet cleaner, mopping up in the corridors and shower area, but was told I could go outside of the prison to do my community pay-back charity work. If you had no risk factor against your name, you were allowed to work in the charity shops in the local areas around Preston and Blackpool.

I was posted to the Barnardo's shop in Kirkham town centre, just a short walk from the prison. I was taken down for an interview and started work there on Monday, July 9.

I hated every minute of it.

I'm all for putting something back into the community but to be sitting around among old women in a shop all day wasn't for me, and I resented the experience. Give me a fence to paint or a hole to dig any day of the week.

It must have shown on my face because, after a month of working in the shop, an old lady called Pam said: 'Mark, you don't like it here, do you?'

I admitted to her that I hated it. She asked if I would be interested in working at her local church, looking after the grounds. I'm not at all religious but I replied: 'When do you want me to start?'

Pam had a word with Father Giles Allen and I began my charity work at St John the Evangelist C of E Church in Clifton, on Monday, August 6. It was a great job. I'd walk three miles to the church every morning, and then three miles back in the afternoon.

I had full use of the church hall to make myself a cup of tea and lunch in what was a beautiful, isolated spot. I enjoyed caring for the grounds and, within a few weeks, had them in pristine condition. I was so proud when I eventually got on top of the long grass and had the graveyard looking perfect. Father Allen showed me some letters from church-goers who expressed their pleasure at how well the grounds were looking.

The screws would often come down to the church to check up on me but I told them that I wouldn't jeopardise my home leaves by not being there. I also had a visit from a local newspaper photographer who had been sent to get snaps of me going about my chores, but I spotted him approaching from the adjacent fields and told him where to go.

It was tough work in the winter, walking six miles in the snow, but I look back on that job as a fantastic experience. I was left on my own, in a position of trust and felt a real sense of achievement.

Having a charity job meant that I was moved to the green billets. The cells there had their own en-suite toilet and shower, which made life so much easier and more comfortable.

* * * *

My home visits each month were great but I think Nicola was finding it hard to understand why I fancied going out for a few pints and socialising with friends on my days out of the prison. After being banged up for three years, of course I wanted to socialise as soon as I got the opportunity – it certainly beat sitting at home on the sofa holding hands. It was the start of a decline in our relationship, although I didn't realise it at the time. I was also forever falling out with Melissa and, looking back, I think I was a bit misunderstood by the women I loved most.

Further hospital tests failed to reveal what was causing me to lose my balance, which was at the root of my upsetting behaviour.

My first Christmas at home with the family in three years felt fantastic in one sense but I still wasn't feeling right in myself. Nicola and I had Christmas dinner at my brother Billy's house but I was finding it hard to hold my drink. On one occasion I went out for a few drinks with my mate Peter McGuinness. We'd only drunk four pints, which would normally be no problem to me, but the beer affected my balance and I fell over and cut my head.

What Nicola didn't know, and it's so difficult to explain properly to other people who can see no outward physical signs of a problem, is that I had spells of feeling dizzy and light-headed. I wasn't feeling well all the time – 24/7 – and so when I was coming out and having a few drinks, the alcohol wasn't agreeing with me. Little did I know at the time but the booze was only making my condition worse.

I obviously enjoyed relaxing with a pint of ale but the beer just made me feel worse, which in turn sparked anger in me, and this undoubtedly had a damaging effect on my relationships with the people closest to me.

I felt frustrated that as well as falling out with Nicola and Melissa, my general fitness levels were also suffering. I've always prided myself on my fitness, so it hurt that I didn't feel well enough to do the things that I'd always taken for granted. I remember breaking down over it with Nicola one night.

It wasn't until early in 2009, when a friend looked up my symptoms on a medical internet website and he handed me the print outs, that I immediately recognised some of them as part of my condition. I also read that patients who suffer these symptoms often have difficulty maintaining personal relationships.

* * * *

It wasn't all bad news, though. I reached another major turning point in prison life when I was told that I'd be able to work on a paid labour scheme for the final year of my sentence. So from May 12, 2008, I could go and find myself a job.

It was going to be difficult, but I met an old mate of mine, Paul Downes, for a coffee during one of my home visits in April. Paul owned Caber Developments, based in Liverpool, and told me that he would give me a start. I earned the minimum weekly wage, although my salary was paid directly into the prison's bank account and held there pending my eventual release. In the meantime, I was given a very basic allowance of £60 to cover my 80-mile round trip petrol costs and expenses.

It was only labouring on a site but I was so grateful. At the time, though, things were starting to get tight as the credit crunch took hold and the building industry was among the worst affected. One or two of the lads had to be laid off as work slowed down but Caber kindly kept me on right up until my release date from Kirkham.

The first job with them was based at the Walton Liverpool building, a Citizens Advice Bureau (CAB), but I didn't have any transport to get there from Kirkham.

I was in regular touch with Tony Gale and I mentioned to him that I was able to go out and work for wages, but had no way of getting to the job. He said he'd speak to the lads from the Boys of '86, and they very generously sent our Billy a few quid so that he could buy me a little Peugeot car to get me to and from Liverpool each day. I've since traded it in for an old Vauxhall Corsa – a red one at that! – but it gets me around and that's the main thing.

If it hadn't been for Paul Downes and the West Ham lads, I would never have got the opportunity to work outside prison.

Back at the church, I said my goodbyes to everyone and thanked Father Allen for giving me the opportunity.

* * * *

There were times during 2008 when I found it very hard to sit down at Kirkham and continue writing this book, even though my editor/publisher Tony McDonald was very impressed and enthusiastic about the hand-written chapters I'd sent him in the post.

The fact that Nicola and I were not getting on was having a big effect on my mentality. With my physical condition and balance also getting no better, I was often left feeling upset and very frustrated.

I loved working with the lads at the CAB, though. We were building the place from scratch and I relished the physical work, carrying the bricks and making the mortar. It put my balance to the test at times – my colleagues mentioned that they sometimes thought I was p****d as they watched me struggle to walk in a straight line – but I was learning quickly and the other lads were all good to me.

The site manager Danny Judge, his brother Jeff, Terry Tosney, Bobby Mac and Paul Downes' son Michael were very entertaining and became good mates. We would play cards – Nomination Trumps – during our breaks and Danny and Terry couldn't understand my competitive nature. I hated to lose and they would wind me up every day, but it was all good banter. I even formed a '100 Club' – if you reached 100 points you made it in. Unfortunately, Danny never joined this exclusive elite – he was rubbish at cards!

There was an extraordinary moment at work which coincided with the sequence of three derby matches involving Everton and Liverpool in the space of a couple of weeks at the end of January and start of February '09. We were refurbishing a big, old Victorian house in Bootle – ironically, a charity-funded £1m rehab place for drug addicts – when Terry Tosney and Jeff Judge were chipping away at the front of the building. Terry went too far into the wall with the breaker tool and when he looked inside the cavity, he was amazed to discover an old newspaper that would create a lot of interest.

I was loading stuff into the skip when the two lads who had found the paper shouted out: 'Come here, Mark, look at this.' I was always a bit dubious of Terry and Jeff, a couple of Liverpudlians who were always playing practical jokes on me, so I thought nothing of it at first.

Then I saw Terry holding a copy of the *Sunday Mirror* from September 19, 1993 and there, under the headline 'It's Bruise Grobbelaar' – a reference to the famous altercation between the Liverpool keeper and

Steve McManaman – was the match report of Everton's 2-0 victory in which Tony Cottee and I scored for the Blues.

My initial suspicion was that Terry had deliberately planted it there, as yet another wind-up and to see my reaction. There was also speculation from the other lads that I'd put it there myself to try and impress them. But, astonishingly, it was a genuine find. The building had evidently had a lot of work done on it over the years and someone just happened to shove that old paper down the wall cavity while working there some 15 years ago.

* * * *

When I started outside paid employment I was put on the NSC (Next Step Centre) at Kirkham, a new building that reminded me of a typical Travelodge. There were 40 prisoners on the billet, the cells were bigger, with an en-suite shower and toilet, and a fridge and television in the cell.

A big kitchen was available where prisoners would cook their own food, and there was also a communal area with a plasma TV that had Sky Sports News. I thought it couldn't get much better than this . . . until I remembered that I was sharing the facilities with a potent mixture of drug-dealers, murderers and robbers.

I'm sure there are plenty of people out there complaining that prisoners are afforded such luxuries. Well, all I'll say to that is, you don't get those privileges if you aren't a compliant and rehabilitated prisoner who is deemed fit to return to normal society.

Kirkham was a good prison. If you behaved yourself, then there were plenty of privileges available to you. Working out in the gym, home leaves and town visits. But if you stepped out of line then you were just shipped back to closed conditions.

I was never going back to closed conditions, but so many others I knew did. In my time there, I never saw any violence or bullying. What little trouble there was remained out of sight of the screws, because the prison staff always hold the trump card of being able to send problem prisoners back to closed conditions and therefore a stricter regime.

HAMMERED

If you do your time correctly, you are rewarded with privileges, charity work and paid employment. I took everything that came my way. I never asked for any favours and served my time, week by week, month by month, year by year.

* * * *

My home leaves were eventually to take their toll on Nicola. We fell out in the autumn of 2008. I so wanted her to be waiting for me on my release in May 2009 but we had drifted apart. I tried hard to keep in touch but she had made her decision and that was that.

37. JORDAN'S TITS

IT WAS Sunday 10 May, 2009. I couldn't sleep. The anticipation of being set free the next morning was keeping me wide awake. I'd spent four years in prison, which amounts to 208 weeks or 1,460 days. I'll always remember a smart arse prisoner telling me how two years equates to 35,000 hours behind bars. Well, the last few passed painfully slowly.

The next morning, I stood with six other inmates patiently awaiting my release from HMP Kirkham. Our Billy was waiting outside with my publisher Tony McDonald. Nick Harris, the journalist from *The Independent,* had driven all the way down from Edinburgh to interview me for a follow up to the feature he'd written in the paper four years previously.

Even though I'd been going outside the prison on a regular basis thanks to my home leave, this was the day I officially became a free man again.

I soon realised that I'd be thrown into the spotlight on my release from prison and the publication of my book in two weeks' time. But I was prepared to accept all the criticism coming my way and hold my head up high. I'd made a terrible mistake and did my time as best I could. I didn't sing like a canary and grass on anyone. I kept my mouth shut, so I had no fears about being accepted back in Liverpool.

Physically, I was as fit as I'd been since my playing days and I couldn't wait to be part of my family and friends once again.

The six other inmates were all let out before me, just after 9.00am, and when it finally came to my turn to pass through the little black door, a screw turned to me and asked if I was okay to walk out with the press outside. I told him I wasn't bothered – I couldn't wait to get out of there and wasn't going to wait a minute longer than necessary.

It was a gorgeous, bright, sunny day and Billy greeted me with a brotherly hug. It was a great feeling to be back on the outside as Mark Ward and not prisoner NM6982 which had been my label for four long years. I left the prison with just a black bin liner filled with a few clothes and masses of paperwork that I'd accumulated over my stretch.

Billy drove me to Kirkby in Liverpool, where I had to see my Probation Officer. I was with her for just half an hour, during which time she laid down the law of the terms of my release on licence. The strict conditions of my release were: one, to reside at a suitable address; two, to report to my Probation Officer every week for the following 16 weeks; and three, not to travel abroad without permission.

If I broke any of these conditions it was possible for her to immediately recall me back to prison. It wasn't going to be a problem for me to see her once a week. I'd never given the prison authorities the opportunity to add more days to my sentence while I was on the inside and now I was out, I wasn't going to give my Probation Officer any excuse to stick me back in jail.

Prisons are full of people who have breached their licence conditions. The conditions are very strict – I am on licence for four years, which is effectively a sentence served within the community. Step out of line just once and I'll find myself back inside. I now see my Probation Officer once a month which is no problem for me. I was really excited about entering a new phase in my life. I felt a sense of satisfaction that I'd come through my time in prison and it had changed me for the better.

In between the visit to Probation and going to my daughter Melissa's house, my mobile phone never stopped with well-wishers. Family and friends quickly made contact and I also received text messages from some of the prisoners I'd left behind.

When I arrived at Melissa she had tears in her eyes – relieved that my prison ordeal was finally over. A get-together was arranged for that evening at the Village Hotel in Whiston, where I stood on the terrace outside the bar with a pint in my hand and soaked up the afternoon sunshine. It felt so much more relaxed compared to my home leaves when prison rules hadn't allowed me to drink. Billy, Tony

Mac and myself were joined there by Melissa, her husband Kevin, Peter McGuinness and Kevin Hayes (The Egg), who all arrived to share in the pleasure of my release day. I was gutted that Uncle Tommy couldn't be there. Months before he'd booked a short-break holiday without realising the significance of the date. Can you believe that!

One of the funniest phone calls I received that afternoon was from my mum. I was driving my little red Corsa when she called and said: 'You're not 'Naughty Mark' anymore!' I realised again the extent of the hurt that I'd inflicted on my family and I was determined to make up for lost time with them.

We met up with other family members and it was decided to end the night in our old pub, The Watchmaker, at Whiston. Even though it was a Monday night, there were plenty of locals in and I was welcomed by them all. Relishing my freedom, I got so drunk that a bird even beat me at pool and, of course, I got loads of stick off the lads. I joked that the last time I'd been leaning over this pool table in the company of a woman, she was straddled over the green baize and hadn't been my cue that she was holding either!

I felt emotionally and physically drained towards the end of the evening and, after a quiet word with Billy, I sneaked off and staggered back to the hotel where I was staying the night. I really appreciated the treatment I'd been given but I skipped the formal goodbyes because I felt so tired and didn't want a big fuss made of me as I left the pub.

I awoke the next morning a refreshed and happy man. At breakfast with Tony Mac, he underlined my busy schedule of media interviews that he'd lined up, starting that mid-morning with the *News of the World*. It was to be held in room 23 at the Hillcrest Hotel in Cronton, a place I knew very well. The Everton team used to eat there before certain home midweek games and, of course, it was also here that I had my last 'encounter' with the infamous Blackmailer.

I felt very apprehensive beforehand, as I knew reporter Tom Latchem was going to grill me about all the aspects of my crime. The reason for doing the interview was the fact that the *NOTW* had agreed to plug my book by showing an image of the front cover plus details of how readers could order a copy from my publishers. I considered it worth an hour of questioning in return for the free publicity in Britain's biggest selling Sunday tabloid.

While photographer Peter Powell took lots of pictures of me, Latchem tried to get me to say if I knew of any current professional footballers who used drugs. I pointed out that while I didn't know of any players who took drugs during the football season, which would be madness on their part because it would destroy their career if they were caught, I said it was feasible that some do dabble in substances during the close season, when they go off on foreign holidays to party with their mates. Let's face it, drugs are rife in modern society, so why expect footballers not to dabble in them to some extent? I wasn't being sensationalist, just stating an obvious fact.

I also told Latchem that it was inevitable some high profile footballers would attract the attention of the criminal fraternity who tend to mix in the same social circles. As I said to him, when these people, often wealthy businessman, approach you in a corporate hospitality box after a game or some other function where your paths are likely to cross, they don't come up to you smiling with the words 'Beware – Drug Dealer' or 'Fraudster' stamped across their forehead. That's always been the case and it still is today. The *NOTW* interview lasted around two hours – Tony Mac was alongside me to record everything I said so that I couldn't be misquoted – and the article was expected to run over a double-page spread in their following Sunday's edition.

The rest of my first week of freedom was basically spent catching up with family and friends, including my four grandchildren. I had to get myself a diary because the various interviews came thick and fast and I found myself in the media spotlight again. My book, published on 30 May, had attracted great interest from all sections of the media – television, radio and the written national press alike – and I was amazed to hear that I was required to appear at three different branches of Waterstone's for book signings

Any slight apprehension I had about being the subject of more lurid headlines associated with my crime was eased when the *NOTW* article appeared on page 15 of their main news section. It had been cut to just half a page, because dominating the rest of the spread was a story alleging that West Bromwich Albion striker Roman Bednar had been photographed buying drugs. The piece on me was quite tame by comparison and when I opened up the paper, I remember thinking to myself: 'I owe Bednar a pint!'

It wasn't just the Bednar article that took the heat off me, though. Jordan's tits kept me off the front page, as the world's media tracked the former Page 3 model to the Maldives, where she'd gone to ground following her very public split from Peter Andre.

I was still in prison mode and by 8.30-9.00pm every night I was ready for my bed. And no matter what time I did get to bed, I was up sharp at five o'clock the next morning. I was told by other prisoners that it takes a long time before you finally get out of this mode. Even after nearly a year of freedom, I'm still up bright and early every day.

As the day of my book launch came even nearer, I was getting a little nervous about how my family would react to what I'd written. Dealing with personal and family issues had been the hardest part of writing the book. Mum was especially apprehensive about what I'd said about her and Dad splitting up, and our family life, but I just wanted them all to enjoy my story and I'm pleased to say that no-one has expressed any displeasure at what I've written. They have all been fine about it.

My interview with *The Independent* produced a very positive two-page spread in their sports section and a back page lead on Tuesday 19 May, the same day I was invited to appear on BBC Radio 5 Live. Apparently, one of the guests due to appear on Victoria Derbyshire's show, which attracts millions of listeners between 10.00am and midday each weekday, had to pull out at the last minute, so they contacted my publisher and were anxious for me to appear as a stand-in at very short notice. There wasn't enough time for me to travel down to West London, so I went to the BBC Radio Merseyside studios in Liverpool, where they set up a live link to the main studios in the capital.

On the flagship station for live news, sport and debate, I followed Tory leader David Cameron on air and was introduced at the start of the show as the main guest and 'ex-Premier League player given an eight-year sentence for drug dealing'. I felt confident at first and answered Ms Derbyshire's probing questions as best I could.

After ten minutes the BBC went to a news and weather bulletin and through my head phones I heard a bloke ask me if I'd mind taking phone calls from the general public. Without thinking, I said, 'Yes' – after all, I had nothing to hide and wanted to give an honest interview.

But I had left myself wide open and vulnerable to attack. The first two callers were West Ham fans who spoke well of me, saying how good I'd been as a footballer and that I deserved a second chance in life. I felt humbled and grateful on hearing their words of support.

After that, it went rapidly downhill.

What sounded like a middle-aged woman from Devon called and was adamant that I should have served the full eight years. She felt so strongly because her daughter had died as a result of being addicted to drugs. I felt awful. Paralysed with guilt, I could only say 'Sorry', although the woman wasn't interested in anything I had to say.

Another caller, I think he was a Man United fan, said he thought I was 'as bad as a paedophile'. Again, I let it go and stayed quiet. I didn't want to get into a heated debate on Britain's biggest radio show.

I knew that there was always going to be divided opinion about me following my release but this felt like being thrown to the lions. It was a shock to the system, no doubt. Leaving the recording studio in Liverpool, I felt like I'd been kicked all over the pitch by Stuart Pearce, Pat Van Den Hauwe and Mark Dennis combined! Friends of mine who'd heard the interview all agreed that I'd handled it with dignity but it was a harrowing experience and much more daunting than having to face any of those three uncompromising fullbacks in their physical prime.

After I'd gone off air, a lad who admitted to being a heroin addict phoned Derbyshire and told her and the listeners that he didn't blame me or any other 'foot soldier' who has been caught up in the drugs network for the mess he'd got himself into. He held his hands up and admitted it had always been his choice to take hard drugs and that no-one was to blame for this but himself. Fair play to him.

I should have stood up for myself and told the lady from Devon that I would still serve the remaining four years of my original sentence in the community under licence and that I would always regret making such a terrible mistake. I should have said that I'd taken my punishment and done the time. I treated her with respect and genuinely felt sorry for what she must have been through with her daughter. But I realise now that there are still many people in this country unwilling to give people a second chance in life.

Not all the radio interviews were an ordeal, though. The one I did with Ken Early on the national Irish radio station Newstalk was entertaining and relaxed, with balanced questions about football and my time in prison. My old mate Mickey Quinn invited me on to his talkSPORT show and he reminded listeners of some of the crazy things we got up to at Oldham in the early 1980s.

While in London, I also did a pleasing live radio interview for Liverpool-based Radio City's *Terrace Talk* show co-hosted by my former Everton team-mate Ian Snodin and Reds' legend Ian St John. 'Snods' is a great mate and he sounded very humble when he said to me that it was difficult for him to ask some of the more awkward questions. The interview went well, though, and I've since done some Q&A forum nights with Snods and enjoyed his company immensely.

On most of my frequent visits to London and the south-east to promote my book I stayed with my best mate Mick Tobyn at his place in Romford. It was a great feeling to be sat in the garden with him, reminiscing about the good times we'd had together while taking phone calls from different newspapers and magazines.

Mick and his sons Gary and Danny joined me at a mini reunion held in the Hammers pub in High Street North, East Ham on 22 May. My former team-mates Alvin Martin, Tony Gale and Tony Cottee had organised a coming-out party. Les, who owns the pub, had kindly let the lads use his premises for what turned out to be a fun night.

Getting off the train at East Ham tube station, I thought I'd arrived in another country – it was wall-to-wall foreigners and a stark contrast to Liverpool. I was feeling very nervous as we walked to the pub when Danny Tobyn pointed out to me the big, black A-board outside the pub entrance which read: 'Innocent – Mark Ward'. I laughed my bollocks off!

The pub was empty when we arrived but within the hour it was rammed full. It was great to have a beer with Galey, Alvin and TC, members of the Boys of '86 who had been unbelievably loyal to me.

It was also good to see Trevor Morley – one of the players involved in the swap deal that took me from West Ham to Man City in 1989 – who was with a group of Norwegian Hammers supporters. Tony Gale had clearly not lost his cutting wit and went on to slaughter everybody, including me.

I'd demolished about eight bottles of Becks in fairly quick time before Mick told me to slow down. He said I'd soon have to get up and do a bit on stage, where Galey and Tony took it in turns to interview their ex-team mates. When it was my turn to face the small audience, Galey didn't try to ease me in gently with a couple of sensible questions about my time at West Ham or anything else to do with football. He got straight to the point: 'Did you bend down in prison to pick up the soap?'

I was prepared for Galey, though. Before I took to the little stage, Gary Tobyn gave me a line – no, not that sort! – for me to use when it was my turn to speak. I explained to Galey and the assembled crowd how John Lyall came to sign me from Oldham. I told them the scouting report on me read: 'Mark is a little winger with bags of speed!' Nice one, Gaz – it got a laugh too.

At the end, I thanked the magnificent Hammers supporters who were there to greet me on what was a very emotional evening. I just wanted them to remember me as the little right-winger who always gave a hundred per cent for them, not the bloke who had been banged up for something he did wrong, and every one I met had only kind words to say. I ended up in some flat with Danny and a couple of his mates until the early hours of Saturday morning – it was a great night.

On the Sunday, the last day of the Premier League season. I was welcomed back to Upton Park by Phil Parkes, Alan Devonshire, Geoff Pike, Bobby Barnes and Stuart Slater, who were also attending Hammers' game against Middlesbrough. It was great to watch the

Hammers again, although I just wanted to turn the clock back and be running down the wing. How things had changed for me since those happy and unforgettable days in claret and blue.

After the match I bumped into Ray Winstone and Perry Fenwick who both made a right fuss of me. They were asking about my book and when they would be getting their copies. Me and Mick went with Ray and Perry to The Cricketers pub at Woodford Green before ending up at Ray's house in Hertfordshire for more beers. I sent both Ray and Perry a copy of my book and Perry texted me to say he hadn't been able to put it down. He said he read it in two days and thought it was brilliant.

He also said that if a movie was ever made of my life story he would love to play me! Ray slaughtered him, saying the *EastEnders* actor didn't have a Scouse accent and couldn't kick a ball either! Actually, Perry is quite a good footy player. I'd played against him years earlier in our annual Boys of '86 football tournament at Upton Park, where I gave him a right kicking!

I was pleased that my release meant I was able to play in the 2009 Boys of '86 tournament on the main pitch. Nearly everybody who played in that historic season was there, although Tony Gale feigned an injury and appointed himself manager. He was his usual sharp-witted self as we were all getting changed in the dressing room before the tournament began. He confirmed the starting line-up and announced that Frank McAvennie and me would be joining him 'on the line' as subs for the first game. 'Oh sorry – I shouldn't have said that,' he sniggered. Our keeper was Tommy Walsh, one of the stars of BBC TV's *Ground Force* gardening show and Olympic gold medal-winning rower Mark Hunter joined the ex-Hammers team.

A few weeks before the football tournament I'd arranged to meet up with Alvin in The Ship, his local pub in Gidea Park. It was great seeing my old captain and fellow Scouser again after all those lost years. Just like we did on my first day at Chadwell Heath in August 1985, we hit it off straight away and he seemed very concerned about my well-being. The trouble I'd got myself into obviously came as a tremendous shock to him and all the others I'd played with. We reminisced about the good old days over a few pints and he kindly promised to help me get work on the after-dinner circuit.

He mentioned that I'd become a little more articulate since my incarceration and he was surprised by that. Maybe I am. Perhaps the long nights and hours of boredom had shown me a different way to express myself.

Even though the BO86 tournament was held on a boiling hot day, people were saying how fit I looked. But just from kicking the ball back and forth to Alvin in the warm-up, I wasn't feeling right – my balance was all over the place.

I still played in all the games on our annual corporate day at West Ham and the fun continued afterwards in one of the main lounges, where it was good to catch up with all my old team-mates. I spent the night in one of West Ham's corporate boxes that convert into bedrooms on non-matchdays. HMP Upton Park has better facilities than its Romford counterpart (aka Travelodge) and the view out onto the pitch was better too!

I was commuting by train between London and Liverpool for weeks following my release. On Tuesday 25 May I returned south for a 90-minute meeting with PR guru Max Clifford and two of his senior staff, his daughter Louise and Denise Palmer-Davies, at their plush offices in Mayfair. Although Tony Mac came with me, I was a little apprehensive at first but the two girls soon put me at ease. They said they had read a synopsis of my book and were fascinated about how I'd managed to conceal my mobile phone SIM card while in prison! I didn't get to speak to Max for long – he was busy outside giving a TV interview about how he was representing Britain's first known swine flu sufferer.

The meeting at MCA was also attended by management representatives from a television production company who indicated there could be scope to adapt my story from book form onto the screen. We talked enthusiastically about the possibility of me 'starring' in a one-hour documentary titled *From Premier League to Prison*.

Later that day, the busy round of interviews continued at the Hilton International Hotel in Euston, where I met Jim White (*Daily*

Telegraph) and Alan Fraser (*Daily Mail*). These two educated, experienced men are proper journalists and I enjoyed their intelligent questions.

As I boarded the 6.00pm train back to Liverpool, I felt shattered and still couldn't believe all that was happening to me since my release.

I was on the train once again on the Thursday to visit my publishers in Hornchurch to sign copies of my book that had just been delivered from the printer. I was delighted to see the result of all those hours I'd spent writing away in my cell over the past few years. And then, with the ink barely dry on the hardback, I was off to a local hotel for an interview with Dave Evans of the local Recorder newspaper group that covers West Ham. Ken Dyer of the *London Evening Standard*, who I've known since my Hammers playing days, also met me for a chat.

Back in the north-west, Granada TV wanted to do an interview for their *Granada Reports* news programme that goes out every night. I was apprehensive but it was another great opportunity to get my point across and obviously it would be great exposure for the book, too. I pre-recorded the interview by the dock-side, a stone's throw away from the Liver buildings, and it went really well. It was strange seeing myself on the news that evening.

Naturally, the *Liverpool Echo* wanted to talk to me and I was very pleased with the coverage Dave Prentice gave me in a series of extracts. It made a nice change to be headline news in my local paper for the right reasons! I also had a lovely chat with Paul Hince, who covered Man City for the *Manchester Evening News* throughout my time at Maine Road. When I was first sent to prison, he wrote one of the most sympathetic pieces and, four years later, it was nice to be able to read it on the internet and thank him on the phone.

Despite my increasing confidence in dealing with all the interviews for radio, television, newspapers and magazines, I really was dreading the book signings at one of Waterstones' leading London outlets - the Leadenhall Market branch in the City. I kept saying that nobody would turn up but my publisher assured me they would. To try and ease my nerves, I jokingly asked Mick Tobyn whether my book would be placed on the shelves of the crime or the sports section. As we approached the beautiful Victorian building I could see posters of myself displayed in the windows and was gobsmacked to see that a queue of people had already formed.

The staff at the shop were very welcoming and sat me down at a table to sign loads of books that had been on prominent display at the front of the busy shop in the heart of London's square mile. The customers were mainly West Ham, Everton, Manchester City and Birmingham supporters dressed in business suits who worked in the City. They came out during their lunch break to buy the book and get it signed but some of them also had replica shirts and photos that I was also only too pleased to autograph. I must admit, it was nice to be remembered for the good things I'd done in my life.

Just weeks previously I'd been pacing my prison cell and now I was in this flagship shop signing copies of my book. It felt unreal.

The warmth from customers was overwhelming and the girl from Waterstone's who was looking after me said that some very well-known celebrities didn't get half as many people turn up for their signings.

I must also express my gratitude to everyone who has sent letters or emails to me, via my publisher, to say how much you enjoyed the first hardback edition of this book. I was overwhelmed by the response from all corners of the country and I read every word of them. No-one has slagged me off and I can only say a genuine big 'thanks' now for the many kind words of praise and encouragement that have been a big source of comfort to me in my first year back in the community.

Probably the biggest public event I attended in the first year following my release was the invitation to speak at the Liverpool Festival of Culture on 15 October. It was a daunting prospect. The annual occasion is an international literary festival which runs over five days. I was talking at their Football Stories event that evening with Jonathan Wilson, who had written a book on tactics and it was hosted by respected broadcaster John Keith of *City Talk*. The event is held at The Blue Coat Chambers, the oldest surviving building in Liverpool which has received millions of pounds of investment for restoration.

All the media interviews and media work I'd given in the previous months had stood me in good stead, because I felt no nerves as I stepped into the small theatre at the start of the evening. Melissa and her husband Kevin were in the audience of several hundred and it was great to have a well known and respected voice in John Keith asking the questions. Some well known faces were in the audience and Tony Fitz was there and was looking forward to hear what I had to say. He has his own production company and is interested in doing something with the book.

One thing that will always stay with me from that night was the Q&A at the end. I answered the questions as best I could and John Keith was ready to finish the night when Melissa suddenly took hold of the mic. I was momentarily stunned, wondering with bated breath what she was about to say. But I need not have had any concerns. She was very composed and said: 'I'd just like to say that I know my dad did wrong and went to prison, but I love him so much. If my two sons grow up to be half the man he is, I'll be a very proud mother.'

It was a very emotional moment for me. I nearly started to cry, especially as most of the audience let out a loud applause after Melissa's heartfelt speech.

38. TO HELL AND BACK

IT is a very arrogant person – probably a liar – who goes beyond their 40th birthday and claims to have no regrets. But if, in these reflective moments as I look back on my eventful rollercoaster life, I was to write down everything I've regretted doing, this book would be thicker than *War and Peace*!

I've done a lot of soul-searching in the past four years and I'll share those thoughts with you here. In my personal life, I wish I'd worked much harder to make a success of my marriage to Jane that ended in 1996 after 14 years.

Melissa was also a victim of the marriage break-up and was devastated by the divorce. I am truly sorry for hurting her as well as her mother. My daughter has been an absolute rock for me since my imprisonment and without the love of her and other family members, especially brother Billy and Uncle Tommy, it would have been so much harder for me to cope. They've always been there when I've needed them.

Being unable to attend Melissa's wedding day in 2006 and missing the birth of her last two children while I was inside are major causes for regret. I wish I'd been able to celebrate the arrival of my youngest grandchildren Isabella and Frankie on the outside and I know I definitely should have been there to give my daughter away. It was a sad day for me when Jane had to perform that honour instead.

* * * *

Football-wise, I have only a few regrets. I was bitterly disappointed when I'd finished playing without having won an England cap, which would have meant so much to me. There was a period – at West Ham in the mid-80s – when I believe I was definitely good enough to have played for my country but two things probably counted against me. Everton right-winger Trevor Steven was a brilliant player with a very successful club at the time. Secondly, perhaps my more aggressive style of play didn't go down well with the people who mattered.

I shouldn't have left West Ham as early as I did. If Billy Bonds – and not Lou Macari – had succeeded John Lyall, I wouldn't have gone anywhere. Who knows, I could still have been living near London and maybe even working at West Ham now?

There are regrets, too, about leaving Everton in 1994, with one year still left on my contract. Yet again, I acted too impetuously in wanting to get away from a poor manager in Mike Walker. I should have been patient and waited for Joe Royle to take over and my hasty decision to join Birmingham City might well have cost me a place in Everton's FA Cup-winning side of '95.

I can't complain, though. I was fortunate enough to play more than 400 senior games, for clubs in four major cities, and there can't be many who can look back on their career and say that they've played in all of the top six divisions of English football. The game gave me a nice lifestyle for a number of years and has also taken me to countries I would not otherwise have had the pleasure of visiting.

* * * *

People ask if I regret having a bet on the horses and drinking as much as I did. Well, I enjoy both pleasures in life. I've always been a sociable person and like to think of myself as a man of the people. I can't change that now and, to be honest, I don't want to. Enjoying a few beers and having a bet has always been a way of life for both my late father Billy and Uncle Tommy. So if it's good enough for them, then it's good enough for me too.

Obviously, my biggest regret dates back to 2005, when I became involved in renting the house that ultimately cost me four years of freedom. You live and die by your actions and decisions in life, and of course I now bitterly regret getting involved in that drug-related crime. I made a terribly stupid decision and I've faced the consequences.

Respect is a great word and, despite the problems I've encountered in my life, some of them of my own making, I've always given respect to people who have deserved it – such as my ex-managers,

Howard Kendall and the late John Lyall, for example. And I believe I've earned the respect of my fellow footballers, friends and prisoners alike.

I'm a great believer in freedom of speech and the freedom to smoke, drink and whatever else you care to do in your own time. Obviously, drugs kill people and they damage the lives of not only those who take them, but also their families.

But I've never forced anybody to do anything against their will. I did wrong, yes, and I've served my time accordingly as a model prisoner. Well, most of the time anyway, if you ignore the concealment of mobile phones and drinking of the odd beer on licensed premises that breached my home leave conditions!

What I still can't understand, though, are the barbaric sentences dished out to offenders in drug-related crimes compared to those who commit far more heinous acts. I've seen lads coming in from the courts with 16-to-24-year jail sentences for their involvement in drug crimes. On the other hand, I've read of evil paedophiles and rapists escaping lightly on four-to-six-year prison terms for systematically abusing children and ruining the lives of their defenceless victims. Tell me how that can be right?

I'm not trying to say that people who become embroiled in drug-related crimes shouldn't be punished. Of course they should. What I would like to see, though, is a much fairer and appropriate sentencing procedure so that the punishment fits the crime. Is that really too much to ask of the British justice system? Or is the system itself corrupt? Maybe it all comes down to money?

As a parent, ask yourself this: Who would you be more gravely concerned about . . . an evil sex offender who could abuse, rape or torture your daughter, wife or son; or someone who rents a house out as a stash? As I've said, I'm not trying to exonerate myself from blame and I realise that two wrongs don't make a right. All I'm asking for is some perspective.

About a month before my release, I read in the paper that the government is set to introduce more lenient sentencing laws for crimes involving drugs. I'm not so much bitter that they hadn't addressed this issue before my arrest in 2005, as glad that at least convicted criminals will be handed down more appropriate jail terms in the future.

* * * *

Four years in prison has definitely changed me as a person. Life will never be quite the same for me following my release. I'll probably forever be labelled the 'ex-Premier League footballer who was involved with drugs and got an eight-year sentence'. Already, just days before my release, news of the imminent publication of my book reached the media and the prison screws at Kirkham showed me a newspaper report that referred to me as the 'shamed soccer star'. That's the media for you – don't they love a sensational cliché? – but I'll live with it.

I think having spent half my adult life in football, 13 seasons as a professional, actually helped me cope with prison. Spending all those years in a dressing room full of bravado, various egos and with all the banter flying around, made it easier to deal with day-to-day life locked up among prisoners who have a lot to say for themselves. You have to live on your wits and stick up for yourself inside, just as you do at a football club.

Footballers have a very structured routine in both training and playing terms and it's not too dissimilar to the strict regime of prison, where meal times and exercise periods remain regimental and a fixed schedule is adhered to. Like I did throughout my football career, I made sure I kept myself as fit as possible in prison. In fact, at 10st 10lbs, I weigh just three pounds more now than I did at the end of my professional playing days. I feel as fit as a fiddle.

It's my burning desire to get back into football coaching, hopefully at non-league level initially, as soon as possible. Why not? The experiences I gained as a player and manager at Birmingham City – where we were champions and cup winners in my first full season as first team player-coach – and later Altrincham and Leigh RMI, will stand me in good stead for future employment with any club.

I honestly believe that, at 46, I could still do a good job coaching or managing at lower league level and, if anything, I'm probably better equipped to do so now than I was four years ago. Managing a group of 20 or so players again, either full-time pros or part-timers, on a daily basis would come easily to me after living alongside and getting on with hundreds and thousands of prisoners.

There were many more volatile and violent characters throwing their weight around on B-wing in Walton than I'm ever likely to encounter at a football club. Prison life, and making your way through the system, is all about managing relationships with fellow prisoners and having the ability to get on with them, to give and take and to handle a myriad of contrasting temperaments. Isn't that essentially what a football coach/manager does too?

I fully appreciate that my CV could have made more impressive reading than it has over the past four years or so! It will take a very big man to offer me the job of managing or coaching at his football club. I hope that, somewhere out there, there is just such a brave character reading this now, who will grant me the chance that I crave. I can't emphasise enough how mentally scarred I was by my bitter Altrincham experience and I still see it as unfinished business as far as my football life is concerned. I know, without a shadow of a doubt, that I still have a lot to offer but the big question remains: Is there a man out there big enough and brave enough to let me prove myself again?

* * * *

It was quickly obvious to me on my release from Kirkham that the financial climate was poor and Britain was in the grip of the worst global recession in living memory – since the Great Depression of the early '30s. Not a good time to come out of prison looking for work.

I'd been so grateful for my year's part-time work which enabled me to leave prison with enough money to rent a flat on the outskirts of Liverpool. I decided to pay six months' rent in advance so I wouldn't have any worries about having a roof over my head for a while.

But the building industry has been one of the worst-hit sectors of the global recession. On 6 May, just five days before leaving prison, I received confirmation that I was being laid off from the part-time labouring job I'd had while allowed out on day release. Work had dried up and there was nothing doing for me there anymore, even though they had been delighted with my efforts and commitment in the past.

Towards the end of the year, thanks to my good mate Tony Murphy, I managed to find some more work as an electrician's mate on a new hotel being built in Liverpool but that stint lasted for about eight weeks before I was out of work again.

Many of you reading this will have been affected by the recession or know of others who have, so I can easily relate to the difficulties many people are experiencing these days. It's doubly difficult when you have a criminal record. I'm more fortunate than many others because I have great friends who help me as much as possible – people like Tony Murphy, who is always looking out for me.

As I've said, it would be a dream come true to get back involved in football in a management and/or coaching capacity. I don't kid myself that I can walk back into the game at a high level or resume the role I had as a successful first team coach at Birmingham City. So I sent out over 50 typewritten letters to more than 50 selected non-league clubs at Blue Square Conference League level and the two North and South divisions immediately below that, making them aware of my past experience and availability in the hope that there might be an opportunity somewhere. I wouldn't be expensive, I would be very realistic in my expectations and I know I can do a better job than some of the people who have been given a chance.

But to this day I've had little response other than a few polite 'thanks, but no thanks' replies from chairmen. Hopefully they will bear me in my mind the next time they are thinking of hiring a new manager or coach.

Meanwhile, I press on and try to find work wherever possible, but it's a tough world out there – in the real world. For several weeks in the summer of '09 I appeared on Peter McDowall's City Talk radio show in Liverpool. It was enjoyable and a good experience but they were unable to pay me anything for appearing.

Another area that has been very badly affected by the recession is corporate hospitality events which most companies and individuals have been forced to cut back on. It's bad news for us ex-pros trying to make our way on the after-dinner circuit. I must say Tony Gale, in particular, and Alvin Martin and Ian Snodin have all been great in helping to fix me up with bookings whenever and wherever they can and I've been fortunate enough to appear at shows with all three of them at different times in the past year or so. The Scouse comedian, Frank Allen, has also been a big help in this respect.

Just before Christmas '09, I was invited to a corporate Christmas lunch at Balls Brothers in London organised by Steve Surridge of Eclipse Sports and hosted by Alvin Martin. Among the other celebrity guests were: Ossie Ardiles, Paul Merson, Mick Hartford, Graham Roberts, Frank Stapleton, Martin Chivers and ex-England cricketer Ronnie Irani. I must say they all treated me very well and no-one shunned me because of my past.

I was shown to a table of nine West Ham fans and they couldn't have made me more welcome. Mark Dougherty was the host of the table and he immediately put me at ease and broke the ice by handing me a badge that he'd had specially made and which all nine lads were wearing. The badge showed four prisoners tied to a ball and chain with the words 'Ball and Chain Gang!' at the top! It was their little way of showing their support for me and it was a lovely touch. As was my dinner name card that I spotted behind my plate, which read: 'Mark Ward NM6982'.

Later that afternoon, I had my photo taken with Mark and his friends beside a replica of the FA Cup. It brought back memories of how gutted I'd felt at seeing my team, Everton, lose to Chelsea in the final at Wembley the previous May. I watched the game with the Tobyns in The Sun pub in Romford but after Louis Saha put us in front with the fastest goal in FA Cup final history, Chelsea went on to win 2-1.

I've enjoyed appearing in public on stage, answering questions about my football career and the less happy periods of my life. I won't duck any issues and will always give an honest answer to a straight question. You know me, I always tell it like it is and the audiences I've appeared in front of seem to have gone home happy with their night's entertainment. I've regained my self-confidence and without wishing to appear cocky, I know I have something to offer.

But it's a sign of the times that I counted 12 – yes, a dozen – shows that I was booked to appear in that were subsequently cancelled by the organisers due to a lack of ticket sales. Hopefully, as the economy improves, so too will work opportunities.

* * * *

In taking the positives from my story and without wishing to sound pretentious, I hope this book will in some way help others in the future. It could inspire youngsters to overcome obstacles, such as height and weight issues, and go on to become a professional footballer against all odds.

I'd like it to serve as a warning to vulnerable people of the dangers of getting involved with drugs and other criminal activity. They should learn from my mistakes.

For those who do fall foul of the law and end up in prison, perhaps reading this will help them to show the strength and character to cope with their sentences and do their time in the best way possible – and I don't mean tips about how to hide SIM cards and mobile phones in places where no screws care to look! By the way, they were the only two prison rules I broke.

I hope you've enjoyed reading my story. I've been as honest as possible within the libel laws – my publishers did have to chop some bits out! – and hopefully that comes across throughout these pages. I've really enjoyed the writing process – it helped keep me sane throughout my time in prison.

Thanks to the love and support of my family and friends, I have been given this chance to rebuild my life and I'm determined not to waste it. My family are there for me and I know how lucky I am to be able to count on their love and support, as well as that of many friends.

We all make mistakes in life and it's how you respond to them that matters.

On the morning of Monday 11 May, 2009, I left behind my prison identity of NM6982 and reverted to being Mark Ward. I'll never forget my prison number - it's ingrained on my brain – but I couldn't wait to walk through those gates at HMP Kirkham for the last time.

I've been to hell. And I'm never going back.